THE LANDSCAPE DESIGN
ANSWER BOOK

Published by Cool Springs Press, a Division of Thomas Nelson, Inc., P. O. Box 141000, Nashville, Tennessee, 37214.

Library of Congress Cataloging-in-Publication Data

Bath, Jane, 1942-
  The landscape design answer book : more than 300 specific design
solutions for your landscape / Jane Bath.
     p. cm.
  Includes index.
  ISBN 1-59186-250-7 (pbk.)
  1. Landscape design. 2. Landscape gardening. I. Title.
  SB473.B37 2006
  712'.6—dc22

                        2006006277

First printing 2006
Printed in the United States
10 9 8 7 6 5 4 3 2 1

Managing Editor: Billie Brownell
Art Director: Bruce Gore, Gore Studios
Copyeditor: Jamie Chavez, Word Works
Interior Designer: Bill Kersey, KerseyGraphics
Cover photograph by Alan and Linda Detrich; Design: Cording Landscape Design, Inc.
All other photography by Kimberly Brown

Cool Springs Press books may be purchased in bulk for educational, business, fundraising, or sales promotional use. For information, please email **SpecialMarkets@ThomasNelson.com**.

Visit the Cool Springs Press website at **www.coolspringspress.net**

THE LANDSCAPE DESIGN

ANSWER BOOK

MORE THAN 300

SPECIFIC DESIGN SOLUTIONS

FOR YOUR LANDSCAPE

JANE BATH

Dedication and Acknowledgments

The seeds of gardening were planted by my grand-mothers, one of whom gave me an iris rhizome for my birthday. I still remember my excitement opening the package. My other grandmother was such a dedicated gardener that she asked for a new wheelbarrow for her 95th birthday! My mother saw every part of life guided by beauty *and* function. From her, I have come to understand that to ignore function or beauty will be a negative but to combine the two will be a joy.

Thanks to my many gardening friends: Jim and Martha Herod; Marsha and Dan Sichveland; Liz and George Tedder; Barbara and Mitch Mitchell; Carol and Fred Dyer. The Daylily Society gave me access to some of the most outrageous, wonderful people anyone could wish to meet.

Steve Bender, editor and writer for *Southern Living* and his entire staff truly love educating and inspiring the public. To allow me to be even a small part of the process has been most gratifying. Mark Kane, past writer and editor of *Better Homes and Garden,* was my true inspiration to write this book.

Erica Glasener, Martha Tate, Walter Reeves, and Tara Dillard are media celebrities but they are also my friends who share in the madness of the gardening world. Who does not know of Dr. Michael Dirr and Dr. Allan Armitage, perhaps the most generous horticulturists in the world? They and many others share their time and talents. Of special note to me in the nursery industry are Rick Berry and Mark Richardson of Goodness Grows Nursery. Their dedication to search out those plants best suited for my area and making them available to the public is amazing. I revere them.

My customers allow me to come onto their property and into their lives. I thank each and every one for giving me this opportunity. For more than twenty-three years, and after thousands of jobs, walking onto a site still excites me as much as it did the first day.

My photographer Kimberly Brown is a love. Every day, I would send her out to sites to shoot but only someone with a creative eye could have known what I needed her to shoot. I deeply appreciate her talents. I thank all those people who allowed us to photograph their landscapes for this book.

Special thanks to my editors, Hank McBride and Billie Brownell, of Cool Springs Press. They took on this project and made it come alive. They have been a constant source of assurances and help to bring this book to you.

My brother Charles has been delighting people for years with his drawings. I knew when starting this book he had to play a part because only he could best illustrate the thoughts I was trying to express. His wife Anne also gave me the best advice on the personality this book should take. Thanks to them both.

My husband Nick has been my backbone. We share a love for each other and for our professional lives. His support is the only way I could have enjoyed doing what I do over the years, as well as his support during the writing of this book. Our three kids—Ginny, David, and Catherine—have each in their own way contributed to my world of horticulture and enjoy it in their own lives.

The impact of these people is sometimes overwhelming to me. Thank you.

Contents

How To Use *The Landscape Design Answer Book*

My design philosophy is based on the idea that each landscape design element can be considered part of a giant puzzle. Once these elements are understood, the homeowner can use them to achieve desirable goals, and avoid unappealing or unsatisfactory results.

Each chapter in this book is composed of individual, distinct *elements of design* expressed as *one thought*. This allows the reader to concentrate on the importance of each idea and see its relevance to the whole.

Each design element is numbered sequentially 1 through 316. At the end of each design element, any related elements of design of similar importance (including photos or illustrations) are listed for easy cross reference. The index can also be used by their *page numbers* to look up particular items of interest.

Chapter 1: Getting Started
Is It Low Maintenance?

Low maintenance is everyone's number one goal. Making thoughtful decisions at the beginning of any project will allow you to reach this goal because good decisions are vital to achieve a unified, functional landscape that integrates fully with the home. Topics in Chapter 1 include: low maintenance; the size and uses of land; the importance of views and focal points; setting goals; the need for enclosure when designing landscapes; decisions about clearing and grading; choosing plants for their mature size; limiting small plantings; using non-invasive plants; the importance of level spaces; designing to accommodate utilities; the power of the sun; how to avoid adding problems to the landscape. A Planting Guide is in this chapter.

Chapter 2: The Foundation
Designing with Trees and Shrubs

Trees and shrubs are major components in every landscape. Knowing how to use them effectively as well as taking proper care of them is essential to achieve the best from each plant for a progressively beautiful landscape. Topics in Chapter 2 include: Significant, Ornamental, and Trash Trees (and how to tell the difference); choosing plants for a specific purpose; avoiding excessive screening; proper pruning and shearing; the importance of an interrupted view; the China Cabinet approach to design; the use of natural materials; natural litter; limbing up and other pruning techniques; the use of evergreens; use of formal and informal plantings; using local resources; the pros and cons of symmetry. A Pruning Guide is in this chapter.

Chapter 3: Adding Drama
Flowers and Containers in Landscape Design

Flower gardening is every person's dream and passion. The most important elements needed to achieve the best results in the landscape are included in this chapter. Topics in Chapter 3 include: plants for maximum visibility; the five major attributes; incorporating herbs and wildflowers; growing for cut flowers; why perennials can be problematic; the tried and true; general care.

Chapter 4: Creating Rooms in the Landscape
Beds and Paths

Just like a home, the landscape contains distinct "rooms." Identifying them, turning them into special spaces, and most important, providing circulation for easy movement between and to them are the most basic elements of landscape design. Topics include: every landscape has four rooms; the inclusion and proper design of guest entrances, car areas, and utility areas; outdoor living spaces; defining rooms by the use of bed lines, plant groupings, and fencing; proper fences; the need for circulation; paths and walks, including using grass as paths; designing for safety, endurance, and attractiveness. Two full-page illustrations, Builder's Choice and Better Choices, are in the chapter.

Chapter 5: First Impressions
The Front of the House

From the mailbox to the front door, a visitor's first impression of the homesite is important. Each one of these elements must be considered to effectively create a wonderful introduction to the landscape. Topics in Chapter 5 include: how to direct guests to the proper entrance; guest parking and exiting; parking pads and their problems; the importance of level spaces; the excessive and poor uses of hard surfaces; the importance of wide, straight walkways; designing coverings and landings for all doors to the outside; why one does not want to line walkways; separating the utility features from the focus of the home. A full page illustration, Standardized Measurements for Parking and Exits, is included.

Chapter 6: Indoor and Outdoor Transitions
Steps, Porches, and Decks

Porches, decks, patios, and their steps are major transitional elements to the natural world outdoors. Many considerations should be addressed for these to be truly effective and to ensure they will enhance a fully integrated landscape to the home. Topics include: the importance of single level outdoor spaces; the influence of the sun; selecting appropriate outdoor furniture; how to hide the grill; the impact of arbors and summerhouses; problems with daylight basements; the importance of consistent heights of risers and treads and avoiding the single-step; pre-

serving the view; the benefits of patios vs. decks; considering the hardscape; the importance of avoiding semicircular steps and those alongside structures; incorporating planting spaces in hardscapes.

Chapter 7: Form and Function
Structures in the Landscape

All structures are part of the landscape. Their prominence means they must receive special attention for any landscape to be attractive. Topics include: the importance and siting of outbuildings; why a separate workshop is important; designing for the detached garage; the value of easy access to a toilet; garden sheds and their important features; why fences are better than plants; the appropriate fence heights; why fences should always be perpendicular to the home; framing architectural features; hiding utility elements; water meters, power lines, and electrical elements; lighting for safety and mood; irrigation.

Chapter 8: Having Fun
Grass and Kids

Common sense advice about grass and kids, suggestions every parent should know in order to create an inviting landscape for the family to enjoy. Topics include: the importance of fencing the swimming pool from access from the house; why large yards are not essential to foster play among children; allowing children to plant; selecting the proper type of grass; preparing the soil for seeding and sodding of grass; caring for the lawn.

Chapter 9: Our Primal Needs
Water, Fire, and Critters

In the hierarchy of wants, dogs seem to be first, then a pond, then fire. Each one of these can provide so much enjoyment to homeowners. Topics include: planning a landscape with pets in mind; needs of other creatures; identifying pests and how to deal with them; the natural world; locating ponds; taking sunlight into account when siting ponds; the advantages of gas and/or wood fireplaces; moveable fireplaces.

Each landscape design goal is numbered sequentially throughout the book.

Each landscape design solution summarizes the main thought in the first sentence (shown in green). Any supporting sentences are shown in black.

Real-life examples are provided to explain the primary landscape design goal. This is where I explain why a particular element works (or does not).

Cross-references to other pages direct you to other design solutions if they relate to the featured one.

Photos of real-life homes show you the ideal landscape goal.

 The architectural design elements of the home should dominate all other elements in the landscape, especially hardscape elements, which should complement the whole.

Hardscapes in the landscape encompass many different elements in the overall design. A few examples include paving, workshops, gazebos, arbors, fences, barns, sheds, swimming pools, and pool houses. These are all "hard," are permanent, and quite prominent. When adding each one to the whole, they should complement each other but, more important, complement the main structure, the home, in many different ways such as in color tones and architectural features.

When a homeowner finds himself floundering in this category, it is time to call in an experienced professional landscape architect or designer. Too often when talking to contractors and suppliers, a homeowner might be drawn into making a decision on a fence or perhaps a shed that looks quite good standing alone but does not complement the house. These are expensive and permanent mistakes.

For example, a Victorian-style gazebo is installed behind a classic Williamsburg-style home. A workshop is built with a low, unappealing roof line and inexpensive metal siding behind a 4000-square-foot home. Sidewalk stone has color tones of orange, pink, and coral, but the stone on the house is a subtle gray. A stamped concrete driveway leading to a beautiful home is distracting because the home contains a great many patterns already.

Decisions in building a home are hard enough though usually people have a professional architectural layout to help them. But these plans do not include decisions in the landscape, especially hardscape elements. My advice is to consider the whole—each element should contribute to the main event, which is the house. And, if in doubt, seek professional guidance. It will be money well spent.

See **Structures** *292*
Rooflines *302*
Paths and Driveways *194*
Walls and Borders *180*
Color of Plantings in Relationship to Structure *86*
Photos *196, 220, 244*

This open carport is a major architectural complement to the beautiful home.

Proper thinning and limbing up of these Ornamental Trees add immeasurably to this landscape.

A certain degree of enclosure creates a much-appreciated space. The addition of the railing at the carport accomplishes this beautifully.

Learning the Language

This book, *The Landscape Design Answer Book,* has evolved over many years as I've worked in the field of landscape design and architecture. Every day has been a challenge facing totally different landscapes, buildings, and the people who would use them; the goal was to satisfy each homeowner's personal vision of beauty while working around problems inherent to the land. Increasingly, I discovered that even though the diversity of the landscape never ceased, the *solutions* to important problems were recurring.

The turning point in this problem-solving process occurred when I read Christopher Alexander's architectural book, *A Pattern Language.* It impressed upon me that all problems must be reduced to their simplest form before satisfactory solutions can be reached. I understood that once basic landscaping rules were examined and repeatedly tested for their validity, they could be applied to endless situations, even though the projects—cottages on small plots, large estates or ranches with many outbuildings, suburban lots with country French, Georgian manor, or other style homes—might be completely dissimilar.

Nothing I recommend in this book is new. Many books are available that address landscape problems—but important usable solutions are often buried in lengthy discussions that fail to explain why a certain point is important. In other cases the landscaping book becomes a "How To" book with lengthy lists of plant materials (often relevant only to a specific region). Again, those books do not address *why* a particular element works or why it does not. The most beautifully constructed fence or wonderful plant specimens in the world can detract from the overall landscape if they are misapplied. If used correctly, the landscape is enhanced.

What *is* new in *The Landscape Design Answer Book* is that I've reduced the subject of landscape design to a number of solutions that can be universally applied to specific problems the reader faces. These solutions are numbered sequentially, with many containing simple cross-references for additional information. For instance, if the homeowner is installing a fence, certain solutions come into play that ensure an attractive, functional outcome. Since fences are expensive, these solutions help save money and time and ensure that everyone is happy. Consulting the solutions regarding driveways and walks can also prevent costly mistakes. There are solutions governing decks, walls, and even the mailbox. Of course, plant materials have a long list of solutions explaining how to use them for positive results in the landscape.

Many of my clients are repeat customers; I landscape a home for them—and then their next house, their neighbor's house, even their church. I've spent more than twenty-two years designing over 4000 sites, from cottages, million-dollar estates, farms, and suburban homes to churches, courthouses, and other public places. And still I am asked the same question over and over: "How do you succeed in making so many customers so happy?" The answer is I do not reinvent the wheel. Each landscaping site is a giant puzzle; as each piece of the puzzle is put in place, the picture—pleasing and functional for the customer—emerges. This book is my desire to share that process with others.

So, welcome, to *The Landscape Design Answer Book.*

Jane Bath

CHAPTER  1

Getting Started

Is It Low Maintenance?

Each homeowner must identify major design elements in his landscape with a special emphasis on low maintenance to ensure that the dual goals of beauty and function are achieved.

Whether it's a new home or a fun project, the homeowner needs to know what to consider not only when enhancing his home, but also how to reduce the chores necessary to keep it in good order.

Decisions made at the beginning often determine the project's destiny. Small details that are missed often become major problems. Identifying some of these might save the homeowner a great deal of grief down the road when he is occupied with juggling the demands of the building project.

1 **The number one low-maintenance consideration is the actual size of the land you choose. Plants are a dynamic life force and need maintenance for every square foot you purchase.**

Outside, every day brings an ongoing growth pattern as small seedlings become giant trees in your sidewalk, one foot from your house. Ivy climbs in your windows and up into trees. Weeds quickly take over every inch of space if no one bothers to contain them. Perhaps in more arid locales, this process is less intense, but Nature still will get in the last word if no one pays attention.

This all means that *when purchasing property, every square foot is yours to consider.* The garden will always need to be weeded. The lawn must always be tended. The trees will always get bigger, some will die, and some will fall down. On larger properties, these activities just multiply.

Am I trying to scare you? Well, not exactly. I am just trying to be realistic. Because if your Number One priority is low-maintenance, land is not low-maintenance. And the more land you have, the more maintenance you have.

Think of the process of getting an estimate for any work. Estimates are calculated by how big the job is or by the square footage. Think of the property you are considering buying. Every square foot must be accounted for—as the size increases, so does the workload or your cost to maintain. Over the years, I have seen more and more people move to smaller and smaller lots, especially as they grow older. Even vigorous young people often have lives too busy to cope with the demands of large spaces.

Being realistic to your aspirations is probably the number one key to low-maintenance. Ask yourself, just how much space do you actually need and can take care of?

See **Separate Structures** *292*
Fences, Walls, and Gates *306*
Enclosure *50*
Significant Trees *96*

The foundation plantings were chosen for their minimal height and care.

An attractive fence defines a small easy-to-keep lawn. The land outside the fence can be kept as a lower maintenance field.

Fun but limited high-maintenance flower beds were located in their backyard everyday living space for personal enjoyment and ease of care.

An architecturally complementary separate workshop/car space was built for hobbies and storage.

2 From the largest farm to the smallest homesite, how one uses his land will determine its level of maintenance. **The most important consideration is: What comes next for each planned project because it is the cumulative effect that pushes many over the edge.**

Package size is a major consideration, but more important is what a person chooses to do with his purchase. One owns a forest and periodically walks around looking at the surrounding wonder. Another gets busy cleaning out poison ivy and honeysuckle and starts planting new and interesting shade plants. If one chooses the latter, will one be locked into keeping this area free of invasive plants over the years?

Another has a home on a lake. Next come the sea wall, docks, boats, and a well-manicured landscape. As long as this person is willing to maintain these wonderful additions, then all is great. But if this is a home away from home, then trying to escape these chores…well, you can see what I'm getting at.

Around the smaller home landscape this same principle applies. A person might build an entertainment patio and want that Old World look of stone interplanted with interesting specimens. But who will keep the uninteresting weeds at bay? If a lovely specimen tree is desired, why install a messy, short-lived mimosa? We will not even discuss swimming pools except perhaps to note that the cleaning tools need to be stored close by. It's the same with fish ponds—they are high maintenance, but if you plan to have them, at least install them away from too many trees.

Not one of these projects is out of bounds for most homeowners' ability. It is just when the homesite is a collection of too many of these desirable features that maintenance chores overwhelm and supersede enjoyment of the site. There's only so much time.

Reducing maintenance chores is a valid goal. Choose your projects carefully and plan them wisely, but the main goal is to enjoy them enormously.

This landscape was designed and installed over 20 years ago with only a few minor modifications since. Ease of maintenance and a pleasing front of the home were key elements important for this homeowner.

Note the importance of Significant Trees both as a backdrop and as providing a lovely, interrupted view of the front of the home.

This lovely home with extended gardens to the side requires a great deal of work, but it's worth it for this homeowner.

The front walk was widened to 5 feet to accommodate everyone for an easy walk to the front door.

Sun now reaches this front yard. Major thinning of excessive Trash Trees on the boundary line eliminated a dark, mossy front space.

3 **Decisions for clearing your building site within a forested area will have a major impact on future low-maintenance. Nonessential as well as inappropriate clearing adds immeasurably to a high-maintenance situation.**

Many homeowners look for a wooded space to build their home not only for wooded sites' natural beauty and air-conditioning attributes but also because they are inherently low-maintenance. But too many times I have seen sites transformed into a wasteland with the beautiful and cooling trees mostly gone; then, the homeowner is faced with an uphill battle of a high-maintenance situation.

Before buying land or settling on a house plan, realistically evaluate the repercussions of the building process on the much-valued surrounding trees. Consider not only *how many trees must be removed* but discuss with your builder *what does not need to be cleared*. At this juncture, a decision needs to be made. Will the integrity of the site be destroyed by the building process, or will the site support your dreams of the perfect house surrounded by the trees you desire? Because once existing trees are gone, an intense landscape installation must follow.

Just as important is the clean-up of the surrounding woods for a low-maintenance situation. Tragically, in a matter of hours a bobcat can create even more stress to the remaining trees by destroying twenty or more years of accumulated natural mulch, mutilating surface roots, and often tearing bark. Consequently, the health of each tree has been marginalized. The homeowner is now faced with a costly, labor-intensive struggle to remedy the situation. He must supply incredible, endless amounts of mulch to help these trees survive and will not know for years what will eventually recover and thrive.

See **Importance of Choice of Architect and Builder** *37*

Learn Names of Trees *104*

Trees – Three Categories *106*

Climax Forest *109*

Succession of Trees *102*

Natural Litter *106*

Photos *205, 345*

The amount of clearing is a major factor for low-maintenance. This homeowner, architect, and builder were all on the same page.

Mother Nature took 60 to 80 years to create this forest, laying down about an inch of topsoil. A bull-dozer takes only a few hours to remove it all.

This represents a nice thinning of trees for balance of light and the health of the forest. Natural litter has been left undisturbed for the continued health of the remaining trees.

Yes, they do have some lawn, just large enough to cut within 20 minutes. Then it's off to enjoy friends or remain home to putter in their garden.

4 Determining a proper final grade includes decisions regarding water drainage, identifying level areas for usable living space (including level walking paths around your homesite), and planning all fencing where mowing is expected. **Once these operations are completed, absolutely no construction debris should be left behind.**

First, grading *all* water away from the foundation of your home and off your property is *imperative*. When correctly done, the basement will be dry and plants will be ready to take hold in your landscape. If your site is not graded correctly, the basement or crawl-space will remain wet and plants will suffocate in water-saturated soil. Trying to overcome this obstacle is high maintenance of the first order. In many cases, a grader must also deal with water from surrounding properties. Just as you must deal with another's runoff, you will be sending your runoff downstream to your neighbors. (This is the time to ask your grader or contractor if he uses a transom because water runs only downhill.)

Second, grading out level spaces is essential for outdoor living spaces and walking paths. Any fencing which also requires mowing must also be considered. These decisions must be conveyed to your builder or machine operator right up front as part of your landscaping plans. Otherwise, attempting corrections later is nearly impossible and you will be left with undesirable sloping, unusable space and unmowable fencelines.

The last item should be spelled out in your contract. After all grading has been done, absolutely *no* debris (dirt piles mixed with other stuff) should be left on your property. Often these are found on the edges of woods or property lines. Most homeowners have no way to correct this situation, and these unsightly areas become some of the highest maintenance sore points I see.

The sidewalk was installed at a proper grade with sufficient backfill to create good surface drainage away from the house.

Buried drains past the sidewalk eliminate another potential water problem.

An extended plant bed allows a nice division from the guest parking and the Car Area.

The Car Area and front walk are essentially level but have just enough of a grade for good drainage.

Water drained underground is necessary, if not essential, in some situations as it is on this site. The problems can be many, but an inadequate size for both the intake opening and the underground drain pipe is often the biggest problem. Don't skimp on this decision.

This new construction is ready for water, both on-site and from neighboring sites. More plants to help stabilize the soil are being planted. Aboveground solutions to drainage issues have the least problems.

The parking spaces and lawn have been kept level for their best use.

No piles of debris were left for the new owners to deal with.

Note the beautiful, complementary choice of rocks in the drainage area.

Water coming off the bank behind the pool is easily directed to the right via a natural downward grade. However, due to the wall's height, drainage pipes were professionally installed behind the high stucco wall to relieve continual water pressure.

Water enters on the left and travels under the wood deck, emerging into a bed of flowers and a water-loving tree, and flows around the house. The decision not to use a pipe under a solid patio eliminated potential problems of 100-year flood rains and a continually clogged intake drain.

The choice of a deck made it necessary to build one step at each end. But many visual aids took care of this hazardous hardscape item.

This entire Outdoor Living Space was carved out from the steep backyard. Without this level space, enjoyment of the backyard would have been limited.

Another water drainage problem solved with an aboveground solution that will last over many years.

5 Limit plant selections that mature at less than 2 to 3 feet in height, especially ones with a sparse growth habit, to support a low-maintenance situation. **Even most groundcovers should be avoided unless they fulfill a needed role in the landscape. This means limiting gardening space for flowers and vegetables.**

Many plants less than two feet tall will not grow thickly enough to block out enough sun to prevent weeds from growing in large numbers. If there is a need for such plantings, choose those that naturally produce a thick mat. Often this means planting them rather close together to allow the growth process to mature quickly. Avoid plants that are naturally always loose. They will never block out enough sun, which allows weed seeds to germinate year after year.

Groundcovers are especially problematic. Often they are recommended to cover large expanses because someone thinks a particular space needs to be covered with plantings or the space itself will not support a healthy lawn. But when a groundcover becomes the home of every progeny of the surrounding natural world—weeds or otherwise—one has to think again whether this is a solution or another endless problem. Controlling large expanses from becoming a weed bed, which only hand weeding can control, is not low-maintenance. Again, the homeowner must think of how the chosen plant grows. Even if the "right" plant is chosen but somehow does not thrive in a particular site, rip it out and start over with one that will. Either do that or buy some of those knee pads, because you will need them.

By their nature, flower beds and vegetable gardens are high maintenance. The whole scene becomes one of constant change, planting, grooming, and especially weeding. For many, this activity is acceptable because caring for the garden is part of its joy. But if getting down on your knees and filling buckets with weeds on a continuous basis is not your thing, then remove these gardening activities off your list.

6 The solution to the need for color in the landscape can be found in the blooms and foliage of many shrubs and trees. **Removing most flower beds does not mean there will be no color for the homeowner to enjoy throughout the year.**

Every landscape professional always receives two requests from homeowners. The first is low-maintenance, and without exception, the second is color. I always find this an interesting problem because just what does a homeowner think when the word *color* is spoken. Often they are puzzled by their request. Most realize the Disney World-look is perhaps out of their reach—they just know they want color.

So if the homeowner also wants low-maintenance, then that means eliminating any major flower beds, especially ones with annuals that need to be replanted once or twice a year. Just how does this request get answered? Easy.

Many shrubs and trees bloom, and just as many have interesting foliage with all kinds of textures, color tints, and even flashy spring and fall displays. Others can be loaded with berries that attract birds each year looking for a good meal. For some people, even a plant's bark can produce a euphoric experience. (Trust me, that's true.) After eliminating those plants that take extraordinary care to thrive, the list is quite long in most areas. And if not, then a few tubs of annuals will satisfy your need for color.

The most important factor to selecting shrubs and trees that provide "color" throughout the year is to remember that most blooming plants seldom bloom for any long period. But then again, some do, so emphasize those types. Pick foliage for its interest; add some berried plants and throw in a bark type here and there, and any homeowner will be guaranteed "color" all year without the high maintenance of flower beds.

7 **Basic planting beds need soil that percolates. A site that holds too much water drowns plants; a site that holds too little water allows the plant to dry too fast, which kills it. Break up compacted soils to allow water to pass through. Add organic materials to loose soils to help water stay longer. If you have beautiful soil already, just feel lucky.**

Let us exclude the bog garden or the sandy, by-the-seashore garden. The basic, run-of-the-mill planting site needs the soil prepared so water filters through it like a coffee pot. The basic way to change this situation is to dig a proper hole (see the illustration on the next page) and possibly add organic material. The kind of organic material you choose to dig in will depend on your region and what you can get to your property handily.

The reason there is no basic recipe for these additional materials is that there is no basic soil condition found everywhere, even within a site or even a few feet from another site! Some people are blessed with old homesites and the soil is quite lovely. Others have new construction where there is absolutely no decent soil and every square inch has to be dug properly. In many cases, soil must be amended for any success (meaning bags or truckloads of organic materials added to the soil).

The end product must be a soil that both readily absorbs and releases water. This means organic materials *might* be added if the soil is dense; organic materials *must* be added if the soil is too sandy. In the first instance, pulverized soil and additional organic matter help break up the dense soil; in the latter, organic material helps hold the soil together.

Any added organic matter must be dug in deeply (get your pick-ax out if your soil is dense). I can't help but think of baking a cake but instead of mixing, the ingredients are dumped right into the pan; do you expect success? Well, you can't dump organic material on top of some pretty bad soil and expect any better results. Take a shovel and turn it over, crank up your tiller, or use a mattock, but somehow turn the soil with the added organic materials.

In the worst cases, you might have impenetrable subsoil. The shovel, tiller, or even a mattock will not go deep enough to break through this barrier. Perhaps you have heard of double digging? The soil is removed to a depth of a foot or two so that you can then dig even deeper to break up the compacted soil below. However, few of us can accomplish this feat. At the Barnsley Garden, the staff horticulturist—after being warned repeatedly of the need for percolation in our heavy, Georgia clay soil—used a backhoe to break up the subsoil. The rest of us will do well to get out our pick-ax and swing mightily, piercing the subsoil as deeply as we can, bringing up big clods of compacted soil and creating fissures for the amended soil to fill. This will allow rainwater to pass through instead of settling a few inches under your beautifully amended soil. You have broken the imperturbable plate and have created a sieve allowing your soil to percolate.

This is called preparing a bed, and it will often put you to bed! But once done, plants will thrive into lush, healthy specimens allowing the homeowner to get on with other chores or maybe take a trip to the beach.

I am often asked just what an amendment is. Usually it is organic material even though inorganic materials such as coarse rocks or expanded shale are considered an amendment. Organic material is any living matter or the remains of it. We are organic, leaves are organic, our food is organic, cow and horse manure is organic; rocks and metals are not organic. Amenders are often found in bags at your local nursery. They will be called Soil Conditioner, Sterilized Cow Manure, Composted Worm Castings, Composted Pine Bark, and so forth. They are used to change the composition of soil. They are *not* fertilizers but can often have some nutrients. It is their chemistry (you know, the class you avoided in school), which creates the necessary environment for plants to thrive. You do not need to understand the complex chemistry of the situation any more than you understand why aspirin works. Just know that by amending or changing the soil composition with organic materials, you will dramatically increase the viability of all your plantings—which means you will also dramatically increase your chances of getting a low-maintenance situation.

See **Water – Irrigation** *340*

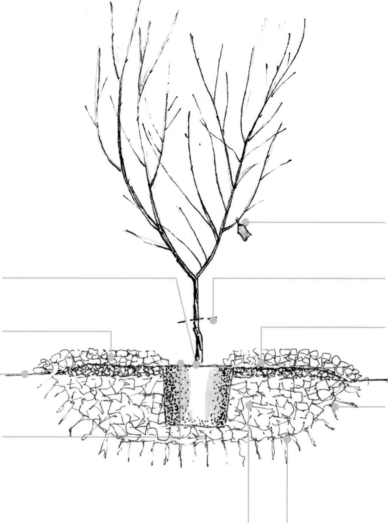

Remove the plant from its container and plant it immediately. Do not expose the plant's roots to sun or wind.

Upon planting, water the tree or shrub copiously. After digging the hole, fill it with water; as the soil is replaced, flood the site to ensure good contact between the new plant and the surrounding soil.

Do not mulch at the trunk base.

Spread two to four inches of mulch over the root area.

Soil Line

Never add soil on top of the existing soil in the container or root ball. It will smother the plant's roots.

Break up any compacted soil; then add it back with no amendments. There are a few exceptions to this rule.

Do not build a water well except on hillsides. If you build a well, tear it down after a few months; otherwise, the plant could drown in this pool of contained water.

Remove all cords, tags, wires, and similar items. They can girdle the plant and kill it.

If the plant is grafted, remove all suckers that are growing *below* the graft.

Plant the tree or shrub 1 to 2 inches high, adding soil to its sides.

Dig a wide hole, not so deep except when it's necessary to break up compacted soil. Most roots grow outward, not downward.

Slant the sides of the planting hole. Never leave the surface slick; it can create a barrier against good root penetration.

Initially, you should use a water hose or similar water source directly onto the plantings to keep them moist; automatic irrigation is often inadequate for the plant's initial needs. Water only as often as the plant needs it, allowing adequate time for a drying period for oxygen needs. If irrigation is used, you should continue the same pattern, timing the irrigation for a deep watering period then shutting it off for a drying out period. Otherwise, the plants will drown and die.

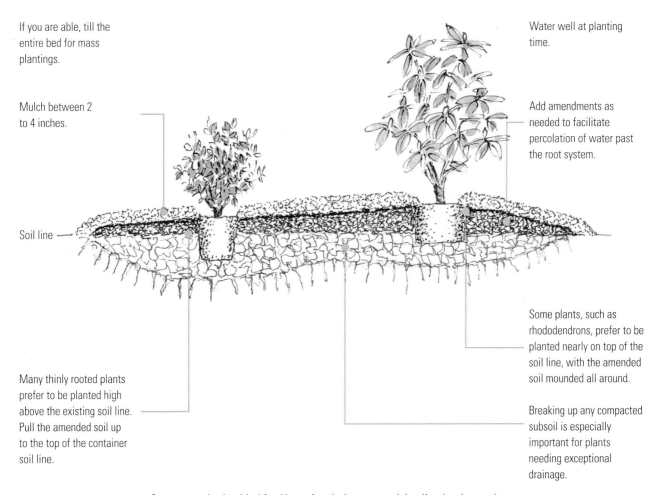

If you are able, till the entire bed for mass plantings.

Mulch between 2 to 4 inches.

Soil line

Many thinly rooted plants prefer to be planted high above the existing soil line. Pull the amended soil up to the top of the container soil line.

Water well at planting time.

Add amendments as needed to facilitate percolation of water past the root system.

Some plants, such as rhododendrons, prefer to be planted nearly on top of the soil line, with the amended soil mounded all around.

Breaking up any compacted subsoil is especially important for plants needing exceptional drainage.

Correct watering is critical for thin, surface-loving roots to thrive. Keeping them moist but never overly wet or soggy is the key to success. Once established after the first two or three years, with roots that extend farther out, these plants adapt to more variable conditions of dry and wet.

10 **Keep plants properly mulched until they are well established and eventually provide their own natural mulch. This will directly affect your maintenance chores.**

About two to four inches of loose natural materials such as pine straw, pine bark, and other locally available materials are essential to even out the effects of the sun, wind, and rain. Otherwise, plants can quickly dry out, even in a few hours, leaving the homeowner with a mess. The plants might die but usually just struggle. With mulch, soil stays at a more even temperature and remains moist, allowing plants to begin growing in their new environment.

Mulch also directly combats the detrimental effects of erosion. The impact of smashing raindrops is diffused, allowing water to be absorbed more easily by the ground. Without mulch, the smashing raindrops further pack surface soils so that absorption is thwarted even more. Eventually, many minor or major gullies develop. Trying to correct these numerous gullies or replace dying plants is truly a high-maintenance chore.

Finally, mulch can reduce weeding because it shades out a great deal of sunlight and the evenly moist soil makes pulling any weeds actually doable, especially after a good rain.

The best mulch is the natural litter found under established plantings and the trees on your property. Leaves and other debris collect on the surface and interact with myriad other organisms to provide the perfect mulch. This means a homeowner should *not* rake leaves from under trees, or bag or burn them, leaving the ground bare. And bringing in "pretty" mulch to replace those "ugly" leaves is contrary to every ecological tenet we know to be so important to our environment. Plus, leaving the existing natural mulch is cheap and is quite effective as a perfect low-maintenance situation.

See **Erosion** *108*

Birds – Food *374*

Flowers – Need for Mulch *154*

Photos *97, 205*

11 **Improperly applied mulch increases maintenance chores. Likewise, a poor choice of mulch increases the potential for problems.**

Burying plants under too much mulch will produce a negative outcome. What two to four inches of mulch does is diffuse and ameliorate the elements. More can suffocate and kill the plants.

No mulch should be applied at the bases of tree trunks any closer than three to six inches out. Many critters, bugs, and diseases thrive under these wonderful conditions and could perhaps harm the tree in the process. This unmulched, "clean" area allows good visibility to quickly assess whether there are any problems. Plus, it's drier for better bug and disease control. But what should not be ignored is mulching the tree's root space, which could be two to three feet or more in all directions. Roots in this surrounding area need that all-important equalizer—mulch.

The wrong mulch can also be detrimental. Some homeowners try to use grass clippings or other products that pack down, creating another situation that is dry and suffocates plantings. This mulch might be the necessary depth of two to four inches, but because it creates a tight mat, water does not penetrate.

(12) Fertilizing is a major component of a low-maintenance landscape. This is especially true for the first years of new plantings, lawn care, and any annuals. But too often because of their perceived complexity, fertilizers are avoided, leaving plants to struggle, which forces a homeowner into a high-maintenance situation.

Plants need food to thrive. Obviously a healthy plant growing right along is what every homeowner wants. Less time is spent trying to administer first aid or pulling weeds between anemic shrubs. So why does this neglect occur? Besides the time factor, another reason might be the endless, confusing choices. Flower food but what kind? Shrubs, trees, and specific fertilizers such as ones for hollies and azaleas? Lawn food? The wrong answer here has big repercussions.

The basic underlying principle is to feed plants when they are *actively growing:*

- When winter ends, shrubs and trees are waking up and putting on new growth. Feed them. Pick a general all-purpose fertilizer and throw it out. Do not worry about a particular plant; just feed them all.

- Notice your lawn's growth habits. Some grass types like to grow only in summer, and other kinds prefer to grow in fall, winter, and spring. Feed each of these only when they are growing; otherwise, you will be stressing them.

- Flowers are either perennial (which come back every year) or annual (which last six to eight months). Perennials don't like much feeding; annuals thrive on good doses throughout the season as they burst forth with constant blooms. If they are planted together, just dish out the food as best you can.

Many homeowners keep it simple. Every winter or early spring they buy a certain number of bags of a slow-release all-purpose fertilizer and broadcast it over all their shrubs and trees, and even throw some on perennial beds. Their next concern is the lawn. Once they know the type of grass they have, they watch for that good new growth and feed, maybe once and maybe some more throughout the season. When annuals are planted, they mix in some more slow-release fertilizer to feed continuously for the next several months of active growth.

The goal, of course, is low-maintenance, and I have just told you to buy bags of fertilizer and spend time throwing it out. But the alternative to *not* doing this is to spend even more time trying to nurse ailing plants, perhaps replacing them, and figuring out what to do about all those weeds where lush plants should have been. Those are the high-maintenance chores we are trying to avoid.

I have two important things to share. First, *broadcast* all fertilizer because it is often caustic and any concentration of it will burn. Have you ever spilled some and watched the grass immediately die? It is hard to get anything to grow there afterwards. Have you ever felt its caustic burn on your hands? Have you seen it burn the leaves of plants that were damp when the fertilizer stuck to them? So throw it out, but never pile it up around anything you are trying to help. Second, fertilizer needs of most shrubs and trees will diminish as their natural feeding program kicks in. This might take a few years. But the need for food every season never goes away for your lawn or annual flowers.

See **Grass** *353*
   Perennials, Annuals *151*

13 **Watering for successful plants begins at the planting site.** After the hole is correctly dug and properly amended, flood it with water before, during, and after the plant is in the ground. Monitor to assess how often it must be watered during the first growing season until it is stabilized in its environment.

The medium that is used to grow a plant for a nursery is quite different from the soil in your garden, plus the roots are growing in an unnatural spiral. Your goal is to combine the growing medium and the surrounding soil so the plant starts growing.

Start by watering the hole to make sure it is fully saturated; once the plant and soil are added, trying to water this underground area will be next to impossible. As you shovel soil back in around the nursery plant during planting, water some more, forcing a direct contact between these two completely different mediums. When all soil is shoveled in around the plant, finish with one more watering. This means have a hose or big watering cans available for each planting.

The frequency of watering afterwards depends on the time of year and how quickly your soil dries out. Obviously, most homeowners prefer to plant when the weather is cool and the plants are in a more dormant stage of growth. Watering is lessened because the climate is not wicking away all moisture on long, hot days during active growth. When you do water, which could be often in hot, dry months, check the nursery-grown root area for dryness, not the surrounding soil. After one or two checks, you can determine just how fast your plants tend to dry out, and water accordingly.

Note that rainwater will seldom be adequate for new plantings. They must be watered *by hand directly on* the nursery-grown root area. This means standing at one plant with a hose for about one-half to a full minute (think how long it takes to fill a bucket of water). Don't water again until the plant needs it because all plants need to dry out some between waterings or they will drown. I see more plants die from too much water with the overuse of an irrigation system or unprepared waterlogged soil than from any other factor. But once firmly established and with correct watering, these plants will survive on their own, creating as low a maintenance situation as anyone could ask for.

See **Irrigation** *339*

Locate plants where they grow best; otherwise, you will endlessly fight for their health and viability. Identify peculiarities of your plant choice (sun, shade, dry, wet, etc.) and try to match the plant to your site.

Plants really can talk. If you plant them where they don't like it, they pout, turn nasty colors, get sick, refuse to bloom, and can even die. People will return to nurseries and ask, "Why did my plant die, or why does it look so sick?" The same reasons apply to why some plants die or look sick at the nursery. Something is going wrong with its environment, affecting its roots, which control the top part you see.

Every plant has a built-in tolerance for cultural conditions. Some are so picky that it is a wonder they grow anywhere. Others are so tough they will survive the lowest bid on the job. One prefers a concrete crack; another would prefer a lot of boggy water. Some take only shade; their friends will go either way—just please give them a little time to adjust. Why do you think gardeners are always moving their plants? They are looking for the perfect, happy place for their beloved flower or shrub. And by the way, as the nearby tree matures, that sunny spot will be in complete shade a few years hence.

But if you're a low-maintenance guy, pick plants that you know are happy campers wherever you plant them. But read the label and know that if the plant tag notes "shade," then hot broiling sun will not make it happy. And if the tag reads "sun," don't walk around to the north side of your home and plug it into a dark corner. Even the hardiest plants can die from the old standby—too much or too little water while they are getting established.

The main point is that plants that are happy in their appointed environment are usually quite healthy, leaving you the homeowner with a low-maintenance situation since you are not their nurse maid. If you have turned into Nurse Nancy, the choice is yours: Either move the plant to a site it prefers or remove it.

Part of the job description of a landscape architect or designer is to tell a homeowner it is perfectly alright to throw away a plant. This is really a big struggle with many homeowners. They will hang on to the ugliest plants that have no place in their landscape and just cannot bring themselves to do what should be so obvious. In their struggle to salvage certain plants, they bring on themselves an unending high-maintenance situation. Learn to bite the bullet and get into a low-maintenance mode of operation by removing plants that are not thriving no matter what you do.

See **Plants Make Liars Out of You** *89*
Planting Zones *28*

Some like it hot… Some like it cool…

15 **Memorize your planting zone (hardiness zone) along with your Social Security number. This information should be found on the tag of every plant you choose to buy for your garden.**

Many government and private entities worked together to formulate the Hardiness Zone chart, which actually is constantly being evaluated for any necessary changes. Additionally, horticulturists evaluate plants as to how they will succeed within certain zones. Since plants are so variable, their ability to thrive in many different situations varies also. This information is printed on a plant tag to take some of the guesswork out of the decision to buy a plant for your particular Hardiness Zone.

Planting zone charts are found in nearly every plant book. Where you live determines your zone. Zones range from 1 to 11; Zone 1 is very cold such as parts of Alaska while Zone 11 is in Hawaii. I live in Atlanta, Georgia, so I am in Zone 7. Hardiness zones are based on the range of average annual minimum temperatures—how cold it gets.

Of course, we all know that the biggest dividing line is the freezing point of water—32 degrees Fahrenheit. Obviously this is a big factor with many plants. Just a degree above or below can determine the life of a plant. If only it were just that simple in the plant world! Instead, many plants, even those within the same group, such as camellias, can be affected by temperatures up and down the thermometer. The 32-degree point is not the only dividing line. Some will live with some more cold, but at some critical point, a particular plant will not be able to live. In fact, many hybrids are cultivated to extend the survivability of a plant into colder and conversely warmer regions than normally expected.

But in all of this confusion, just know that buying a plant out of your Hardiness Zone will be risky. This information is to help avoid this costly situation *unless* you are knowingly willing to try the plant anyway. Gardeners do that all the time.

USDA Plant Hardiness Zone Map

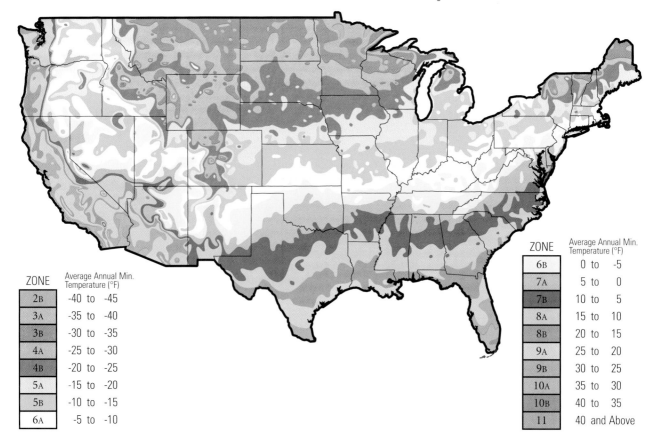

ZONE	Average Annual Min. Temperature (°F)
2B	-40 to -45
3A	-35 to -40
3B	-30 to -35
4A	-25 to -30
4B	-20 to -25
5A	-15 to -20
5B	-10 to -15
6A	-5 to -10

ZONE	Average Annual Min. Temperature (°F)
6B	0 to -5
7A	5 to 0
7B	10 to 5
8A	15 to 10
8B	20 to 15
9A	25 to 20
9B	30 to 25
10A	35 to 30
10B	40 to 35
11	40 and Above

16 **Although planting zones are associated with cold hardiness, other factors are now deemed as important for a plant to succeed.**

Planting zones often appear in diverse parts of the country. My own Zone 7 appears in eastern California, down into areas of Utah and Arizona, crosses a large area in Texas, appears again through the South, and is found again upward in Virginia and Maryland. But if anyone travels in these areas, you know the climate is certainly different in many respects. Some of them have hot days and cool nights; others have low humidity. Sometimes soil composition is quite different from others in the same zone, and rainfall comes at different intervals and amounts. That is a lot of stuff to consider besides average temperatures, especially freezing ones.

Over the years I have tried to grow many different flowers. I look at the planting zone first, but more often than not, I look to see how the new plant performs in my neighbor's garden or at a test garden. The same flower in the dry, hot days and cold nights of the West often will not stand up to my muggy, hot 24-hour-a-day climate. An area that has hot days and cool nights gives plants a chance to recover for the next day. But other regions have nights that are never cool. The same plant is never given that much-needed rest in those regions.

Humidity can vary from very dry in the Southwest to a sticky wet in the South. Constant high humidity gives diseases and insects a great environment to thrive, and culturally many plants just don't enjoy all that heavy moisture in the air. Even season length can influence results. Obviously the more northern latitudes have shorter growing seasons while the more southern latitudes have seemingly endless months to enjoy many of the same plants.

Additionally, microclimates can be found in pockets of a region and even in one's backyard. Somehow a combination of factors creates a climate that allows a gardener to grow something that perhaps his neighbor cannot.

But for most of us, learning our planting zone gives us a big step up in deciding on buying a certain plant. If your budget is tight, why spend time and money on a plant that very pointedly says on its label that it does not survive in your area.

If a much desired plant is not listed for your zone, the best advice is to try it and enjoy the gamble. A few good mild winters could be in your future and the enjoyment of a great plant in your garden. I've had many customers tell me of certain lantanas that reappear each summer; the same with agapanthus, and for others begonias. I know and they know that one hard winter will cut them short, but in the meantime they are enjoying these repeat performers.

Just a reminder, planting zones do not address freak weather situations. The acceptance of our natural world is all part of gardening. Many years ago in my area, a severe freeze of 6 degrees below zero devastated many plants. My garden club happened to have scheduled a wonderful old lady who was to discuss her collection of camellias, some fifty to sixty years old. She sat there very composed and very much a lady describing their wholesale death. But somehow, I got the feeling that as a true gardener she expressed hope. I remember hearing a couple of years later that many of these fine specimens had sprung from seemingly dead roots and were recovering mightily.

See **Use Local Sources** *90*
Tried and True *150*
Native/Tough *37*

You never know where it will grow!

17 Check the habits (blooms, fruit, roots, etc.) of your plant choices. **A beautiful plant in the wrong place can greatly affect your maintenance chores.**

This is one high-maintenance item that more and more homeowners are homing in on. "No crape myrtles near my pool—what a mess." "The roots of that river birch will cause too much of a problem near this driveway." "I don't want rotten fruit on my patio." "Those leaves will get into my gutters."

The problem in my job is that nearly all plants are messy in some way, with some messier than others. Just how far does one narrow the category of "messy" to fit the person who wants a low-maintenance landscape on a daily basis?

The only answer I can give is to move a beloved plant but obvious offender to the background to be seen but not experienced. And put those plants that are better behaved in more high-use areas. If the property does not have a good spot for that desired but messy plant, remove it from your "want" list or try to find a good substitute if low-maintenance is a high priority.

In my area, the huge, old-fashioned magnolia gets the biggest reaction. "Don't ever put that thing in my design. It's a mess. I had to rake those leaves all year long." But of course this same beautiful tree planted just inside a forest edge where its offending leaves are of no concern makes it a wonderful choice as a large evergreen screen. Plants just need to be situated where their habits are acknowledged. Maintenance chores can then be greatly reduced.

See **Trash Trees** *100*
    Character Trees *82*
    Photo *39*

BOINNGG!! Some trees are dangerous and messy!

18 **Invasive plant materials should be carefully evaluated before planting. A bad choice here is probably the Number One cause of a high-maintenance situation.**

Many plants have a rampant growth pattern or self-seed mercilessly. You know many of these culprits such as ivy, bamboo, and certain lawn grasses. With every landscape choice, the first question you should ask is: How does this plant grow? If the term "invasive" fits in the description, do not think in your wildest dreams that you can control it easily. If you must choose them, place them where their uncontrolled habits are—if not exactly welcomed—at least properly sited for the least damage with the option for future controls in place.

The biggest dilemma I have owning a nursery is making plants available that I know are considered invasive. One person takes home English ivy and designs a lovely container garden. But just as certain this same person will use it in her landscape because she just can't throw anything away. Years later, the mess is there to be cleaned up. I want to carry only the tidy American wisteria, but seldom is it even available. Perhaps the customer who buys the Asian type knows to keep it under control; many do, but many don't. Even in the natural world around us, my dear dogwoods and oaks self-seed unmercifully. And my gloriosa daisies have spread like wildfire over a bank, joining other rampant growers. In fact, most plants will become invasive if the situation is ripe for their peculiar needs.

The trick is to not knowingly introduce anything that will take over. You know bamboo is horrible. You know ivy and wisteria are troublemakers. So don't allow them on your property. Believe me, you will have enough to keep you busy without adding troublemakers.

See **Perennials – Invasive** *136*
Tough vs. Exotic *37*
Grass – Invasive Types *354*
Borders – Mortared Solid *182*

Mother gave me that little piece of ivy twenty years ago.

19 **Slopes and banks are major high-maintenance situations. Your first choice is to leave any established slopes undisturbed. If they must be cleared, vigorous plantings are emphatically recommended over thin, very low plantings.**

Slopes and banks laid bare by construction must have immediate, intense attention if the area is to be controlled for erosion, be made attractive, and eventually be a lower-maintenance situation. I often see little plugs of creeping stuff such as ivy and thin, low-growing junipers massed over huge spaces. But light and water quickly bring life to dormant weed seeds, and these unwieldy slopes must then be weeded. The homeowner hopes that the bank will soon be covered with vegetation to choke out the weeds. But because the chosen plants are small and sparse even at maturi-ty, the problem never goes away and only intensifies.

One must recognize that the way to accomplish all of these goals—control erosion, increase beauty, and encourage low-maintenance—is to choose tough plants that mature at least one to two or more feet in height and also grow thickly. Most plant selections should be even taller to block out the sun reaching weed seeds. Even when some weeds do grow in this environment, it's possible either to pull them or to spray with a selective herbicide. Maintenance chores continue to be reduced as this thicket takes over, blocking out the sun and controlling water run-off. If a little thought is put into this whole situation, the site can be a really beautiful addition to your landscape.

See **Slopes Planted** *180*
      Photo *272*

This slope is maintained with partly controlled native materials and a few new tough additions. Herbicides are used sparingly and selectively to control certain destructive weeds such as briars and alders. But like most slopes and banks, it is never a low-maintenance situation.

22 **Know the mature sizes of plants before planting. If any plant grows too big for the space you have, your maintenance chores will never end and in fact will accelerate as the plant matures. Correct choices are particularly critical for foundation plantings and those under power lines.**

There are two groups of homeowners: One is new to the landscaping world and looks in wonder at every plant in their yard. The second group has lived in their home for several years and is aghast at how big and overwhelming all those cute little shrubs have grown. The first group needs a crash course on the horticultural world—watch out, plants grow! The second group wants to do as much damage control as possible—remove, move, and anything else to get out of their mess. If starting over, they do not wish to repeat what had happened before.

Plants are genetically coded to reach a certain size. If a plant is programmed to be fifteen or so feet tall and wide but you want to keep it three to four feet, here is what happens. The first few years keeping the plant about this size is fine because it's young. But the plant's roots keep growing, trying to fulfill its destiny. The trunk gets bigger and bigger, the root system keeps expanding, and it starts putting out more leaves. The once or twice a year shearing now becomes an every other week affair. The homeowner is now in a high-maintenance mode just about the time he wants to go into low gear.

To eliminate this mess from your life's chores, research all plants, especially ones planned around your house or under a power line, and select something that will best fill that space. Nothing is perfect, but you should try to get within the ballpark. Tipping back a five- to six-foot plant to three to four feet is quite acceptable. But if the tag says it matures at fifteen to twenty feet, well…choose your poison.

Plants are not precise in their growth habits. When reading about a plant, a homeowner might note a particular plant will be described as maturing at six to ten feet, sometimes as tall as twenty four feet. I have seen some species struggle in one spot but in another site grow far beyond what anyone could have imagined. This is definitely not an exact science, but

you must still make the best decision possible. For instance, a 'Nellie R. Stevens' holly located three feet from your carport when it requires a minimum ten-foot diameter space will not work—*ever*.

The other problem is the limited number of plants that grow less than four feet tall, which is the requirement for many foundation plantings. Compound this situation by considering their cultural needs and whether they are evergreen or hardy. All of these factors limit the choices even more. This often results in making the best choice with what is available, knowing some maintenance will be necessary. I often have to tell homeowners I can name four plants for their site and only two of those will be acceptable.

The biggest obstacle is the need for homeowners who are not willing to wait for the "what comes next" axiom to have "real" plants out front—something big—for immediate impact. But homeowners who have witnessed an overgrown, high-maintenance situation do not wish to repeat this mistake. They take a deep breath as they look down at their tiny little bushes and know they will be just fine; they just need a little care and a little time to grow. They want low-maintenance.

See **Pruning, Shearing** *114, 115*

    Local Sources *90*

    Utility – Power Lines *331*

    Shape Desired *121*

    Photo *230*

Maybe we should trim the foundation plants this year!

23 **Weed control during the first three years is imperative.** This maintenance chore will never go away but should lessen as plants establish and fill in their allotted space, covering as much bare ground as allowed.

Besides mulch, what are the different controls for weeds? I must say that putting down a weed barrier is not a long-term control. They allow water and fertilizer to pass through this mesh, *but* as the years go by, the mulch decomposes into topsoil. The roots below try to reach up into this wonderful stuff but cannot. I often see these massed, dried-out roots and the suffering plants as a result. In the meantime, weeds are growing in the mulch on top of this weed barrier with their roots stretched out in all directions. When they are pulled, half the mulch comes with them. The expense and effort trying to remedy the situation is incredible; the weed mat is now buried and enmeshed with the dying plants and their roots.

The alternative? Spread out newspapers over newly planted beds. Spread the mulch over that. The newspapers will block out the sun, cutting out weed production, but these papers will slowly break down and join the soil in a natural mix.

There are enough chemicals on the market that one would have to write another book to describe them all. Some chemicals are applied before weeds appear—they are called *preemergent.* Other chemicals are applied after weeds appear—they are called *postemergent.* Added to that are chemicals that are selective and kill only what is listed on their labels, meaning you can spray an entire bed. There are nonselective herbicides that kill every green plant they touch.

A very important point for low-maintenance is to allow plants to grow more naturally into the shapes and sizes for which they are destined until there is no space between them. This denies light to the soil surface, and many fewer weeds will emerge. By trimming plants into individual specimens, the spaces in-between are fair game for weeds—forever. This motif might be fine when there are ten or fifteen plants involved or one has an outstanding maintenance crew coming by weekly, but not for the normal low-maintenance situation.

24 **Set stone or gravel into concrete for low-maintenance drives or walkways.** Loose stone or gravel drives and walks are high-maintenance items. Loose stone or gravel used as mulch will also become maintenance albatrosses.

Only nostalgia or necessity makes loose stone or gravel surfaces appropriate. Weeds will quickly mar the beautiful natural look these stones afford in the landscape. If one is looking for low-maintenance, press these stones into concrete where weeds cannot add another chore to your too-long list of gardening needs.

Usually these architectural elements hark back to days-gone-by, but behind each of these old stone walks and driveways was a maintenance man making sure they stayed weed free and neat. If you have one of those rare persons, pay no attention to me. But if you are the typical, hardworking homeowner I see every day, do yourself a favor and put that loose stone, gravel, or bricks in a bed of concrete.

Loose stones are also used as mulch. I cannot say too much aesthetically because that is a personal decision, but on the maintenance scale of 1 to 10, this will become a 10 except in arid regions. Elsewhere, debris will constantly collect between these stones, decomposing and allowing little unwanted things to grow. One can pull and one can spray, but one will always be pulling and spraying. And as the stone discolors, it will need refreshing. But stone is heavy and even matching your previous selection might be a problem. People have often come by my nursery looking for this and that color stone, only to find that each manufacturer has changed its mind about what they want to carry, which leaves homeowners with a real time-consuming dilemma. Perhaps building a quaint stone wall will satisfy this need for stone.

See **Loose Materials** *192*

25 The use of native plant materials is often mentioned as an important ingredient for low-maintenance. **However, most homeowners are confusing the terms** *native* **with** *tough.*

There is no magic in the use of native plants for a low-maintenance landscape. Native plants, just like all plants around our world, are site specific and have various degrees of hardiness. Thankfully, native plant societies are creating a much-needed awareness of what they are and how to use them. By using their websites, any homeowner can download a list of suggested plants for a bog, a hot dry hill, or a woodland glade and hopefully find these plants in a local nursery. He can then decide if and how he might use them in his landscape. As he looks closer at the issue, he will discover a truly complex world and begin to wonder where they all are since they are native. (Actually those were some of the plants the bulldozer took away.)

Of course the answer is that many natives have been overrun by nonnative plants. Many books have been written describing how these invasives—both by accident and transplanted—have transformed our landscape so that it has little relevance to what our forefathers saw. Even now, newer invasives are pushing around our landscape as we know it today.

So can we push back the clock four or five hundred years and recover our original paradise? No, but we can all be aware of saving what we have and even push the envelope back where possible. It means to be aware of nonnative plants that threaten to be so invasive and disruptive to our landscape that eradication might be in order. I hope you will decide not to use them in your landscape.

The reality of this dilemma is that there are many fine nonnative plants that most homeowners want on their site. They have various degrees of hardiness, and most are not detrimental. They also can be tough and just as important as many natives for a low-maintenance landscape. Carefully studying the attributes of plants from either group should be your guide.

26 The selection of a builder and an architect (if using one) will be a major determining factor to achieve the goal of creating a low-maintenance situation.

There are many fine architects and builders, but some have more awareness of how land should be used to maximize its qualities with the house to be built. If you are quite serious about your forest or open spaces and how your home will relate to your land, choose this person carefully.

These professionals should be able to advise you on how a particular house plan will work, what adjustments need to be made to get good outcomes, how to work with your particular piece of land, and how to maintain as much of its integrity as possible. These considerations will markedly affect the outcome of creating a low-maintenance situation.

What you do not want is to say: "I bought this lot because of the beautiful trees and not one is left!" "That stream out back had loads of native azaleas and ferns; now they are gone." "I had this nice natural area with trees but they cleaned it up and now I have mud everywhere!" "I had no idea the steps to my front door would be so high!" "There is not one flat area for us to enjoy the yard." "Our basement and backyard stay wet all the time." …And so on.

Find a builder who demonstrates an ability to work with your plans and with your site to leave you with the best possible scenario. This part of the puzzle is extremely important for creating a low-maintenance landscape. Remember, this person is on-site and directs workers throughout the building process. If you two are on the same page, many maintenance problems will be eliminated upfront.

27 **Not maintaining a landscape creates a high-maintenance situation. Remember, plants and the hardscape are quite reactive and dynamic. To ignore them is to allow problems to get bigger and much more expensive to correct.**

Too many times when a homeowner does not correct problems in his landscape, he thinks the problems will lie dormant until he sells or decides to respond. Unfortunately, this is not true. Instead the landscape actually continues to deteriorate, causing increasingly more drastic measures necessary to remedy the situation.

For instance, tree seedlings are Nature's way to refurbish the earth. They emerge everywhere—sometimes in sidewalk cracks, too close to a driveway or a house, or too close together. They might also be the wrong tree for the site. I have witnessed massive trees totally overpower a house, creating a horrible situation. If only the homeowner had recognized these tiny little sprigs were really the wrong plants for that location. Now he is paying thousands of dollars to have them removed and thousands more to repair broken concrete and a mildewed house. If he had only pulled or cut them down when they were small. Oh well.

Another problem occurs when landscape plants are left to simply survive. No mulch and no fertilizer are applied; therefore, the plants decline and weeds take over. If you have ever had to remedy a situation like this, you know how terribly difficult it is. A great deal of labor and money is expended to just get back to square one. In fact, when homeowners get a price for clean-up, they are appalled that this cost is often more than that of their expected new landscape.

Ignoring other environmental concerns also adds immeasurably to high maintenance. For instance, by refusing to address a problem such as bare earth washing downhill and downstream, which dumps choking raw earth into all the wrong places, you'll soon have a problem of monumental proportions. I have seen all kinds of corrective measures using large, expensive equipment taken just to get a site back to some kind of order. Often the damage is already done and all one can do is stop it from continuing.

Even keeping miscellaneous items picked up—either storing them in a proper site or throwing them away—is a major concern if the beauty and function of your beautiful landscape are important. Maybe it is time to get that storage shed built or make a few runs to the local dump. Otherwise, you'll constantly be dodging items while mowing, containers will become mosquito maternity wards, and too many out-of-use things will become a burden. Then, the landscape is no longer enjoyable.

Many books abound with glorious photos, but the reality is that all ideas for your landscape must stand the test of time. low-maintenance starts with recognizing the best site for your personal lifestyle with the knowledge that you must maintain the land. Without vigilance, your dreams will be buried.

See **Too Much Land** *12*

Too Many Projects *13*

Trash Walls *110*

Invasives *31*

Succession of Forest *102*

Unnecessary Fences *34*

Outbuildings – Need for Storage *292*

Items Dotted Over the Landscape *34*

Plant Choices – Bad *30*

How a home relates to the outdoors is personal. Be sure your house plan and the choice of your site come together to unify this relationship.

Every house plan must relate to the outdoors. Every door exits *somewhere* and how each exit relates to the outside is very personal. Making sure your exits meet your needs should be a number one priority before you start building.

For example, one couple has a house sitting up high overlooking a mountainside. They have no plans to actually walk on this rather steep hillside except for casual maintenance. An interior staircase to the basement is just fine, so an elaborate staircase from their deck to the land below is left off their plans. More important for them will be a quick and easy access from their parking area into their living space.

Another family may have kids who need easy exits to go outside to play. The exits are located off the major living area and kitchen with only a few steps to the ground level. If the exit is too intimidating, such as long, narrow steps at the end of a long,

narrow deck, casual departures will be greatly diminished, much to the mother's chagrin.

This is the time to sit down with your contractor and landscape designer/architect and ask this question: Are my needs of how I want my home to integrate with the outdoors going to be met with *this* design on *this* site? Remember, adjustments in design can be made by entertaining different approaches. In many cases, money can be saved because the unplanned-for-problems were averted upfront and expensive down-the-road corrections were avoided. But more important, your ideas for your house plan and the outdoors have come together to be all you wanted them to be.

See **Distance to Supplies** *296*
Distance to Restrooms *300*
Lighting *334*
Entertainment in One Place *243*
No One Step *274*
Exit Doors to Outside *263*
Circulation *186*
Photo *210*

Downsizing for this maturing couple included some important features: Room was found for an on-grade entrance and main living space; a small garden site was located on the corner; a lovely outdoor patio in back and a side play yard were included for grandchildren.

A large Significant Tree with Trash Tree qualities was removed and a better choice planted in this constricted space. There are plenty of shade trees in back shading the hot southern exposure.

Incorporate all essential outdoor uses of space into an overall design before making any decision to buy a piece of property and especially before siting the house and starting construction.

Most elements for outdoor uses demand enormous amounts of space. Usually the first consideration is space for cars. The square footage for this element alone is often *more* than the square footage of the house. When other elements such as patios, play-scapes, swimming pools, and workshops are added, their space requirements and interaction with the home become additional major considerations.

The accommodation of cars is of primary importance. The essential elements necessary for a satisfactory outcome are quite numerous: space to enter and exit; auxiliary parking for family and guests; level landing pads; driveway access to the home for function and beauty; how the drive relates to the front walk; and so on. These are both expensive and critical decisions that—once made—can seldom be changed. Hoping everything will "just work out" might force corrective measures that will be very costly and give unsatisfactory results.

Because of its magnitude and how it profoundly affects your overall landscape, be sure you sit down with your contractor to evaluate the whole parking picture to eliminate unwelcome surprises at the end. The additional input of a good landscape designer/architect can aid in this decision-making process. It is important to note that contractors build houses and landscape designers/architects deal with outdoor space. Both are concerned with its function and beauty. Combining the expertise of both should help achieve a good outcome.

Other space allocations could include a workshop or barn, dog pen, play area, swimming pool, or maybe a vegetable garden. Sit down and make your own list. Then see how a particular house design will work on a piece of property and how it works with your wish list. I'm thinking of some of the situations I have been asked to help solve. The workshop was going to be perfect "right there," but the covenants of the subdivision didn't allow it. The dog pen needed to be on one side of the yard, but the doggy door was built on the opposite side of the house. A steep grade made having a level play area a Herculean and very expensive task. The swimming pool and the septic system were not coordinated. The too-wooded lot made vegetable gardening only a patio venture.

We all expect to make compromises. But if the essential outdoor elements plus your wish list were considered at the initial planning stage and not left to chance at the end, the number of compromises could be greatly reduced.

All elements were planned at the beginning of this construction. The screened porch means there's no open deck facing the hot sun. The secondary carport/workshop is located to one side and is architecturally complementary. The ornamental pond is set back from the upper porch for good visibility and enjoyment of the sound of water. The enclosed lawn was built with a low wall and shrubs for the grandchildren to play.

No items such as these bird houses should be out in the lawn where they create a lawn mowing nuisance.

This wall was specified to be built about 17 inches high to double as seating.

The bed lines are broad, easy to maintain, direct traffic, and create rooms in this landscape.

Additional seating is provided by the wall surrounding the putting green.

Tucked up on the far side of the lawn, the putting green and the summerhouse are for all to enjoy.

30 **The architectural design elements of the home should dominate all other elements in the landscape, especially hardscape elements, which should complement the whole.**

Hardscapes in the landscape encompass many different elements in the overall design. A few examples include paving, workshops, gazebos, arbors, fences, barns, sheds, swimming pools, and pool houses. These are all "hard," are permanent, and quite prominent. When adding each one to the whole, they should complement each other but, more important, complement the main structure, the home, in many different ways such as in color tones and architectural features.

When a homeowner finds himself floundering in this category, it is time to call in an experienced professional landscape architect or designer. Too often when talking to contractors and suppliers, a homeowner might be drawn into making a decision on a fence or perhaps a shed that looks quite good standing alone but does not complement the house. These are expensive and permanent mistakes.

For example, a Victorian-style gazebo is installed behind a classic Williamsburg-style home. A workshop is built with a low, unappealing roof line and inexpensive metal siding behind a 4000-square-foot home. Sidewalk stone has color tones of orange, pink, and coral, but the stone on the house is a subtle gray. A stamped concrete driveway leading to a beautiful home is distracting because the home contains a great many patterns already.

Decisions in building a home are hard enough though usually people have a professional architectural layout to help them. But these plans do not include decisions in the landscape, especially hardscape elements. My advice is to consider the whole—each element should contribute to the main event, which is the house. And, if in doubt, seek professional guidance. It will be money well spent.

This open carport is a major architectural complement to the beautiful home.

Proper thinning and limbing up of these Ornamental Trees add immeasurably to this landscape.

A certain degree of enclosure creates a much-appreciated space. The addition of the railing at the carport accomplishes this beautifully.

The restored gardens of this historic Greek revival home include a rotunda of complementary classic columns viewed from the homeowner's main living area.

30

The major removal of large, unattractive, dying trees blocking the view of the home and major pruning of the classic boxwoods required a stout heart on the homeowner's part. But the results demonstrate that what seemed drastic paid off with a stunning landscape. It did take the boxwoods several years to fully recover, but the wait was worth it.

30

31   Incorporate permanent "borrowed views" into your design plans.

Many times a house site will overlook lakes, large lowlands or mountains not suitable for building, easements, a city skyline, or just a pretty neighborhood. Mark these views to be incorporated into your plans. Don't ignore a million dollars' worth of incredible real estate. Sit down with your architect or your set of plans and have this on the top of your goals—a free million-dollar view.

I suggest taking a ruler to draw a line on your plan. Begin where you will spend most of your time inside the house and extend this line to your view or multiple views beyond your property lines. Work on that plan until this line connects these two points.

But there is a catch—this view must be permanent. One person I know built a "glass" house overlooking the Atlanta skyline. The open area that allows this vista incorporates a large park. He is quite sure no changes will ever obstruct his view and his whole house has been completely oriented to it. In another situation, I helped a couple from the foothills of the Georgia mountains. They showed me a picture of "their" mountain but also in the picture was a row of cypress trees their neighbors had planted on his property line. Soon "their" view will be gone. So the keyword is *permanent*.

See **Unnecessary Screening** *68*
    Fences *309*
    Duty of Plant Choice *64*
    Symmetry *92, 94*
    Plan Use of Outdoor Space *40*

A combination of different plantings gives interest to the landscape.

Screening was necessary both on the left and right, but the center looked on the neighbor's lovely back yard allowing for a borrowed view. The bed lines pull the eye right on through.

The view is open from the house to the neighbor's backyard.

This formal garden was constructed on a level space.

Never share a project with another property owner. If you must, do so with detailed legal accountability in place.

From time to time, I have observed various projects shared by property owners. But here's what usually happens: years later, the history of the now-deteriorating fence is lost; a lake owned by several people needs its dam repaired for safety; a retaining wall between two properties is now falling down.

Many of these jointly owned projects are initially costly and have inherent safety and monetary problems down the road. Because relationships change, make sure you have "what if" scenarios in place *before* entering into these type projects. My advice is that one should personally bankroll projects on his own property and let a neighbor do the same. This way you can stay good neighbors.

Built-in shared projects are a particular concern. The main ones I see involve landscapes at subdivision entrances. In some subdivisions the developer made plans for an association to be formed and funded by the homeowners. When this is not done, the entrance is usually doomed. But even with an association, the details can leave the entrance a mess. Is membership mandatory? What does the fee cover, and how much can the association assess? Who gets to vote, and how is the association set up? It's another example of joint ownership with its usual built-in problems that ends up leaving a poor-looking landscape.

 If you have a choice, find the most beautiful sites you want to see above all else but never build there.

Your goal is to design and site your new home to have the most beautiful views possible from every major living area. I often watch homeowners walk all over their property and, after identifying the most beautiful spot, decide to build there.

They need to keep walking to locate less desirable sites that look out to what they consider beautiful. If they are *viewing* their sweet spots, the location of their new home has been found. Now the beautiful sites have been saved for viewing and the less desirable site has been given a better use—building the house (which, of course, destroys the site).

This is a design principle discussed in *A Pattern Language.* Homeowners forget that a homesite permanently disrupts the land on which it is built. Whatever beauty was there is now replaced by permanent structures.

Once, I had a client envision his house nestled in a large grove of old trees. Just east of this grove was a nondescript field. I explained the grove of trees would be virtually destroyed once all the necessary grading was completed. By moving the homesite to the rather dull field, he would still have a wonderful view of the lovely forest to the west and also retain a view of his lovely lake.

This design principle is for people with perhaps several options, especially on larger tracts of land. Always save the view and use the leftover space for building.

See **Clearing** *100*

Significant and Trash Trees *96, 100*

Marking Trees *105*

The Power of the Sun *56, 57, 58*

Decisions for Clearing *15*

Borrowed View *44*

34 Design and site your home to consider views of adjoining property as well as your own landscape from all major sitting areas. The goal is to enhance all views and avoid any unpleasant ones. Be sure your hardscape decisions will be part of the solution, not add to the problem.

Every homeowner has a homesite with at least one major view and perhaps several. It might be a future garden planned with fountains, a lawn, and some flowering shrubs and trees. The view might be a forest or a particular specimen tree or a small side yard.

These two major factors—your favorite living spaces and what is viewed from them—must come together for the maximum enjoyment of your home. Usually the living spaces on top of everyone's list are the living room, kitchen with a breakfast area, master bedroom, and outdoor spaces. Just by drawing lines on the plan from the living space to the views, the homeowner can visualize what he will be viewing for many years.

But the problem is two-fold. First, the homeowner must identify what he will see on *adjoining property* that might constitute an eyesore: a neighbor's air conditioning unit or trashy shed, an unkempt yard, or a flashing tower. These need to be dealt with in some way. Of course, adjoining property might be part of a beautiful vista and incorporated with one's own visual landscape.

If the house plan cannot be adjusted to eliminate a particularly ugly view, landscaping must be expected to correct the problem within the confines of the homeowner's property. It is important that the solutions are at least entertained upfront. For instance, if a fence is needed, will there be room for its installation? If major shrubs and trees are planned, can any concrete work be adjusted to allow this important addition to the landscape?

The second part of the problem are the decisions made on *one's own property* that end up being major eyesores where a beautiful vista should have been instead. Some examples include a utility item that should have been placed elsewhere, the dog pen built outside the breakfast window, the shed whose unsightly contents are in full view. But the worst offender is the misuse of concrete. It is found displacing much needed planting beds, squeezed up to boundary lines with no space even for a fence, poured up against an overbearing retaining wall with no place to plant a screen, or even taking up whole backyards.

But these disagreeable results do not have to be. Here's an example of seeking alternative solutions: I met with a gentleman who wanted a concrete drive to his backyard for his boat. He also wanted to fence in the whole back area for his dogs. But his backyard faced an incredible grand vista. "Wow," I said. "Just what kind of boat do you own and what kind of relationship do you have with your dogs?" The boat was just a small fishing boat and the contractor assured me that a side entrance was entirely doable. The dogs also were found to need a much smaller fenced area, which we placed off to the side with silent fencing taking care of the larger space. By attacking this problem *before* construction, the homeowner eliminated a huge expanse of concrete across his back as well as a rather unattractive fence for his dogs. His incredible view was saved, but his boat and dogs were still taken care of.

Strange as it might seem, this basic design principle is often not noticed until the house is built. Instead, homeowners concentrate on interior spaces. Once the walls are up, they are quite surprised to learn where they plan to spend most of their time might not have the best views. They realize that the landscaping is going to have a big job to make this spot more appealing. As ridiculous as it may seem, in some cases the carport or other utility spaces sadly have the best views in the house.

Get out that pencil and ruler, and mark out your views from your favorite spots. Camouflage a neighbor's unattractive elements and make decisions for your own property that will add to, not subtract from, your own situation.

The view from the upper story dominated this design. There's no deck on the top level because it would have blocked the inside view of the gardens below.

This site has lots of good circulation with steps and paths all around.

The entertainment space is all on one level.

The homeowner has a choice of in the sun or covered summer house.

Heavy screening and open areas were adjusted along the sides as necessary. The summer house is located to the side to keep the view open.

34

35 **If a homeowner wishes to maintain or even enhance a natural landscape, the design should not force inappropriate or contradictory elements onto what is an otherwise beautiful natural setting.**

An invisible line exists between the natural world and that created by man. We all know when we have entered a forest and left behind our manicured landscaped yard. We look out over a meadow that is quite different from our perfect lawn. The streambeds meandering through the forests differ from the one we built in our backyard, no matter how natural we tried to make it.

The natural world has its own look, its own presence, and its own integrity. Just by its sheer majesty it will dominate. Any person wishing to add elements to this environment must do so with some careful considerations. The natural environment will make a mockery of any trite and inappropriate attempts to compromise its grandeur.

So exactly what is it I am talking about? Let me give you some examples.

One young man led me along a very long path into a light, airy forest. At the end of the walk was a small manmade clearing. He had marked out some very formal designs with many plantings. But the plantings were ones found in manmade gardens such as begonias, pansies, 'Otto Luyken' laurels, and gardenias. All around us were magnificent pines and oaks. A few sparkleberries could be seen here and there, and I saw a buckeye or two. I could not make these two elements come together. The plant choices in this formal setting in the midst of the forest would look quite lovely back in this young man's garden but not surrounded by those grand trees.

Another site was at an institution where children played. Out back was a large area that became rather like a bog—actually a retention pond—after some construction. Everyone began to study what plants would grow naturally in this permanently wet site. Someone suggested a controlled, definite design with a planting of some trees. It was a simple design, but anyone observing nature would know its power would quickly consume whatever anyone had in mind. Why direct so much energy "controlling" nature into some sort of human terms instead of time spent learning to appreciate the beauty of the natural growth in just such an area?

Learning to appreciate our larger world will often release us from making plans, spending money, and using up our energies on projects best left to our own home landscape. That leaves Nature to do what it does best. If we must embellish, take clues from the grand Master and do so naturally. In the meantime, learn to enjoy its own personal beauty.

See **Walls and Borders – Use Natural Materials** *180*

Ponds – Natural Fall of Land *360*

Learn Your Native Trees and Shrubs *104*

Marking Trees *105*

Clearing *100*

Photo *185*

No railroad ties or cinder blocks here. No little beds of begonias, either. However, a seat full of chiggers might accompany you as you stroll this native forest after a nature talk.

As a forest matures, pay attention to all proper procedures for its health as well as its beauty. Constant attention must also be paid to controlling any destructive invasive plants, especially exotics.

These rocks were here when construction began over 30 years ago. Thankfully these homeowners knew to enjoy their natural position and not try to arrange them into a little circle or some other formal configuration. A few plantings scattered about is all they needed to add their timeless beauty to the landscape.

A certain degree of enclosure is necessary for outdoor living spaces to attract people to visit. However, too much enclosure will have the opposite effect and cause the space to go unused.

Like many creatures, man prefers a certain amount of enclosure in order to feel comfortable relaxing. When this need is not fulfilled, a space left too open will go unused. But what does one mean by *enclosure*? Is it a wall, a tall hedge, just what?

Enclosure is anything in the landscape that creates a separation from the entertainment space and the space beyond. It can be quite dominant like the house itself or a summer house at the edge of a patio. A wall or fence either quite tall or one quite low could be effective. An interesting mixed shrub border or just a grouping of Ornamental Trees could be used. But in every case, something is worked into the landscape design that helps every entertainment space—large or small—come together as a whole and not spill out endlessly into vacuous space. We all like elements to give us a small feeling of belonging

to a certain space and perhaps a little something to our backs.

But too much enclosure will also destroy a space. If a wall or shrubs are too high and too encompassing and the exits are narrow, the homeowner will become wary. The enclosure could also be buildings that enfold too much. The air becomes stagnant, the space gets hot and airless and, in many cases, sunless. A person feels trapped in a cage—and wants out.

So how do you know if you have too little or too much enclosure? If you are drawn to a certain spot, you know it is right. But if it is avoided because it is too open, start adding some "walls" to give it more comfortable parameters. If you feel surrounded and the space goes unused, tear something out until you eliminate that feeling of entrapment.

See **Ornamental Trees** *78, 99*

Fences *306, 309, 310*

Wall – Extra Seating *268*

Screening *68*

Power of the Sun *57, 58*

Porches and Decks – Recessed *259*

No Built-in Seats *261*

Photos *193, 323, 362*

Note the small wall circling partway around half the circumference, the choice of low shrubs, and the very open exits to either side of this summerhouse. The right degree of enclosure will attract anyone for a visit; a person feels comforted but never trapped.

"Borrowing" the neighbor's tall cypresses to use for screening allowed this homeowner to install more interesting plantings next to the patio.

The entertainment area is all in one place and all on one level.

36

The patio was positioned to face the warming rays of the southern exposure with plenty of trees to soften the hot sun. If the patio had been situated on the north side of the summerhouse, it would have been avoided for any real use.

Before any plans for this landscape were considered, all trees were thinned. All Significant Trees were tagged to remain, and all weak Trash Trees—plus many invasive, nonnative plants—were removed. After this careful operation was over, a wonderful balance of light and shade was restored to the site. Because nature is a dynamic force, attention to the forest is a continuous project.

36

37 **It's important to provide seating in your landscape because of the strong psychological effect of drawing people out into the landscape by promising a respite. Otherwise we might not make the journey. Even if the journey is not made, the promise can be just as important as the journey itself.**

I worked with one site that had a tight narrow lot backed by a tall wood fence. A small constricting low deck came just off the kitchen where the mother was often surrounded by several active children. We removed the deck and added a more expansive patio, in addition to three wide brick steps up to a small space above. We also included a little sitting area punctuating the new circular path. As she stood at the kitchen sink, the mother of the family could see this little sitting area. Maybe she didn't have a lot of time to actually go there, but she knew she *could*. Even in the most hectic times, she could visualize going to this retreat.

That is what seating does when placed strategically in the landscape. Just seeing or knowing they are there allows the homeowner or others to venture out knowing they can sit down—if only for a minute—before walking on or starting some important gardening chore. That bench or swing provides a destination so important for humans, a place to rest awhile in this busy world of ours. We can be comforted just by their presence.

See **Seats and Benches** *269, 322, 325*

Any outdoor space begs to be explored. Knowing a place is provided to relax along the way makes exploring all the more inviting.

A strong arbor is needed to support a heavy vine.

Success with perennials or annuals gives that "wildflower" look.

Lights in a bed provide visual aids but do not create hazards for the person mowing the lawn.

37

Some level surface space should be provided outside the home. When all land surrounding a home is sloping, the space will not be inviting.

Many homes are built on beautiful rolling land. It is invigorating to walk up and down these hills. But a person wants his feet to be on level ground when he comes to a resting place.

The land surrounding a home needs level spaces especially where the homeowner would like to go outside to enjoy his yard. Too many times this need is not identified when grading is done. Instead, it becomes a challenge to always be walking up and down, and the homeowner finds there is nowhere to rest. As time goes by, he will find himself looking *at* his landscape but not enjoying being *part* of it.

This design element is very important when building a home or a remodeling. Grading on terracing can be done concurrent to the whole landscape project. Sometimes that means including a simple patio or a small level lawn space off the back. A formal garden must also be level for good effect. Walks around the house can be addressed with all the equipment on-site. The important thing is to recognize the need for some level space because we all know that coming back to add this important element of design is very expensive and disruptive.

All spaces used for parking, including the Car Area, must be level. Yes, they must have some grade to drain properly, but any more slope than is necessary renders the space unusable and even hazardous.

See **Initial Grading** *17*

Plan at Beginning for Spaces for Outdoor Uses *40*

Paths Must be Level for Good Walking *198*

Kids Play Area *346, 348*

All Parking Spaces *215*

Formal Gardens – Must Be Level *316*

 Site anything to be used as major focal points from where they will be viewed. Do not stand in the spot where they are to placed when making this decision.

Often a small tree, birdbath, or even a structure like a shed is placed but no one bothered to notice how it would be seen from major viewing sites. It is very important to actually walk inside and sit at the breakfast table, for example, and direct another person, "Move it over some to the right." When viewed from that favorite seat on the porch, you discover the tree to be planted is in the way of an important object beyond. Another plant was to be used as a framing element, but when viewed from the kitchen window, it is just not placed right for the desired effect. The angle of the shed could have been better as it relates to the overall landscape, but no one noticed when standing on the patio.

So put that tree down and start walking about, especially to those places where one hopes to see this beauty as the years go by. When it pleases you, start digging. Do this for every major focal object in your landscape. Each one should be a part of the larger composition, but because of the complex, three-dimensional nature of landscaping, just go to those few spots that warrant consideration for a good view.

See **Ornamental Trees** *99*

Creatures – Man-made *376*

Containers *156*

Structures *292, 294*

Ponds *358*

Photo *173*

40 A landscape will have multiple focal points (both hardscape and plant materials) of various degrees of beauty and importance. Their use (a positive force) or misuse (a negative force) can have great influence on the perceived beauty of the landscape.

The human eye will roam over a landscape concentrating on one item at a time, take it in, and then move to another focal point. The human brain visually takes in a whole space, will evaluate it, and then place each of the items into the whole picture. Along the way, the person is assembling images that either give him pleasure or will be a negative force that causes a displeasing response.

Each piece of land has its own character. It can be a clean slate, have too many trees and scrub bushes, or perhaps have just a few trees here and there. At every point the homeowner must make decisions regarding what to add, what to clean up, and what to enhance. Along this journey, he is faced with adding new focal points or identifying existing ones and using them to advantage to create a beautiful landscape.

For instance, an incredible outcropping of rocks is revealed; creating a garden with cascading rock garden plants could make this a wonderful vision from the sitting area. Perhaps adding a natural-type pond at the base would be another item of interest. A specimen Japanese maple is planted near the entrance and over the years becomes a great object of admiration. Three bird houses are mounted on posts in a garden area; their selection is quite beautiful and placement is just right. A gazebo is located in just the right space with all elements complementing the whole. A large urn is sited just so in the garden. The result? All eyes are drawn not only to the urn's beauty but also to the beauty of the surroundings.

In each case, the homeowner had a choice either to take what was given to him and expose and add to its inherent beauty or bring in new materials and add to the whole. For a landscape to work, each decision is important. We will look at each item—some small and seemingly unimportant, some of great drama and beauty—and assemble them into a vision that can produce feelings of awe and wonder.

But if various objects of interest are inappropriate and distracting, the visual beauty of the landscape will be compromised because all focal points are seen as part of the whole.

For example, one homeowner invited me to her very small back yard and wanted to know what to plant to make it pretty. But I saw a shed (in direct view from her kitchen) that was in disarray; debris was spilling out and various piles of materials were stacked along the lovely fence line. Her back porch was filled with many broken pots and other works in progress. It was obvious she and her husband loved to work outside but seemed not to know where to go next.

I recommended that she move all projects to a dead space around the corner, out of view from the house. I also suggested giving the shed a good cleaning, painting it, and making it into an attractive feature instead of one to be avoided like a bad relative. The fence was quite nice, but the weedy debris made it a liability instead of an asset. Once that was cleaned up, I drew a design including a few shrubs for accents and interest. All objects that were negative focal points were moved, removed, or repaired, and attractive, positive objects were added.

Objects both natural and man made become focal points in our landscape. By removing the negative, the positive ones will dominate to create beauty all around.

There are multiple focal points of beauty in this landscape. Can you count them? The seat tucked into a small garden; the nearby bird bath; two urns with conifers; an open summerhouse for informal gatherings; two brick pillars welcoming you to the formal garden beyond; a beautiful Ornamental Tree flowering a bright pink for summer enjoyment.

41 **Identify the areas of sun and shade in your landscape. Structures create defined areas of intense sun to areas of no sun, but these areas can change markedly from the longest day to the shortest day six months later—and then back again. Surrounding plants also provide every kind of shade that can change for any number of reasons. Therefore, "Do you have sun or shade?" can be a tricky question.**

Shade given by a structure can be accurately identified even though the variables are rather complex. Of course the height of the structure will define just how much the sun will be blocked out permanently. In addition, where you live will determine just how much the angle of the sun will change as it moves higher in the sky starting December 21 and lower in the sky starting June 21 (it's opposite for latitudes south of the Equator). At the equator there is virtually no movement throughout the year. As one moves northward (or southward), the arching becomes more dramatic until at each pole, summers have endless light and winters have little sun. But each one of these elements is dependable. The structure is permanent and the sun can be counted on to move just so each day of the year. Therefore you can determine your shade and sun situation with a good degree of accuracy from permanent structures.

The sun/shade situation given off by plant materials is quite different. The variables are endless, and there endless changes are created by the types of plants giving shade, time of year and just what the latest storm, or maybe a chain saw, took out. Then of course plants keep growing and adding shade to a former sunny situation.

Working with all of these variables makes gardening interesting. Many plants can adjust to more or less sun, but some don't. None like abrupt changes, but some will finally adapt; others never do. Gardening will have you noticing the sun's powerful influence on your planting world in many different ways.

See **Plants – Sun or Shade Loving** *27*
Thinning a Forest *100, 114*
Pruning – Thinning, Limbing Up *123*
Grass *352*
Photos *87, 143, 172*

42 **All major living spaces should be situated to receive some sun during the day. Man is inherently drawn to this powerful, dynamic force and will avoid any space that has too little sun.**

If there is any choice, a person will be drawn to a warm, sunny site and avoid places that are cast in darkness. In other words, he will prefer the morning sun (east), the noonday sun (south), or the afternoon sun (west). A person might not actually sit in the sun, but the space is influenced by it.

This means when planning a house, mark where the sun will come up in the morning and set in the evening. At some point, the sun should be shining in your bedroom, kitchen, living space, and any other room where you plan to spend a lot of time. Reserve utility rooms, the carport, extra bedrooms, and other "dead" spaces for the darker, north side.

Too often I see a beautiful plan for a home sited with no concern for the sun's power. Many of the living spaces end up on the north side or trapped by interior walls. Unless there are other architectural features that allow natural light to flow into these areas, the homeowner will never know why he is not attracted to these spaces…no matter how beautifully decorated. The bedroom is never cheery, or the porch is always rather damp and forbidding. Eating out is more appealing than cooking in a dark kitchen, or the breakfast nook never became the destination spot you thought it would be. I have actually watched a person fold clothes in a utility room awash in sunlight rather than sit in a gloomy living room trying to find a good light to read the newspaper.

Just recently a couple described their new home to me; the wife said they somehow always ended up in their formal living room. The first thing I asked was, "How much natural light is there?" They looked at each other and they both exclaimed, "Only the formal living room gets a lot of natural light." Their answer was right there.

Look to the sun for its rays to influence every one of your important living spaces.

See **Arbors and Summerhouses** *253*
  Common Concerns for Patios and Porches *242*
  Decks *256*
  Significant Trees *96*

The aboveground deck to the right and the one nearly on the ground both have a wonderful proper balance of good sunlight and delicious shade, making these Outdoor Living Spaces inviting and well used.

The fence design is very creative and a major complement to the house architecture.

The choice of 4-foot fencing next to a public sidewalk indicates a welcoming atmosphere.

43 **Ignoring the power of the sun can ruin the best of homes. Carefully choose your design on a particular site with its force in mind, or its potentially unbearable penetrating light and heat could ruin a comfortable living space.**

Many new house designs coupled with the placement of the house ignore this factor to create a very negative situation. Mainly it results from the use of large, tall windows and perhaps a deck facing south or west. Unless very tall trees are in place or can be planted for necessary shading, the living space becomes unbearable. Often the homeowner tries to add a porch, awning, or at least an arbor, but the architecture might not allow it or it can be done only at great cost and effort. Of course, some modern techniques such as tinted windows help a great deal and some people even use heavy shades or curtains to help (although this blocks the view), but these do not solve the problem completely.

The answer? Look at your plan. Mark the spots where the sun comes up and sets. If its power will be a problem, either make changes in your design or how you site the house. Porches can be a great addition to help with a hot western sun, even cooling the breeze some. Awnings and arbors can also be added to the initial design. And of course, nothing can replace the effects of shade trees and shrubs. Are they already on site or do you have a place to add some more in strategic spots?

Only through a combination of a good architectural design appropriate to the orientation of the sun coupled with a plan for the effects of the landscape will this problem be avoided and instead, a comfortable and sunny home will be enjoyed by all.

See **Common Concerns for Patios and Porches** *242*
    Significant Trees *96*
    Pruning – Thinning, Limbing Up *123*

43

Design problem: This originally was an open deck with no trees and high windows facing directly west. The living spaces inside and outside were unbearable.

Solution: An arbor and porch were added and a tree planted for shade.

Additional set of steps help direct circulation off the porch. The other stairs are at the far end away from living space.

Iron was used for the rails, giving better visibility to the formal garden and extending the view.

Note the comfortable wide steps with backings and contrasting paint on the treads.

44 Require all utility systems to be shown on your plans before construction begins.

Utility systems can be your powerbox, gas meter, air conditioning units (and their water drains), gutter downspouts, trash cans, and so forth. They are all essential, but they do not need to greet us every day when we arrive home. Do you want to sit on your terrace and hear the air conditioning unit drone? Will water gush from your downspouts across your front beds and walkway? Is there any place to keep your trash out of sight and away from animals?

Ask your contractor to place each one of these items on your plan to your satisfaction and even spell them out in your contract. Unfortunately, they are often last-minute decisions made by installers who have been given no directions. Unless you take charge, the aesthetics or even good common sense of their placement will not be factored in. I have seen homes with beautiful architectural details with a power box squashed up next to their edges. The beauty of this site is forever marred and remains a daily reminder in full view when the homeowner arrives home.

When these systems are poorly placed, the homeowner is faced with the job of softening their harsh effects. Sometimes solutions are made nearly impossible because only major surgery can correct the situation. For example, a bank of power and gas outlets are too close to windows and solid concrete underneath them makes this situation nearly impossible to soften. Air conditioning units are placed next to the patio; even if it's possible, they can be moved only at great expense. And believe me—tunneling under concrete to move downspouts is very expensive if not impossible after the fact.

Think ahead because the final stages of building really heat up fast and solutions are easily overlooked. You'll be left trying to correct the appearance of these unsightly utility elements. This is money and effort that could have been better spent beautifying your garden.

See **Air Conditioning Units** *325*

Too Much Concrete *218*

Irrigation and Septic Tank/Field Layouts *333, 341*

Power Meters *319*

Utility Systems *169*

45 Locate and permanently mark the boundary points of your property.

There are many reasons why homeowners do not know where their boundary lines are. But every day I must try to figure out just where the space to consider for a landscape plan *is*. Until this is done, decisions are on hold. Where does the fence actually go? Did you know your driveway is on the other person's property? (I see that all the time!) Who owns the dead tree (and must pay to have it removed)? I worked with one property owner who was desperate for extra parking space. Even though he paid a great deal of money for his lot, he did not know he owned another 100 feet up the street. Was he ever glad to find that out!

Until you know the exact location of your corner posts or points and draw lines of demarcation, any project can be jeopardized. Even an error of a few inches can make a huge difference if installing a wall or planting a small tree for privacy. On larger properties, land owners can be just as exacting. I have visited farms where the lines are carefully noted so no one will have any misunderstanding where to work.

This is one area that is exact: All boundary lines travel straight from point A to point B and never curve to accommodate a particular concern. Knowing your exact boundary lines at the beginning of any project will settle any such issues with your adjoining property owners.

See **Fences, Walls** *306*

Standardized Dimensions for Driveways *216, 217*

Design All Essential Uses of Land *40*

View from House *46*

46 **Consider a contractor's price for building a house carefully.** Many items for outdoor space will not be listed or will be priced so low as to be almost irrelevant to the realistic final cost. The result often means the homeowner has a beautiful home surrounded by an unappealing, nonfunctional landscape.

A homeowner should consider hiring both a professional landscape designer/architect and a landscape contractor at the *beginning* of the project to come up with a general plan and its cost. The landscape designer/architect can quickly come up with a general plan for all of your outdoor spaces such as where the driveway and walks go, how the decks and patios figure in, fence placements, and so on. With a fairly exact plan, a landscape contractor can come up with a pretty good estimate for implementing his part of the deal. He can estimate the costs of earth moving, grading, drainage, irrigation systems, soil preparation, mulch, grass, and plants. He should be expected to work with your general contractor because these two job skills often shift back and forth according to their individual expertise.

For instance, a general contractor is expected to do the general clearing and grading, decking, patio, even all concrete work. With a plan, he can also give a more accurate cost to you for your final bill.

Many in my profession of landscape designer/architect are asked to visit properties after most decisions, which are often minimally functional and often unappealing, have been made. Additionally, we are told that everything is over budget and are asked if we can we do everything for a fixed price. The compromises often leave a beautiful home looking stark and short-changed. The homeowner had hoped the landscape designer and contractor would be able to do much more for much less. The fact is their participation in the building process was never in the budget from the beginning.

If the whole package is important to the homeowner, then budgeting for *all* components is essential for a great outcome. The cost of building a home is the largest budget item, but it is not the entire amount needed.

See **Low Maintenance – Choice of Contractor and Architect** *37*
Clearing Your Site *100*

CHAPTER **2**

The Foundation

Designing with Trees and Shrubs

Most people think choosing trees and shrubs is *landscaping.* These important elements are planted with little thought except how they look in the nursery!

So what's wrong with that? Nothing—as long as a homeowner is armed with some knowledge of basic design elements. Using this information, he can design attractive plantings that fulfill their role. But ignoring good advice might lead to a landscape that has negative outcomes and even create high-maintenance situations.

Some people plan ahead, study books, and read every label. Others walk through a nursery and are compelled to buy something wonderful. Either way, how plants are incorporated on a site and how they are maintained over the years will determine their positive or negative effects on the landscape.

Choose each plant to perform a specific job. Additional attributes will increase its value in the landscape but the primary goal for it should always be considered first.

Plants should be used first and foremost as *problem solvers*. Each plant should be chosen to perform a prescribed job. Will it give shade? Will it be a good evergreen for winter? Will it provide flowers for enjoyment? Will it be fragrant? Control erosion? Screen a neighbor's view? Will it make my house look good?

Throughout this book are my recommendations and ideas for considering the various elements of design problems or challenges. The trick is to learn the attributes of the plants you will be considering so they will best match the tasks that have been identified. If this concern is ignored, instead of finding solutions, you will find your problems have just begun.

The Number One problem is—of course—*low-maintenance* choices as discussed in Chapter 1. This means selecting plants that will not outgrow their designated space and that are culturally compatible. The job description might go something like this: "Dwarf Burford holly—that looks just like the perfect evergreen to go under our bay window." Then, after reading the label: "Fifteen feet tall—I thought it was a *dwarf*." It is, considering its mother grows to thirty-five feet or more. After a little looking around, the choice is perhaps a Carissa holly, which reaches only about four feet tall and is a better choice considering the desired mature height needed for this site. Problem solved.

"I love weigela with its beautiful blooms in spring." But, after talking with the nurseryman: "I didn't know it got so big and needed cutting back every few years. But look at this cultivar; it stays much smaller and needs very little care. I'll plant that larger variety back in my mixed border." You found one with blooms but at a size to fit the space. Problem solved.

"Don't you just love that Indian hawthorn? It has great foliage and it even blooms. Deer…did you say deer? Yes, we have deer…right in our front yard. And deer love this plant?" This couple needs to move on by selecting a better plant that deer do not eat. Problem solved.

"Our site is so open; we need shade. How about an oak tree? Acorns? Yes, the location is right next to our patio. Maybe an elm or maple would be a better choice. Of course the elm has a less invasive root system but the maple has great fall color. OK honey, which of these trees do you want?" By looking at the attributes of each tree, the best choice is made for this situation. Problem solved.

As you move about your site marking down what you want in your landscape, remember that plant choices should be made to solve a problem. If you are really lucky, that plant choice will fulfill many needs all in one package. In just one plant, the homeowner might find his necessary screen, but this same plant may also be evergreen, bloom, and might even have fragrance. Another plant might give essential shade, but it also has wonderful fall color and distinctive bark that add even more interest in winter. The homeowner must first and foremost establish the primary goal each plant will solve. All additional attributes are just icing on the cake.

47

This Ornamental Tree will need thinning as it matures to expose its beautiful, structural winter form. It also provides shade from the hot, western sun in summer.

Mature heights of foundation shrubs are minimal, requiring little pruning. Also, they are evergreen, which is important for winter interest.

A generously sized covered landing with evenly spaced steps.

This tree was chosen for its bright leaf color as contrasted against the dark red brick of the home. This particular tree also has a small mature size, plus its winter silhouette adds interest.

Strong bold lines and a large blank wall are wonderful backdrops for Ornamental Trees and shrubs.

This Ornamental Tree was carefully chosen because it will mature at the right size to suit this small front yard, it will not grow into nearby power lines, and it will not block the view to the home. Because of its prominence, it also needed to be a plant that will develop a lovely shape.

A friendly, 4-foot open fence has just the right degree of enclosure and architecturally complements the home.

The use of a formal fence motif demands a level space.

This brick surround gives both visual weight and architectural beauty.

This angular space is greatly enhanced by the soft, cascading form of this Ornamental Tree. Because of its airiness, plenty of light filters through for a more enjoyable downstairs space.

48 **Shop throughout the year in order to have something blooming or some other element of interest at all times. Nurseries market plants at their best—when they bloom, when they are fragrant, when they have colorful leaves or berries, and even when they have striking bark color.**

One of the greatest joys of a landscape is walking outside *anytime* and finding different blooms, berries, colorful leaves, delicious scents, and even dramatic barks. In fact this is one of the most frequent comments from homeowners after a successful landscape project. "I just love discovering something blooming in my yard year-round!" They say this with a big smile and come into the nursery and want more! They now see the possibilities open up to a broad spectrum of wonderful plants, not just the usual three-varieties-azaleas-fits-all, which bloom in spring and then the show is over.

Every month or so, browse through your local nursery. They will be highlighting something that will attract a homeowner with a "must have" plant. If you are not there, you will miss the scent of the fra-

grant tea olive or the experience the beauty of an electric-purple beauty berry for your fall garden. Drop by in winter to see camellias with just that right color or maybe discover a daphne or some hellebores to add to your shade garden. Of course, summer visits are a must to round out any garden.

There are literally hundreds of plants that expand the visual palette to be as extensive as one wants. Once the homeowner actually sees that perfect color or smells that heavenly scent, he will be assured that he really *must* have that plant in his garden. But this means visiting nurseries or botanical gardens when their show is on—summer, fall, and winter—not just during those few short weeks in spring.

Shopping for your landscape is like going to the circus. If you go only in spring, you will miss some of the most exciting acts in the show because you left after the first act. Nurseries are in business for the full show; acts come onstage throughout the year.

See **Local Sources** *90*
   Photo *55*

This famous restaurant in Atlanta is open year-round, and landscape interest is important for each day. Both the center island and the necessary screening to the left host an array of plant choices with each selection taking its turn to display its best attributes throughout the year.

No boring row of six or seven identical trees or another row of hollies here. Something is blooming or fragrant, has berries or fall color, and displays dramatic texture nonstop.

49 **Avoid unnecessary heights in screening since most unsightliness is at ground level. A mass of too-tall plantings can consume a landscape, creating an unfriendly feeling of entrapment. Use tall plantings only where they are needed.**

We cannot control another person's use of his property, which might not be as pleasant as one would desire. Screening immediately becomes a solution. But too often the solution becomes overkill. A fence built like a tall fortress or plants that will reach to the sky creates an overbearing enclosure.

What needs to be understood is the phenomenon that most of the unpleasant stuff in your neighbor's yard is *scattered on the ground,* such as trash cans, junky stuff, and untended weeds. Once this ground view is obscured—to about five feet or more—only the architecture of a neighbor's home, the tops of trees, and of course the sky can be seen.

The best place to start is by assessing your problem. Just what do you need to screen? If the problem is on the ground, construct a fence about five feet tall or choose plants that mature to less than ten feet tall. If a particular problem sticks out, such as an ugly shed, plant specifically to solve that problem. But to plant an enormous hedge where none is warranted will often backfire after the homeowner discovers he has created an overbearing enclosure and a dark, sunless backyard for his own landscape.

In another situation, planting the tallest plant possible is warranted. For example, a deck might be situated one to two stories high and look right into the next door neighbor's own sky-high deck. A tall cypress growing thirty to forty feet tall will solve the problem, as would a tall-growing sourwood or a tulip poplar tree. Still, planting too many tall screening plants only becomes a detriment to one's own property.

The most difficult situations are found when screening is needed for sites that are both tall and far away. No plant will ever be tall or thick enough to totally block the view. This is the time to mix up the plant selections—all very tall choices—and, with this mix, create a natural, muted setting of a mixed forest.

See **Enclosure** *50*
Fences – Height Matters *309*
Symmetry – Avoid Too Much *92*

A loose mixture of wonderful Ornamental Trees and Shrubs creates just enough privacy for full enjoyment of the backyard. The center island is even more sparsely planted, allowing some screening but permitting a view around the homeowner's landscape

The use of bed lines creates mystery and depth.

No boring straight lines are found along this back.

A long row of extremely tall and unnecessary shrubs would overwhelm the homeowner's own garden, even create unwelcoming, excessive shade.

Because of the good neighbors, much less screening is needed on this corner. A few large evergreens create just enough enclosure to give some degree of privacy.

The slight curve of these large evergreens creates a sight line an eye will follow into the homeowner's landscape.

Planting for symmetry is always chancy, but the cultural site is identical and few trees are planted. Even if one is compromised, its removal will not destroy the effect of the remaining trees.

50 **Break up the strongly horizontal architectural lines of a one-story home by planting an occasional medium-sized tree or shrub. This will add interest and dimension since the foundation shrubs and groundcovers must be kept low and unobtrusive.**

Too often, homeowners are afraid of hiding their ground-hugging home if any tree or large shrub is placed out front. This unfounded fear often causes homeowners to plant a whole string of little shrubs and groundcovers, leading to the absence of any vertical interest. Worse still is the selection of many large hedge-type shrubs that smother the home instead of dramatizing its best features.

With some careful thought in plant selection, these vertical elements can add great interest to the overall scheme. The beautiful bay window or the front entrance can be greatly enhanced with some framing plants chosen for their appropriate mature sizes. Other areas might be rather blank, windowless walls. Certainly a selection of interesting structural plants will do wonders for this mass of bricks or stucco lying close to the ground. In fact, the strategic placement of plants playing off each architectural element can create a most interesting landscape.

See **Ornamental Trees** *78, 99*
   Winter Branching *118*
   Special Interrupted View *74*
   Pruning – Thinning, Limbing Up *114, 115*

"Let's see. What do I need for this tight spot? Something that's pretty, stays small, frames the window, and is not messy." Many homes sit close to the ground and need just the right plant or the foundation shrubs will grow too big. The whole facade is boring when there is no sense of height anywhere.

Many interesting plants and other features all lie low, never to grow up and cover this beautiful home.

Container gardening allows for great flexibility each season.

The homeowner read about this tree and selected the correct cultivar for its particular growth habit.

This tree has been correctly thinned and limbed up to allow it to frame the window.

51 An interrupted view provided by strategically planted trees and shrubs (correctly pruned and thinned over the years) will provide some privacy. **More important, they provide the depth perception necessary to enjoy particular views up close as well as distant ones. Understanding physical dynamics will help homeowners understand the importance of this design concept.**

People need objects to establish depth perception, which in turn creates interest. The human eye roves around the landscape, allowing the brain to take in all of the features. A person looks for something to focus on for interest and beauty. If successful, the eye will again focus on some more beauty. The brain assimilates this vista using these visual clues at different distances to greatly enhance one's enjoyment.

At the opposite extreme are large vacuous spaces with no visual interruptions: an ocean; endless, rolling cornfields; a desert. Each of these situations is greatly enhanced by visual interruptions—the ocean has boats or islands in the distance; vast cornfields have a farm site with comforting trees sitting in its midst; a desert has an oasis with palms.

So why does this information apply to the home landscape? Because many homesites are devoid of necessary visual clues to create interest and beauty. The house might have been built on what was once a field or is now scraped clean for construction. What is important is that the homeowner should design his landscape by establishing strategic visual clues or it will be like the empty oceans, boring cornfields, or lonely deserts.

Why wouldn't a homeowner do this? Because he doesn't want to block his view of the golf course, the lake, the sky, or his house. He thinks any trees or structures will be detrimental to his enjoyment when, in fact, the view is sterile, flat, and uninteresting when nothing is planted or constructed. Adding some strategically placed trees, shrubs, and perhaps some structures will allow the human brain to better assimilate the whole with greater appreciation of the view beyond. Essentially by looking *through* these elements, the whole landscape becomes wonderfully interesting and beautiful.

See **Pruning – Thinning, Limbing Up** *114, 115*
Balance of Light and Shade *56*
Succession of a Forest *102*
Significant Trees *96*
Thinning a Forest *100*
Photos *96, 205*

51

Look out your window. Too many trees left bushy and messy indeed hinder a beautiful view. But if these same trees are thinned and limbed up, the results are totally positive. Not too open, not too closed is the balance that makes a view come alive.

Note the tiny seedlings in the grass. If this pasture is not kept mowed, it will revert back to a primary forest.

The grouping of Significant Trees in the far right distance has been cleared of underbrush and thinned for a healthier growth pattern.

Place plants just outside a viewing window for the intimate watching of animals and the extra joy of seeing plants in great detail throughout the seasons. It's called a special interrupted view.

I often design a landscape so that a tree or shrub is situated just outside a window. With proper pruning and placement, it should not block the window. It is there to add a special point of interest to the home-owner because the outdoors landscape is often rather far away. Birds can be seen but only at a distance.

When a tree or shrubs are located just outside a window, the homeowner can observe his bird friends only a few feet—even inches—away. The added benefit of seeing particular leaf patterns and colors enhances this intimate view. Once a cardinal has lighted on your own little tree and you have experienced the electric glow of a Japanese maple in fall colors right before your eyes, you will never again question the importance of interrupting distant vistas from your best viewing windows.

At my home, the living room overlooks a small pond where many birds visit my husband and me. They keep their distance, and we keep binoculars handy. But right outside our windows we planted a 'Winter King' hawthorn tree. As soon as we hauled it off our truck, a bird lit upon its branches even though it was still in our carport lying on its side. He proceeded to flit on and off while watching us dig the hole. Even as we dragged it over to the site, he still was on and off as if to tell us to hurry up and get it in! Before we could get the tree completely watered in and mulched, many more birds started doing battle for the best perch…we called it "king on the mountain" when we were kids.

Since then we have stretched out on our sofa in freezing weather and watched one bird after another feather himself, pluck berries off for a snack, and just have fun like birds do. Without this close-up bird play set, we would never have such an intimate viewing of some of the most joyful creatures on earth. And the bright red berries and the rustling leaves only add to our pleasure. Yet every day, homeowners resist siting any plant up close and protruding because it will block their view, when in fact an incredible view could be added to their vista.

See **Pruning – Thinning, Limbing Up** *114, 115*

Plants – Correct Choice for Site *35*

Creatures in the Landscape *374*

Photos *62, 165, 223*

52

The structure in the distance is angled with its "pretty" side in full view and the open work area facing west for warmth in winter.

A little shade from the noonday sun is provided by this strategically placed tree. Plenty of Significant Trees to the west take care of the hot late afternoon sun.

With a little thinning and limbing up, this tree will enhance the view beyond. When the birds come visiting and the tree displays its beauty, both can be observed with great intimacy for even more fun with the landscape.

This tree was chosen for its mature height and its open, vertical growth habit that will require minimal maintenance.

53 **Arrange collections of a wide variety of plant materials, especially ones with distinctive shapes and colors, into cohesive groupings when they do not have special stand-alone places in the landscape. Even one selection of many plants will show off better when massed than when randomly scattered.**

This is the "China Cabinet Design Element" (or why a mixed border and flower beds work). Everyone loves to collect, and gardeners love to collect plants. The problem arises in deciding the placement of each selection to show off its beauty. But think of the qualities a china cabinet affords. It takes a wide selection of doodads and by arranging them within this *attractive defined space,* the collection takes on a whole new dimension.

Planting within defined spaces allows some big changes and many smaller ones without compromising the beauty of the whole. In fact, problems within a defined space are greatly diminished because any ailing plant is not standing alone for all to see. It is the arrangement within these spaces that will keep you busy gardening the rest of your life if you choose. Always out there is the Holy Grail—the perfect combination—the search for which includes

trying different combinations, maybe adding some conifers, rearranging your prize daylilies, substituting a different shrub rose, tweaking your herb garden, or adding a "must have" viburnum to knock out a "has been" in a mixed border. These same plants scattered about without any rhyme or reason will be quite diminished in their beauty. Together, they will create a beautiful landscape. Sometimes the plants of choice are all one type. Planting a mass of forsythia or a grove of fruit trees in a field will show off these plants far better in this cohesive grouping.

Gardening is creating visions of beauty. Individual plants in their own special place are one part of this picture. But just consider pond gardens, herb gardens, rose gardens, flower borders, mixed borders, foundation plantings with specimens, groves of trees, and on and on. These plantings are a combination of many different and often odd plants and even a mass of one kind. But when congregated into a whole, their beauty is magnified far beyond the beauty of any one plant.

See **Ornamental Trees – How to Use** *99*

Bed Lines *170, 172*

Walls and Borders *180, 182*

Grass – Invasive Types *354*

Shrubs, Trees – Evergreens *151*

Low Maintenance – Choose Plants Over 2 Feet Tall *20*

Avoid Odd Items in Lawn *34*

Photos *89, 131, 133, 182*

53

The garden is in full view for maximum enjoyment, but far enough away that imperfections are not easily visible (which, by the way, is just part of gardening).

Notice the use of many bold, large, blooming shrubs. Dollar for dollar, these shrubs provide the best color and interest in the landscape.

Instead of scattering the choices about, planting them together as a whole makes a beautiful statement.

The convenience of maintenance within a defined bed is another overwhelming reason to congregate plant choices. Incorporating one circular border instead of dodging multiple plants in the lawn is a low-maintenance decision.

54 Plant "stand alone" shrubs and Ornamental Trees in relation to structures and defined spaces. **They will then be greatly appreciated and will enhance the beauty of the landscape.**

Just by their size, Ornamental Trees and shrubs are best suited and complementary to human-sized structures and living spaces—not when they're located in large vacuous spaces where Significant Trees would be better choices. Humans stand about five to six feet tall; their living spaces are around ten to eighteen feet tall; and most Ornamental Trees and shrubs range just slightly taller. These three considerations come together to make a whole—the person, his spaces, and shrubs and Ornamental Trees.

For instance: How does one soften a blank wall? What about adding an accent tree such as a Japanese maple at the front entrance? Would a line of crape myrtles help direct traffic to some other area? Would a scattering of dogwoods and other native plants soften the nearby woods? Would a "just right" plant at a bay window bring birds closer? How would a pee gee hydrangea look at the corner of the vegetable garden?

These same plants and many more dotted about the lawn with no purpose often look odd. A forsythia here, a crape myrtle there, some favorite roses just planted wherever, but if each of these lovely plants is given a role in the landscape, its worth and beauty will be much greater.

Even more thought must be given to the distinctive plant that stands out because of some very pronounced feature. Siting a contorted filbert, or weeping Atlantic cedar, or brazen golden threadbranch cypress can be a real challenge. The problem begins when one goes shopping and you're drawn to the unusual, dramatic, and unique. But just as decorating within the home, how many objects of art can one cram in without going into overload? Just think. A lot of money went into a structure, ceilings, walls, and floors so you can hang one or two pictures on the wall! The same goes for the outside. When deciding on buying that very special, distinctive plant, think where it will be used to show off its decidedly distinctive beauty. The number of these very special places can be quite limited.

This brings us back to the mixed border or china cabinet solution: if the list of desirable but distinctive plants is too long and you can not find any more dramatic settings to show off a particular "must have" plant, go back to the mixed border/china cabinet element of design to salve any plantaholic's soul. Create a large space; within this space, plant that contorted filbert, weeping Atlantic cedar, witch hazel, or whatever, and it will work. A little crazy, but it will work.

See **Focal Points** *54*
Place from Viewing Area *53*
Ornamental Trees *99*
China Cabinet Element of Design *76*
Photos *83, 85, 99, 135*

The fig bush, enhanced by an historic shed nearby, and the lovely grove of trees all come together to create a beautiful composition.

55 Permanent visual statics (fences, hedges, paths, arbors, sheds, houses, barns, rock or brick borders or walls, casual boulders, and water features) are the framework necessary for most flowers and shrubs to become the vision of beauty one desires. **This is especially true for off-seasons.**

We all love artwork—watercolors and oil paintings, collections of china and figurines, throw pillows crafted with cross stitch—the list goes on. However, to enjoy these pieces of art we give them a space that frames them, enhances their beauty, and puts them in context of a bigger picture. Paintings need a wall as a backdrop; figurines look elegant in a china cabinet; cushions are artfully scattered on a sofa.

Your perennials and shrubs are no different. Siting those within a framework of visual statics will set them off to be enjoyed as works of art. Adding a lovely fence or a low rock wall can make any flower bed or a small tree more charming. Flowers scattered about a water feature are quite beautiful. Vines climbing over and about an arbor give a dramatic touch for a wonderful effect. In fact, how many photos just of plant-

ings do you see in magazines? Instead, they are usually accompanied by some lovely bench, historic gate, or perhaps an elegant brick wall. Magazine editors know what everyone should realize—visual statics set off elements to look their very best.

Even more important, many flowers and even many shrubs and trees do not always look so wonderful. To have permanent structures as elements of the whole, you are able to keep the visual picture within some semblance of stability for year-round pleasure. For the off-season, the fence, hedge, path, arbor, or shed gives substance to an otherwise rather bare view. For an illustration of this point, visit gardens in winter. Despite the absence of lots of green and blooms, the landscape will still give a powerful message if the permanent visuals are beautiful and appropriate for the site.

See **Support Posts – Attractive** *263*
Undersides – Attractive *276*
Power Meters *319*
Walls, Borders – Use Natural Materials *81*
Rooflines *302*
Don't Bisect Architectural Features *260*

Flowers and trees are beautiful but the additions such as this arbor, beautiful structures, and some quaint birdhouses allow this scene to be greatly enhanced, especially in winter.

55

56 **For a more effective, beautiful landscape, construct all visual statics from natural materials (stone, wood, iron, brick, even glass or ceramic) or a really good fake.**

Coarse materials such as railroad ties or commercial-looking products such as paving bricks or blocks detract from the beauty of any landscape and should be used only for unseen construction. The more a homeowner can use natural materials such as iron, brick, stone, wood, or even glass or ceramic, the better. There are products that very successfully mimic natural elements and are perhaps cheaper, easier to maintain, or lighter to handle. I have seen some great "boulders" that two men can place without using a machine. Fencing can be permanent white vinyl requiring no painting; cobblestone is really formed concrete. The test is just how well they mimic the real thing. But if the budget allows, go for the real materials. These elements are so basic to man that it is impossible to ignore their inherent beauty.

What can detract from a landscape are materials that are themselves unattractive and even garish.

Some of the concrete retaining wall and edging choices as well as many "paving bricks" are still too commercial-looking. Of course, many customers use chain-link fencing, but one hopes they choose the more subtle black.

Money can be a limiting factor, although I have found in most cases that the price difference is very minimal. The homeowner's lack of knowledge of the effect these unnatural materials have on the whole landscape is more a factor than anything else. In many cases, additional money is spent trying to soften their unappealing presence. Often, I am asked to cover a bright, silver chain-link fence and plant shrubs to rid a view of a railroad tie wall. Worst are the pale pink, commercial-looking pavers and retaining wall materials that blend with nothing. These products might be handy to buy and install, and might also be "cheap," but one can hardly ignore their negative dominance in the landscape. And in many cases, their use is not even necessary.

See **Natural Landscape – Use Natural Materials** *48*
   Photos *18, 133*

A Significant Tree limbed up over the years with a beautiful canopy for dappled shade.

This 4-foot tall open fence creates a perfect enclosure on this busy street.

Stone, brick, and wood are all wonderful natural materials that add warmth and earthiness to this already soft, welcoming landscape.

56

57 **There is a fine line between a tree that is ugly and one that has character. Trees or shrubs with character can have a unique place in the landscape; ugly ones should be removed.**

Everyone seems to want perfectly shaped plants. But a certain plant might have a certain twist, a crazy bend, even a malformed shape over its whole being. A decision has to be made. One farm I visited has an old gnarled cedar in view of the front drive. The homeowner is quite the gardener, with a creative spirit. She built a low rock wall surrounding the cedar, added some plants, *cleaned up the dead and damaged limbs,* and this odd creature became a wonderful focal point. Its very character sets the tone for entering a wonderful garden of equally great character.

Recently, I had a Japanese maple at my nursery with a rather bent shape. I eventually sited it near a pond to great effect. In many gardens plants are carefully pruned (including using wires and braces) to train them into a decidedly twisted shape. I just luck-ily found one already formed by nature.

The decision to either keep a twisted, bent plant discovered on the site or to create one is an artistic choice. But to keep any tree or shrub that is obviously ugly and has no artistic value will detract from any landscape. Too often I have seen a diseased, torn, and twisted tree that a homeowner either wants to save to see if it will eventually recover or just doesn't understand the need for its removal. As the years progress, the tree remains an eyesore as it slowly declines. This plant has no character or any potential of ever becoming a plant of character. It is just ugly and needs to be removed. Otherwise the whole landscape beauty will be compromised.

See **Clearing** *100, 101*
    Trash Trees *100*
    Illustration *113*
    Pruning – Cuts at the Crotch Leaving Collar *122*
    Photo *43*

A makeover of this back garden uncovered an old cedar. Once cleared of invasive vines and broken and dead limbs, this ugly duckling became the centerpiece of the landscape. But not every tree can be recovered; some should be removed as a negative element in the garden.

58 **The contrasting effects of foliage—its color and texture—is one of the most important elements of a pleasing design.**

If you dissect why you like a particular combination of plant materials, you might be surprised to find that the colors and textures of *foliage* are the real reasons. Dramatic blooms will give an exciting edge but most last only a short time. The whole palette is really filled with foliage of wonderful colors that can vary dramatically in sizes and shapes, and that can range from very dull to the shiniest leaf. Arranging plant materials with their foliage in mind can turn an anemic landscape into a dynamic, three-dimensional sensation.

On the other hand, ignoring this element can result in a dull, confusing effect. I have visited many sites where various hollies are planted. The choices were all very much the same in size and color of the leaves, but the effect was not coherent. It reminds me of my father wearing two different checks: one for his pants and one for his shirt. Separately, each one might be attractive but not together. At another site I saw a red, weeping Japanese maple next to a bed of red barberry. Neither looked good as their reds blended together for no real beauty at all.

At the other extreme are flamboyant color choices that assault the senses. It's all a matter of taste, but a brassy gold euonymus or a 'Gold Mop' thread-branch cypress stuck out into a landscape with nothing to draw these electrifying elements into a more pleasing whole is too abrupt for me. You might extend this vibrancy with additional shocking colors to make a real statement. In other words, wow the daylights out of everyone with a real Disney World look. Or one could choose plants to ameliorate the situation and help turn off the sirens with increasingly less intense colors.

Designing with the color and textures of foliage in mind is one of the most exciting parts of design. Each vignette becomes a challenge in creating a work of art. Whole sweeps of a landscape take on a beauty throughout the seasons as leaves unfold, turn colors, and contrast with their neighbors, playing off each other in complementary hues and textures.

See **Photo** *209*

An Ornamental Tree chosen to fit perfectly in this location.

A 5-foot wall keeps unwanted visitors out but is still quite friendly. The iron gate is especially inviting.

Five major textures (including the lawn) make this landscape entrance totally compelling. Three shrubs have lovely blooms but it is the contrasting greenery that makes this work so well.

Evergreens provide some of the strongest and most important elements in your landscape: greenery during winter, camouflage for an unpleasant winter view, and foundation plantings.

Winter is when the importance of evergreens becomes self-evident. Deciduous trees and shrubs lose their leaves; no matter how much a person loves silhouettes of different plants and, perhaps, the bark, the vista is mostly brown and bare. Sometimes in summer I will comment to clients that even though everything looks green now, I know it will be quite stark in the coming months. The response is usually overwhelming. The long winter months become oppressive, especially with my older customers. Everyone seems to desire some green, especially in winter.

Sometimes an evergreen can double as camouflaging material. All kinds of ugly views can disappear during summer, but when fall arrives, it feels like someone took down the curtains to your bedroom. Just be sure your chosen plants fulfill your future needs not only by their mature size but also by thriving where they are planted. There is no use planting a Leyland cypress in deep shade or a Florida anise in hot sun. Although both are evergreen, they will not do anyone much good when they decline.

Evergreens are also essential as foundation plantings. Sometimes a few deciduous plants will be just fine but I have *never* found a homeowner happy with completely or even mostly bare plantings along the front of his house. Evergreens are especially important in the immediate vicinity of the front entrance; this is no place to mass deciduous barberry, daylilies, and spirea. All have great summer color, but for six months the area is forbidding. Either tuck these choices in among some evergreens or move them to a shrub border elsewhere.

Evergreens might connote a boring landscape but many have blooms, and more important, they come in many different sizes and textures that can enrich the landscape beyond just being green. Tall loblolly pines in the distance, the large textured leaves of an 'Emily Brunner' holly, the fluffy leaves of azaleas, the reddish hue of cleyera, and even the purplish cast of the common dwarf yaupon holly all add character and interest to the landscape as well as being green!

See **Screening** *68*

Symmetry *92, 94*

Plants Chosen for a Special Job *30, 35*

Photos *33, 65, 114, 209, 257, 320*

The landing above was extended to hold the grill off to one side—still convenient but out of sight.

These evergreen foundation shrubs soften the entry to this back patio area every day. Even when the other plantings lose their leaves, the exposed view is quite lovely but the footings of this deck are still hidden.

Small concrete bumpers indicate to drivers where to stop. A pretty decorative wall up close would cause problems.

The path to the Utility Area is plain concrete. The second path leading to the patio is in beautiful stone. The choice for surfacing gives strong guidelines where to walk.

59

60 **The colors of plant foliage and blooms should complement the colors of all permanent structures. If plants have no relationship to any structure, their color is a matter of personal taste.**

Except for some wild changes with paint, most color choices of permanent structures are permanent, especially those of brick and stone. Some of these color choices can be quite muted—beige, taupe, and so forth. But even these colors can have overtones of pink, orange, brown, or gray. Other choices can be quite distinctive like a deep mustard stucco and red tile roof. The color tones found on homes are endless, but once certain colors are established, all plants should be selected to complement permanent structures.

Picking complementary plants for more muted colors is easier because of their apparent neutrality. But even here, use caution when considering some color overtones that might go unnoticed. For example, a white crape myrtle might not be the right color to place against a white house; one of them might look like a "dirty white" instead. Sometimes a beige has an orange overtone and the soft-pink azaleas just don't seem to look right when they bloom. Muted

colors on structures also look poor when paired with particularly brassy colors of some plants. One is just so delicate and the other just too bold.

Highly distinctive colors in a structure especially need attention when choosing complementary plants. Will that yellow forsythia look good sited near the mustard stucco home? Will orange azaleas have a positive effect if planted in front of a bright-pink brick house?

I often suggest homeowners take foliage and blooms of various plants to the homesite to see how the color combinations work. Stand back and look. If there are any uneasy feelings, this is the time to look at other choices. Plants chosen to enhance the house and other outbuildings should do just that…be complementary for overall beauty.

If there are plants that you must have but are not complementary to your home, just plant them in the back yard. That includes perennial beds, shrub borders, or just that dramatic piece you just have to have but that would look terrible in the front of your house. Just get these "must haves" situated out back for patio viewing.

See **Choice of Flower Colors is Personal** *138*
   Photo *257*

All colors in this landscape complement the soft yellow tones of the home. The annuals are chosen for their subdued coral colors and are further enhanced by the muted burnt-red tones of shrubs. There are no harsh yellows or a jagged mix of strongly colored annuals; these are found in the back garden.

The bed lines are drawn in simple, bold lines indicating where grass will grow plus creating a beautiful space for the front.

Ample beds for planting are 6 to 8 feet wide. Narrow beds tightly running around a home make it difficult to have a pleasing landscape.

There is a nice balance of Significant Trees and Ornamental Trees. All have been thinned and limbed up as they matured over the years. Also, seedlings have not been allowed to grow up along the property line creating an unsightly and unnecessary "wall" of Trash Trees.

61 **The actual number of plants (odd or even) in a particular setting has no bearing on a planting being termed natural or formal. It is the setting and spacing that makes this determination.**

God has never counted when planting. Believe me, He just throws it out there and lets it grow and He is as natural as anyone can get. When the homeowner is deciding the number of plants he wishes to buy, too often I hear the adage that they *must* buy odd numbers to make the site more *natural*.

Let's first deal with mass plantings. Once the numbers exceed five or six, no one is counting. In many cases, the plants will grow together and the number is moot. More important is to mark out the space to be covered and buy the number of plants needed to cover the intended space. In other words, buy what you need.

When it comes to buying specimen plants for a grouping, the word "natural" becomes even more important to some homeowners. They are sure if they do not buy three of something, then they will be

doing something wrong. First, the site might not actually have the space to hold three plants. Why crowd a beautiful grouping just to have three? If one wants to have a natural look, just plant off-center to erase any formality. And what is so formal about two plants planted off to one side here and there? Second, if three are chosen in order to be natural but the plantings are done in a very precise, formal configuration, the natural look is lost. But if the same three plants are scattered about with a little bit of casualness, then perhaps the natural look will be captured.

To take this a step further, a formal look is actually accomplished by setting plants in precise configurations. The homeowner might first think of a plant on each side of his steps as formal, which equals two plants. But he can also create this same feeling of formality with a row, perhaps of crape myrtles, along his walk and the number required can be two, three, four or whatever the space allows. It is the manner of plantings of precise equal distance apart and from the walk that will make this planting formal, *not* the number used in this sequence.

Even – Odd / Formal – Informal
It's all in the placement.

62 Some plants will make liars out of professional advisors and authors.

The adaptability of the plant world is fairly incredible. As soon as someone tells you that a certain plant will never grow here or there, it does in your garden...and fabulously. Working in Atlanta's long, hot, sticky climate, it is a hoot to walk up on a beautiful clump of *Corydalis* spilling over a rock in someone's garden or see a beautiful specimen of fragrant snow-bell. Obviously a small microclimate permits these successes, but these are definitely not plants to stick in the ordinary garden spot. So don't be afraid to ignore good advice. But if your plant tells you over several growing seasons it does not like that spot, then listen and move it. If you have tried it three times and each time it dies, then don't try it again. However, it is fun to beat the odds…to see success when all advice said otherwise.

This gardener was told this pink hydrangea only grows in the shade. But here it blooms gloriously out in the hot sun next to some sun-loving yellow daylilies. Having fun growing plants out of their prescribed environment is just part of the gardening experience.

Use your local nurseries, local botanical gardens, local garden tours, local plant societies, and regional books to be your guiding lights in choosing all plants for your landscape and to help with problems that will always arise to confound you.

Success is every gardener's joy. Disappointments are downers. Look about you to see local gardens, local nurseries, and local botanical gardens to discover what does well in the area. This will give you a step ahead of what is going to work in your garden. Regional publications also add to your resources, as do plant societies, and radio and newspaper gardening authorities. Because these resources are regional, they have already culled the best of literally hundreds and even thousands of plant choices and landscaping techniques.

Use national publications to inspire you. Enjoy your trip to Nova Scotia or Scotland to increase your awareness of the beauty of nature. Visit the botanical gardens at Longwood Gardens in Pennsylvania or the desert gardens in Arizona and marvel at the creativity of their horticulturists. Drool over those catalogs from all over, and from time to time, push the envelope and order something special. But come home to see the beauty surrounding you of plants that not only survive, but also thrive, in your location. Your local resources are there to help you open up doors to your surrounding natural beauty.

Were these local resources always there to be tapped by plant enthusiasts? All over the United States, interest in gardening has exploded with wonderful results. For instance, in my region, just a few years ago the Atlanta Botanical Garden was literally a trailer sitting in a nest of bushes. Look at it now! The test gardens at the University of Georgia were in the planning stages. What an incredible resource they have become. Local nurseries were few and seldom carried flowers except a few annuals and seasonal stuff. Now there are wonderful nurseries, each with their own flavor of offerings. Books were encyclopedic and tried to cover every plant in one book. Now my shelves actually groan with offerings covering only my region. Planting zones were seldom identified on plant tags; now tags not only give the Planting Zone but also much more information, helping customers make intelligent decisions as to what to buy.

I can't help but laugh at my attempts to garden years ago without all these present-day aids. I was convinced I had to build and use a cold frame. It was in all the gardening catalogs and plant books. No one told me that for our more northern states, with their very short summers and erratic cold snaps, cold frames were perhaps essential. I live in Georgia! Nearly everything I wished to grow can be seeded directly in the ground because our growing season lasts a long time. If I had had local resources available to me then, a whole lot of useless activity could have been avoided and my plant selections could have been more successful too. The "good old days" are past…and that's good.

Just be glad each region has developed its own resources to aid the gardening world. Eliminating a lot of unworkable material and getting right down to what will work in your area will make your gardening experience wonderful and efficient.

Sticky or abrasive plants should never be planted where people are expected to be walking, working, or playing.

Many plants have natural, built-in defensive systems. The leaves have sharp points—hollies, yucca, and barberry, for example. Others, such as many ornamental grasses, have serrated edges that cut if handled. Others have dried foliage or fruits that pierce the soles of shoes and make walking barefoot impossible—more hollies, cunninghamia, and sweet gum trees, for example.

The front walk should be your first consideration. Everyone should be put at ease. A nice silk dress should not be in danger of a snag nor should one fear an abrasion on the arm getting to the front door.

The air-conditioning guy should not have to endure those kinds of plants—so why do people plant them there or anywhere a service man will be working at some time?

I hear stories from customers describing how as children they never played in their back yard because of the millions of sweet gum balls littering the ground, or how they were stuck by dried holly leaves. Many sticky or abrasive plants have a place in the landscape; we can all think of a few right now. I've planted them under windows to deter unwelcomed visitors. I've also planted ornamental grasses near pools for their blousy effect but not close to where anyone would be having fun. Leatherleaf mahonia is great as an accent but not when it's close to an entertainment area. And a barberry might be chosen as a barrier to an unwanted visitor. I even like sweet gum tree—but out in the forest—not located in the play yard or over the driveway.

This is a classic adage to keep in mind: Put the right plant in the right place.

See **Plants with Problems** *30*

Plants to do a Job *64*

Trash Trees *100*

Walk to the Front Door *225-230*

 Repeating certain plants and forms of plant materials throughout the landscape gives continuity and wholeness to the site.

Selecting a theme is basic to good design. Inside the house this is all very apparent as color swatches, paint chips, and tile colors are all coordinated. A basic tone or theme is repeated as one travels through the different rooms.

The same might be said of one's landscape. A way to establish this feeling of continuity is by the repetition of certain plants and certain forms. By interspersing the same choices over the landscape, one creates important neutral sites. This gives the more interesting specimens the necessary background to best display their beauty and not detract from the whole.

Too often I have come onto a landscape with perhaps a dwarf yaupon holly over here, 'Hellerii' holly over there (they look nearly identical), some Carissa hollies on this side, and Indian hawthorn on that side (which also look nearly identical). All are wonderful plants but they are *neutral* plants. By not settling on one or two types, the effect becomes quite confusing when all the other landscape plants are added. Maybe one of the small leaf varieties and one of the large leaf choices would do the trick. These could be used over and over again as the need arises. Another landscape might repeat sweeps of azaleas here and there, giving the landscape a look of wholeness.

Also repeating definite shapes will help bring a landscape together. If the homeowner has decided on some dramatic cypress-type arborvitae, perhaps another similar variety could be used nearby and even around the corner to continue the theme. If a cone shaped 'Foster' holly is used, maybe this same shape can be repeated in other selections, both smaller and larger such as a Steed holly and a deodar cedar.

Just how much one plays on a particular theme is a very individual choice. But when there is some question which way to go, err on the side of repetition. Have fun with all of those must-have specimen shrubs and trees—not the background plants. Even a little repetition with your accent pieces will never hurt.

66 **Use symmetrical plantings for any great distance or over many areas with caution because you are dealing with dynamic, living plants. For many reasons, symmetry can be compromised and never fixed.**

The need for symmetry is very human. It gives a sense of order and, probably more important, a sense of control. Many classic structures follow these rules, and even asymmetrical structures, although more subtle, must follow certain rules of weight and balance to achieve an appealing result. Because the plant world is dealing with dynamic, living plants, some issues with symmetry need to be addressed for good results.

First, confirm the cultural conditions will be the same. Will the location be going in and out of full sun to deep shade? Will you hit a bog after coming off a high, dry hill site? Will you be planting next to a hardy grove of trees that will inhibit growth of your plants? Plants react to their specific site. In one place they are robust, elsewhere they lag far behind, and in other locations, they just die. Take the pulse of your site and be prepared to adjust your selection as the cultural situation changes.

Second, decide your recourse when natural occurrences over time damage, disfigure, or kill a plant. This is the famous question of "What comes next?" Select a plant that is easily replaceable. Also, write down the *exact* name because a different cultivar or variety could be a real eyesore. If many years pass and disaster strikes, what does one do with the oddball vacant space? I don't know.

Third, only the hardiest plants should be chosen for long rows of symmetrical plantings. This is no time to experiment with plants on the cutting edge or ones with disease problems. You want the tough-as-nails variety.

Symmetry certainly has its place in a landscape design. But once a homeowner has left a tight, super controlled small situation of three to five plants in a row and has leaped over to planting a massive row of identical trees and shrubs, another dimension of landscaping has been entered. I would enter it with caution.

See   **Planting Under Power Lines**   *331*
      Even and Odd Numbers in Plants   *88*
      China Cabinet Element of Design   *76*
      Photos   *51, 67, 83, 211*

Five tall cypresses and two matched evergreens at both ends of the wall constitute the only major symmetrical plantings in the landscape. Both selections were chosen for their hardiness and because of their limited use, major problems will hopefully be averted down the road.

These symmetrically planted weeping evergreen trees gave some screening and softened the brick wall when positioned against this far wall. But their use was limited as all symmetrical designs should be because of the potential for inherent problems as the years go by.

67 **Aesthetically, the use of symmetry soon becomes monotonous in the landscape if used too much. Provide a mix of plants to create more interest.**

Many sites cry for a symmetrical design. Perfectly matched plants on either side of a classic front entrance are very reassuring and complementary. A knot garden should have its little English boxwoods in perfect rows and matched in size.

But often symmetry is extended to situations where this motif is not only unnecessary but actually detracts from the landscape. For instance, on one site I visited everything was planted in groups of threes—oaks, Foster hollies, river birches, and crape myrtles. Nothing blended with anything. Another site had beautiful oaks planted as a grove in a field but they were in equally spaced rows. If this was a pecan grove, I could understand it but this symmetry was counterproductive to the ambience desired. Even worse is a large rolling field in the countryside where nearly all sides of a pasture are lined in Leyland cypress. The sheer monotony and vastness of this overbearing plant in this bucolic setting is overwhelmingly oppressive in its symmetry.

If a screen is desired, think how much better it would be to look at several plant materials with differing textures and growth habits and develop interesting compositions. The eye glides from one lovely composition to another, enjoying the effects of the various plant forms. This doesn't mean you would plant one of everything (even though you could); it just means that after ten, fifteen, or twenty plants of the same type, everyone would appreciate a little change, for goodness sakes!

In fact, this is a golden opportunity to create a mix of some of your favorite plants that otherwise are just too big to fit in anywhere else in your landscape. It is called a mixed shrub border, but its presence is also a living screen—or any long line of plants used for a purpose.

At my farm I have a hedge between my home and the parking area for a nearby cabin. If I had a few more pages, I could list all the plants used. Every day of the year, there is interest and beauty. This mix is so much better than a monotonous row of "whatever." Because my landscape need did not require symmetry to be successful, I was more than happy not to go that route.

Instead of planting a long string of identical plants for that symmetrical look, try this instead! The neighbors to the right cannot be seen but look how glorious the screening is.

68 **Long dramatic drives on large expansive landscapes should use plants selected for scale, longevity, and loose forms. Only if the hardiest plants are chosen and the cultural situations are identical should they be planted in a symmetrical pattern.**

If the decision has been made to line a long drive to a grand estate, consider these thoughts.

Trees should be chosen for their eventual massive size. Only an oak, maple, elm, pecan, and other Significant Trees can reach the proper size to be in scale with the grandeur of the site. And only these giants with their overarching branches give a sense of endless time and history.

Small Ornamental Trees will always look anemic and lost, and most have poor records in thriving and even surviving the harsh conditions found along a roadside. It is truly sad to see a long row of dogwoods dying out in bits and pieces. And a Bradford pear becomes a mess after any big windstorm. The grandeur of Significant Trees was mistakenly traded for a few years of blooms.

Even choosing a Significant Tree for its form is important. Some of these giants have very distinct, formal shapes such as dawn redwood or deodar cedar. The trap of perfect symmetry is the same as discussed previously. Anything that goes wrong will be quite noticeable. But if the tree has a more informal shape—as do most oaks, maples, and elms—the occasional misadventure will be forgiven because these giants are not identical meatballs or cones anyway.

The last detail worthy of some thought is whether to plant the chosen Significant Trees symmetrically. Evaluate the site to determine if the cultural situation is nearly identical *for each tree.* Next select that special tree species that you know is extremely hardy for your region and for your particular cultural condition. Then just hope the deer don't chew one down, making a mockery of the whole process.

But who can deny that a grand allée of magnificent trees lining an impressive drive is not completely lovely? I hope these suggestions will make it a grand success as the years march by and that homeowners plant some history in their landscape.

See **Significant Trees, Spacing** *96, 98*
 Ornamental Trees *99*

Although tiny saplings now, these trees are a good choice for this grand entrance. These Significant Trees will grow into magnificent specimens of 50 to 70 feet and live many, many years. Their placement is also staggered, which eliminates problems with a symmetrical design, especially on this dry open field.

68

69 **Significant Trees are the dominant features in the landscape; they create the framework for your home and all other plant materials.** Reaching 30, 40, or even 50 feet, these majestic giants create a feeling of wholeness as they cool and soften the effects of any structure. Using Significant Trees as a design element should be every homeowner's first consideration.

The appeal of large, cool shade trees to any site is universal. In the absence of existing Significant Trees, the trick is to strategically plant these future giants to enhance the beauty of the site as the years progress.

I often run into homeowners who exclaim they do not want to cover up their house. "No trees; I want to see my house." Instead, they plant ornamentals, which are beautiful but as the years go by, their contributions to the landscape remain secondary as the house site continues to look hot and barren.

Another homeowner looks ahead and plants a few oaks or elms to the sides and to the back of the home, providing a wonderful framing effect. If the front space is large enough and shade is needed, he adds a few more there. As the years progress, the outline of his home is softened, cooled, and beautifully framed to make this house more of a home for comfortable living.

This is one design element that is the easiest to solve. Significant Trees are easy to plant and care for. Dollar for dollar, they are a bargain. Planting them will add more appeal and value to a home or other structure than any other element in the landscape. *Siting these future giants should be the first thing on your to-do list when working toward a beautiful landscape.*

On smaller sites, the effects of a Significant Tree can actually be on another person's property but its influence is just as valued.

Every photo in this book demonstrates this principle.

See **Cut at Crotch Leaving Collar** *122*
    Pruning Guide *113*
    Continual Maintenance *104*
    No Topping *120*
    Winter Silhouette *118*
    Photos *12, 79, 81, 95, 197, 322*

Sheltering Significant Trees create a soothing environment for this home. The lovely back garden is opened up to the sun but is framed by more of these cooling trees.

Many trees have been thinned out and limbed up over the years as the dynamics of sun and shade change.

Note the bed lines are arranged away from the trees allowing them to be framed into a wonderful setting.

Don't believe the myth that you'll never see a Significant Tree grow to full size.
This is no excuse for not planting a Significant Tree.

The biggest excuse to planting a Significant Tree seems to be "I'll never see it get big." I am so glad our forefathers were not so short-sighted! In the South, trees fairly bound out of their bark, especially when planted in a landscape that is watered, fertilized, mulched, and in full sun. Even in more northern latitudes, just knowing that a wonderful shade tree is coming along gives great comfort to the homeowner.

I am always amused by a customer's surprise when in a *few short years* he has delicious shade and his home looks truly connected to the land with handsome trees framing the home. This same customer can usually look up and down the street and see house after house still sitting out in the hot sun with a cute Ornamental Tree at the front door and maybe another must-have Ornamental in the front lawn. Now this customer realizes the value of planning ahead and planting Significant Trees!

See **Climate, Erosion Control** *108, 109*
Pruning Guide *113*

This homeowner knew his front yard—facing directly west—needed shade, which he planted soon after moving into the house.

Smaller Ornamental Trees are placed near the home to give more immediate shade but also add beauty to the landscape.

This homeowner is slowly removing a lower limb or two every two or three years to create the necessary canopy.

Mulch beds will increase in size as the trees mature, perhaps one day creating an "island" where low shrubbery can be added.

Significant Trees add value to your property, even if they are young and newly planted.

Nearly every customer I have had was influenced to buy property because it had beautiful trees, even if they were not aware of the different kinds they had, or that some might be considered superior to others. Sometimes trees were only a few years old, but the new homeowner was pleased to know they were already part of the landscape. When I've been called to landscape a property without trees, the homeowner has often said, "I wish I could live long enough to see a big tree," or "Can you tell me where I can plant some big trees?" All considered Significant Trees on their property as essential—even if they had to start from scratch.

The excuse that you will be in the home for only a few short years is truly not a valid reason for not planting Significant Trees. Instead, their presence will increase the value of your home when it is time to sell. In many cases, their presence is a major selling point. Just ask your real estate agent!

 Spacing of Significant Trees and all other trees is based on the goals of the homeowner.

Spacing newly planted trees will confound anyone. They start out small but, as we all know, mature over many years. The problem for the homeowner is to try to visualize or even have the patience to allow for future growth. The solution to this problem is to realize that if the homeowner has planted too many trees— maybe too close together—it's important to thin them out by transplanting a few. What is desired is a beautiful and healthy landscape. If that means culling, nature does it and so can the homeowner. If any tree has gotten too big, well, that's why the chainsaw was invented.

I was once asked at a lecture exactly how far apart oaks should be planted. My reply: What do you want those oaks to do for you? Are they to be planted in an allée so they need to stand alone, or do you want their crowns to mesh? Is the oak to be one specimen tree? Or do you want to recreate a forest effect?

Trees will accommodate the space they are allotted. Take notice of them in the forest; they compete for light and nutrients and grow accordingly. Some are quite close, others are more spaced out, but in no situation is there an *exact* spacing.

Another thought on spacing trees in the landscape is to realize many different trees with many different growth patterns are usually grouped together for a certain effect. Reestablishing a forest should perhaps mimic nature's layering method. For instance, a homeowner in my region might plant a tall, skinny tulip poplar, a few loblolly pines, a maple or two, a few oaks, and maybe mix in a few sourwoods. So what is the proper spacing? That's an interesting question, one best answered by visiting your local forests to note what grows in your area and approximately how they are spaced. Then grab a shovel, dig some holes, and get some trees out for your future enjoyment. Don't allow yourself to become paralyzed with indecision because Significant Trees are often critical in many landscapes that are otherwise barren.

See **Sun, Shade** *56*

Succession of a Forest *102*

Photos *205, 208*

73 **Ornamental Trees are colorful, fragrant, have berries or flowers, and often display distinctive attributes.** As ornamentals, their beauty is best displayed in relation to other features in the landscape; they become lost in large vacuous spaces. Their limited size and odd features eliminate them as substitutes for Significant Trees.

Ornamental Trees of ten or twenty feet tall add charm, grace, and even dramatic interest. Cherries, crabapples, lilacs, dogwoods, Japanese maples, and many more add the texture and color we all desire in our garden, through a succession of seasons.

Don't confuse an Ornamental Tree with a Significant Tree, however. When there are no Significant Trees to help frame the site, the smaller Ornamentals continue to look small and the home-site never acquires a settled look. A big house with little Ornamental Trees will never develop the scale necessary for the home to be as beautiful as it should. Ornamentals are the window dressing of great beauty; just don't forget the main event…Significant Trees!

See **Stand Alone Shrubs and Ornamental Trees** *78*
Every Plant Has a Job Description *64*
Special Interrupted View *74*
Shop All Year *67*
Use Local Sources *90*
Photos *65, 66, 103, 364*

A lovely crabapple perfectly displays its beauty in this nook created by the fencing and close proximity to the parking lot. This same tree planted alone in a faraway pasture would be lost. However, if a grove of such trees was planted as a fruit orchard, then together they would create a lovely composition.

The classic 3-foot-high homestead fencing adds a high-maintenance chore but it's warranted. First, it creates a lovely division between the parking space and the lawn; additionally, it helps direct all driving and walking patterns, essential in this public historic setting.

The definition of Trash Trees depends on where you live and the purpose of the tree. However, there are some occasions when it doesn't matter where you live or what you think the purpose of the tree is—it is still trash.

One man's trash is another man's treasure. An empress tree on a large estate can be glorious; next to a patio, a disaster. I have no use for a wild cherry, but a bird lover might want to keep one or two for his little friends. And let's not discuss a mimosa! In one spot a tree might be an ecological disaster, but elsewhere it's fine—for example, a sweet gum tree is a nightmare where people will be walking, but in your woods it is a grand specimen.

I remember walking up to the most beautiful, perfectly sited wild cherry in front of a customer's house. It was mature, in good health (surprise!), and perfectly formed, so the young couple (with limited funds) who owned the property saw no reason to replace it—a perfect example of a Trash Tree as a treasure.

But some trees are just pure trash. For instance, why would anyone ever plant a silver maple over a red maple? There is no variety of privet that is acceptable. Buying a no-name crape myrtle is just throwing your money away, especially when the market is flooded with superior cultivars. So buyer beware: if a tree is sold as extremely fast-growing and really cheap, what would you think? I recommend that you spend a few more bucks and buy a prize for a glorious, long lasting landscape.

 When thinning wooded land, study and identify the trees to keep and to remove. If in doubt, call an expert to avoid mistakes.

Before removing any trees, identify them. Are they wonderful Significant Trees? Are they less desirable Trash Trees? Do you have too many primary forest trees? Are there some "buried" treasures?

For example, on one site I saw that the homeowner had cut out every sourwood, whose twisted trunks looked defective, while every sweet gum, which looked like a maple, was left. Another customer had someone clean up her forest; the smaller trees were cut out while the larger trees were left to mature. The problem was that the smaller trees were white and red oaks, black gums, hickories, and beech; the larger trees were faulty pines, many large sweet gums, and diseased wild cherries. Lack of knowledge was to blame in both cases.

In every landscape with existing trees, some up-front identification can have a great impact on the future beauty for the site. A forest is a living, dynamic event that is continually growing and expanding. Different trees are filling their allotted time and space. Knowing where your particular trees fit into this picture will help you decide which to remove, which to save, and perhaps what to add in the future or save as seedlings for a continued forest rejuvenation.

76 **If a tree or groves of trees are a critical part of your landscape plan, be sure to have them assessed by a professional for their attributes, their health, and even feasibility before you continue.**

Attributes: A tree of apparent great worth might not be the right one to leave in a special situation. I recall a job site that had two large white oaks overhanging a very constricted circular driveway whose grading compromised their massive root systems. I suggested to the owners that the mass of acorns would make this area almost unusable. The oaks were also quite large and aesthetically overpowering to the low-slung house, behind which was a thick forest of magnificent oaks. Eliminating the two out front would not be missed. In their place, I suggested smaller trees that had only leaves as their litter and were much more pleasing aesthetically.

Health: Many homes are built with a special tree or trees as the focal point, without any thought to the tree's health. After everything is said and done, the tree is found to be in bad shape and dies. Years ago a customer had an oak in a key spot that I was sure was in bad shape; it had smelly ooze that seemed to indicate that it was on its last legs. I suggested hiring an arborist, who marked another oak for removal (but not the one I thought was on death's doorstep). Sure enough, even though it looked healthy, the marked tree was hollow and ready to fall. The "smelly ooze" tree was cleaned up, disinfected several times, and continued on its healthy way in that very special spot. If you really are going to design around a special tree or trees, give them a health check first.

Feasibility: A commercial site was named Grand Oaks because some large oaks were "saved" during construction. But no one wanted to recognize that these oaks were at least five to six feet *above grade* and surrounded by parking spaces. Their roots were cut, walls tightly boxed them in, and these magnificent white oaks became less magnificent every year. If at all possible, save any good trees you can. But if it is unavoidable, remove a tree that cannot be saved and plant another once construction is over.

Originally a large pecan grew in this nook, but when the building was remodeled for a five-star restaurant, this deck was to be a serving area. After considering the litter and staining qualities of the pecan, it was replaced with a tidy but large-growing Significant Tree for the necessary shade on this site.

Limbing up was critical for this tree to perform its described duty. Otherwise it would not reach up and over and would have had many limbs smothering the site.

76

77 **Understanding the concept of natural plant succession for your region is important because most home landscapes disrupt this process.** However, with only the least bit of neglect, this natural phenomenon will reestablish and the homeowner must know what is happening.

Nature has a basic process governing the order of how plants grow; ultimately, the result is termed the climax forest. Although I describe a climax forest for much of the eastern U.S., the principle is the same for all areas. If left to a natural progression, nature will follow this definite growth path. It's slow, it's messy—but it will work. Unfortunately, many non-native invasives have disrupted this natural flow so that *even more* knowledge on the homeowner's part is critical to keep this natural succession moving toward positive results.

Barren Field: The first year after new construction starts or crops are abandoned or whatever event allows light and rain to reach the surface, certain weeds appear. Seeds often have been dormant for years, just waiting for a chance to grow, but they save the ground from erosion. In the home landscape, the barren field could be your unweeded flower bed and the untended edge of your property.

Primary Forest: In the third or fourth year, seedlings of pines, sweet gums, poplars, persimmons, and wild cherries seem to spring up from nowhere and dominate the scene. Their density and distribution can vary widely, but they are ubiquitous. These multiple seedlings will continue to appear in the home landscape and might need to be controlled.

Climax Forest: As a primary forest matures, other trees begin their journey. Their qualities are often what people associate with the grandeur of the desirable climax forest. In my region, these trees might be oaks, maples, hickories, or beech. Because of the competition for light and nutrients, they grow slow but strong. Some trees from the primary forest remain, but their numbers are reduced and added to the forest floor as nutrients. The beauty and grandeur of these Significant Trees increase over the years and create a dramatic forest that has a very long life.

When a mature tree dies, it creates a new open space and the progression starts over. Identifying these giants of the forest on your property will result in having the best landscape possible, especially if you allow desired seedlings to live to sustain a continual rejuvenation.

So how does this affect the beauty of your landscape? By observing the kinds of trees and their approximate age, you can assess where the landscape is in this progression so that intelligent decisions can be made. On a newly graded construction site, obviously you have created a barren field. You will likely establish a lawn, but you should also plant some Significant Trees. Otherwise, the landscape will continue to be "barren." If some of your remaining trees are mostly pines and sweet gums (primary forest), look for some Significant Tree seedlings scattered about. They will already have incredible root systems and—with a little help—will quickly grow into your own climax forest. If no seedlings exist, you might start planting some Significant Trees.

Of course the prize goes to the owner of a climax forest.

The goal is to identify the trees, clear only what is necessary, keep out exotic invasive plant material (ivy, privet, honeysuckle, and such), and make sure heavy equipment does not disturb the remaining forest floor that supports the trees with nutrients and controls erosion.

See **Natural Litter** *106*
     Not Maintaining the Site *38*
     Trash Walls *110*
     Photo *73*

77

A barren field has potentially millions of seeds germinating. Mowing keeps seedlings under control; otherwise, a barren field will quickly progress to the next stage. This is also true for any home landscape.

This climax forest is dominated by certain trees found in my region. However, if the land is cleared either by man or nature (resulting from a severe storm), this open spot will revert to a natural succession of plants.

The edge of any forest is susceptible to the rank growth a mix of shrubs and various trees can create. Sometimes this growth can add to the landscape, but often, this unchecked growth creates an unsightly barrier to the forest and contains detrimental plants. For instance, in this photo several lovely dogwoods and a mass of buckeye are visible— that's good. But an invasive plant, such as privet, would take over, destroying this site.

These Ornamental Trees are perfectly sited at the edge of this forest. But if they were planted in the field, they would not thrive culturally and they would look out of place.

78 Trees require maintenance and attention. To achieve a healthy landscape containing trees, you must constantly evaluate seedlings, thin out brush and trash, and attend to the health of older trees, cutting them if necessary.

Nature is a dynamic art form, continually growing and changing. Seldom can a person buy land with trees—or have a landscape installed—then walk inside the home, shut the door, and expect that nothing will need his attention!

Dead and dying trees need to be removed; they're not only ugly but also dangerous. Trees located too close to the home create a hazard. I have seen hundreds of situations where seedlings were left to grow next to a home, then finally were removed at great expense.

Thin trees to get better air circulation, open a view, and help other trees mature better. Remove lower limbs of trees to encourage the trees to grow up instead of out. Remove trees under power lines, as well as trees that create a mess where they are sited or have never done well for various reasons. Why put up with a problem tree?

Not every person wants or has the ability to manage trees; it is dangerous work and should often be left to a professional. But if you own land and you have trees, expect them to be a part of your life.

79 Do not be overwhelmed at the idea of learning the names of trees and their attributes. It is just not that difficult. A little knowledge can go a long way for personal enjoyment as well in landscaping projects.

Usually, trees fall into a particular pattern in a landscape. Even though identification appears complex, once the basic ten or so types are learned, you'll see they just keep repeating themselves. One quickly learns to identify a poplar, then a wild cherry, and understand the differences between a maple and a sweet gum. Even the Ornamental Trees are relatively few in number and are easy to identify once a pattern is established.

Spend a little time with some regional tree books, talk to your local nursery or extension agents, or hire a professional to help get you started in getting to know your trees. Those little "penguins" will then become individuals, so you can decide which ones to cut down or to leave and which ones to plant. Mistakes of this type are quick to make but nearly impossible to correct, and the results must be lived with for years. I know of one homeowner who discovered—just minutes before a bulldozer would have destroyed them—that he had a first rate, rarely seen giant grove of giant black gums. Another finally identified her unique chestnut oak forest. Her new tennis court site was moved.

So get to know your trees on a first-name basis. It will vastly increase the enjoyment of your forest.

Hi, Mr. Oak, Mr. Pine, Mrs. Palm, Miss Maple…

80 If clearing is to be done, mark all Significant Trees and desired shrubs with bright tape—during a time when they can be easily identified. **Otherwise, they might mistakenly be cleared during a season when even mature plants seem to lose their identifying qualities.**

If you have ever walked through a forest, especially one that still gets a fair amount of light allowing numerous smaller trees to grow, it is a curious endeavor to spot the more desirable trees such as a black gum here, a serviceberry there, and lots of different oaks scattered about. But come winter, they look like identical twigs. Bright tape advises the homeowner and any helpers of their presence, allowing him to clean all around what he wishes to save, giving each special tree space to prosper.

See **Clearing** *100*

81 In the plant world, *cultivar* (a contraction of the words "cultivated variety") is a plant that will share the same characteristics as others of the named cultivar. **Cultivars are selectively bred from plants originally chosen for various compelling reasons such as fragrance, color, or size. Planting a cultivar ensures the homeowner can expect the same features in his landscape.**

A homeowner will see all manner of seedlings emerge where they are allowed. How each one performs might be a little different from the others scattered about. But if these differences have an outstanding quality--leaf color, long bloom period, a wonderful growth habit—a plantsman might propagate a particular plant by taking cuttings or tissue cultures to ensure an exact duplicate of the original plant is available.

Cultivars are usually identified by single quotation marks or perhaps just by capital letters: crape myrtle 'Natchez' or NELLIE R. STEVENS holly. If a cultivar is available, read its description so you'll make a better determination of what you can buy for your landscape.

This tape will last two or three years and is visible for long distances. It is also very stretchy, which is essential as it won't gird the tree if accidentally left on too long.

Nature would probably have this tree win out in the long run, but with a little help from the homeowner (by clearing around it), its growth and beauty will move along at a quicker pace.

82 **Every homeowner should think of trees in three categories: Significant, Ornamental, and Trash.** It will help him make decisions about what to keep on his property and what and where to plant for the future.

 83 **The spongy, natural litter under trees is essential for food, moisture retention, and erosion control.** Severe, if not permanent, damage is done when this natural mulch is unnecessarily removed to produce a sophisticated neat appearance using other mulches.

Oftentimes the homeowner's reaction is to lump them all into one category—when property is bought, he exclaims, "See my trees!" But trees are not all the same. They play significantly different roles in the landscape. These roles can be divided into three parts: Significant Trees are the basic framework to all landscape; Ornamental Trees are the window dressing to the landscape; Trash Trees flit in and out of various roles but their drawbacks must be understood.

An obsessive need for order has done more damage to a natural forest than any one factor I see in my landscaping work.

The spongy litter of decaying leaves and limbs that covers forest floors takes years to build. Sometimes forty, fifty, or more years will produce only one-half inch of this "black gold." If you try to dig into this litter, you will find it is intertwined endlessly with roots and you'll discover it's quite light and airy. This is the food for all plant material, and it obviously acts like a sponge to soak up moisture when it rains. Scientists are just now beginning to understand how complex and essential this litter plays in the overall success of forests.

For many homeowners the problem seems to arise with its disheveled appearance. What is natural and acceptable in a national forest is not so attractive in a rather tight, controlled suburban lot. The homeowner will go to great expense and labor to blow, rake, and bag all leaves, leaving the earth neat as a pin—and destroyed. The "black gold" is often removed along with the "messy" leaves and dumped elsewhere! In its place, neater, more "sophisticated" mulch is routinely applied.

After I explain to the customer what the natural process should be, I can often see the struggle within as he contemplates how to accommodate the natural litter "mess" to a personality that requires neatness. Yet accepting and even appreciating the texture of this natural product is necessary, as it plays such a critical role in the health of the forest.

Significant Trees

Ornamental Trees

1. Got my shade . . .
2. Got my decorations . . .
3. Got my trash . . .

Trash Trees

See **High Maintenance – Incorrect Clearing** *15*
Erosion Control *108*
Photo *205*

In a home landscape, replacing the natural mulch is extremely costly and, regrettably, its effectiveness cannot be duplicated.

With a little information, this homeowner can become knowledgeable about what to value and what to remove. In this picture, the wonderful native buckeyes need to be coveted and the nonnative, invasive jewel weed needs to be removed.

Except in extreme cases, removing fallen limbs is counterproductive to a healthy forest. Once their presence is accepted, the beauty of their contribution can be appreciated, especially when turning up rather interesting bugs and watching various mushrooms explode along their lengths.

83

84 All shrubs and trees play a critical role for erosion control, so maintaining their presence and planting more for the future is vitally important.

The major areas to consider for erosion control are denuded land (especially slopes), river and stream banks and their flood plains, and *large open lawns found in subdivisions*. But how do trees and shrubs help?

Consider the impact rain has on the land. If a man stands outside in a heavy rainstorm, he will quickly experience a stinging feeling from large droplets as they strike his body. As they hit the ground, these same droplets pound the earth, quickly collect on the surface, and travel across it at increasing speeds, which allows the water to carry soil downhill.

If the man stands under a tree during this heavy storm, he discovers the rain is dispersed into a mist or smaller droplets; these droplets are more easily absorbed by the spongy combination of mulch, roots, and loosened soil provided by the trees and shrubs.

Nearly every week I visit construction sites eroded to bare soil. Even after the homeowner has landscaped, he often still experiences severe problems; in every case the primary problem stems from the absence of large areas planted with shrub beds and groves of trees. Obviously this problem is multiplied as whole stretches of subdivision lots and other bare-earth situations produce erosion problems of the first order.

So what is the answer? Move as quickly as possible to replenish the site with trees and shrubs. There are always some slopes to manage, areas needed for shade, and other spaces just needing the beauty of the plant world. Pay special attention to areas subject to erosion. I am amazed that zoning and planning departments have stringent tree planting codes for commercial properties but nothing for the hundreds of acres for home construction. Don't wait to be told what to do—the problem is too great to allow your site to be part of the problem, when every homeowner needs to be part of the solution.

See **Grass – Poor Erosion Control** *354*
 Slopes *32*
 Proper Clearing *15*
 Litter – Natural Erosion Control *106*

Drops hit the bare ground,
picking up dirt.

Drops first hit trees and are slowed so
they are absorbed into the ground.

85 Significant, Ornamental, and Trash Trees are critical for climate control. **They have the size and canopy to markedly change the environment directly in their shade and to affect the surrounding breeze.**

A hot western sun might ruin the use of certain rooms in your home. Visitors' cars might be baking in the sun as they are parked out front. The absence of any cooling effects of some trees is sorely missed especially when the children would like to go out to play. A grove of trees could buffer a howling northern wind. In each case, planting trees can dramatically change the site from a negative to a positive one.

Trees are the ultimate climate control tools. Strategically placed, they can solve a lot of your problems. Even standing under a juvenile tree in summer can reduce the temperature on your body significantly. Just think what it can do for your homesite as it matures over the years!

See **Power of the Sun** *57*

Decks *242*

Arbors and Summerhouses *253*

Natural air conditioning.

86 Establishing a climax (or natural) forest is often difficult because many desirable Significant Trees are often not available in a nursery. **So it's wise to nurture what already exists on your property.**

Most oaks, beech, black gums, and other fine Significant Trees are seldom available to buy, or the varieties are quite limited. They have difficult root systems for a nursery-growing operation to deal with, are slow to mature in a nursery setting, and often have an ungainly look in their youth. Nursery growers know which trees can be grown economically and are marketable, so needless to say they will not be growing ones that have a limited market and are costly to grow!

Knowing this, each homeowner should be very aware of what is already present on his property, because replacing any Significant Trees that are accidentally destroyed will often not be possible. Remember, a bulldozer can wipe out a grove of trees that took fifty to eighty years to mature—your lifetime!—and in several hours they are gone. Your replacement choices will be limited to what growers are willing to market, certainly not the ones found in a good mix of Significant Trees on your site.

See **Local Sources** *90*

87   Trash walls are bands of untended, junky plants growing along the periphery of the homeowner's well-kept landscape. **Control them, or they will get out of hand.**

On suburban and in-town lots this space is often not very wide, perhaps only a few inches to a few feet. Because they abut property lines, many homeowners do not attend to this space for whatever reason—the neighbors, their dog, a fence, ambiguity of the lot line, hard to maintain. The homeowner might even see trash walls as providing some sort of quick, much needed privacy. But they can quickly get out of hand; plants grow, but not the kind anyone wants or needs, such as privet, poison ivy, sweet gums—the list is endless. I can think of a number of examples where this space soon overwhelmed the homeowner and encroached more and more on his limited interior landscape.

I also see the detrimental effects of trash walls when the lot borders the edge of a forest, but the edge is left rough. The trash wall soon springs up with all manner of undesirable plants, creating a barrier to the property owner's forest and closing off any visibility. The reason he bought the lot was because of the trees, which are now nearly impossible to see!

The growth of a trash wall is silent and very quick, and neglect can have serious consequences. These trees are often great hazards to homes, and are removed only at great expense and effort. On larger spaces, this trash wall is just an unsightly mess and makes any real efforts in the landscape very difficult.

See   **Maintenance – Grading** *15*

   Fences – Remove if Unnecessary *34*

   No Maintenance Means High Maintenance *38*

   Don't Share Projects *45*

   Photos *81, 103*

At the edge of woodlands or perhaps along the property line, these barren "forests" seem to take hold, creating a massive problem for the future. Removing this unplanted tree that survived as a seedling years ago is going to cost these homeowners a lot of money.

Getting control of the remaining trash wall will be in everyone's interest.

88 Most tree roots reach out beyond the drip line of the tree and are usually found in the top 12-plus inches of the soil. **Human contact can easily have a major impact on the roots of a tree, and therefore its health.**

To maintain tree health: do not park under a tree; do not wash anything containing chemicals under a tree; do not remove the natural litter under a tree; do not dig significantly around a tree; and do not pile materials under a tree—even temporarily.

Trees are living specimens just like humans and animals. They can be stressed and become vulnerable to pests and diseases and die. They need to "eat" by taking in nutrients and drinking water. They have "body" parts such as their roots and transfer cells located just under the bark. When these major transfer cell systems are damaged, a tree's source of nutrients and water is destroyed. The result is death, meaning there's no time to wait for the construction period to end or to postpone watering during a drought.

Since roots are not seen, they are thought of as being not very important. Plus many trees are viewed as big, tough guys that can be punched around a lot and not really hurt. It reminds me of Houdini's tragic death. An admiring sailor caught him after his act and gave a hard punch to the stomach. Houdini was not prepared for the blow, and his internal organs were destroyed. We often damage our trees the same way. We give them a one-two punch and the tree's vital parts are destroyed. Then, we're saddened to see our "tough guys" leave us.

These tough anchor roots lie right at the surface. Even farther out (but broken off by the fall) are many miles of feeder roots, which also run just under the surface searching for water, nutrients, and oxygen.

88

89 **Proper pruning procedures spaced out over several years are essential for the health, beauty, and beneficial elements for which a tree was originally planted. To ignore these procedures--which are simple and take only minutes every few years—will result in a tree you will not like.**

Sadly for many landscapes, the homeowner views his newly planted tree just like one growing in the forest that requires no pruning care. However, he is comparing apples to oranges because the dynamics for the trees in a home landscape and those of the forest are very different and require attention to their differences.

So let us begin; it's as easy as 1-2-3.

1. Remove only broken or dead branches from newly planted trees. Leave all other branches on the trees for several years to allow the leaves to gather food for good root growth. The only exception would be to remove any actively growing suckers from the base of the tree. Once the tree is actively growing, move to Steps 2 and 3.

Small trees getting started naturally in a forest are buffered by surrounding trees from the hot sun and drying winds and have a loose rich soil to send their roots outward for good growth. Have you noticed how hard it is to try to dig even the smallest tree growing in a forest? It has just three leaves, but it has roots reaching to China.

2. Start removing various limbs from your maturing trees. The most important cuts are called limbing up, which means lower limbs are progressively removed every few years as a tree adds new top growth. Bear in mind that trees do not stretch out as our kids do as they grow. Trees add only on to their top, which leaves the original lower limbs hanging close to the ground—forever—if they are not removed. In that case, the tree becomes a giant "ball" instead of the canopy tree you were expecting. Limbing up until the right canopy is established takes care of this problem.

In the forest, trees reach upward for light, leaving the lower branches to atrophy and fall off because they do not get enough sunlight. This is why you see trees in a forest grow very tall and arch over with such lovely canopies. Nature has achieved this because of the different growing situations found in the forest, which are not found in your landscape.

3. Other important pruning cuts to a growing tree include removing crossing branches, double leaders, all suckers from the base, and even removing suckers along the branches of certain trees. One pruning cut that most people do not do is thinning, that is, pruning out branches in a tree to keep it from becoming too full. This is a big problem in a controlled landscape. For some trees thinning keeps it from becoming a hazard as a giant wind catcher, possibly crashing in a storm. Additionally, thinning creates a more beautiful tree in the landscape.

If these problems do occur in the forest, nature has a way of trimming trees in its own manner. Usually, due to the lack of all-around light, their growth habit is looser and these problems are not as prevalent. But in home landscapes, these growth problems can be very problematic and cannot be left unattended if a healthy and attractive landscape is desired

See **Illustration** *113*

Interrupted View *72*

Special Interrupted View *74*

Trees – Continuous Maintenance *104*

**Pruning the Growing Tree
in Your Landscape**

A few proper cuts every few years equals a beautiful tree!

On planting day, prune dead
and broken limbs *only*.

Trim out any double
leaders

Thin branches

Remove
suckers

A few years later.

Continue
to thin

Limb up every few years.

NOW

LATER

The same limb
years later.

A tree grows by adding to its top. This makes "limbing up,"
or removing the lower branches, essential to creating
a beautiful tree in the landscape.

Well-Pruned Tree

Neglected Tree

A mature tree in the landscape . . .
the choice is yours.

Prune plants to expose their inherent beauty. By understanding the qualities and growth pattern of each plant, the correct pruning method can be used.

Every plant has a definite growth habit and identifying shape. As people we powder this, squeeze that, clip and maybe dye our hair—all kinds of things to make the base project (our person) lovelier. The homeowner should consider doing the same things to his plants. He might cut out dead branches, thin out others, and maybe make a drastic cut-back from time to time. Other plants might get sheared into a definite shape and size. But the goal is to enhance the inherent beauty and purpose of each plant.

In other words, pruning is not one-size-fits-all. Often I see whole landscapes completely ruined by indiscriminant shearing as each plant is put on the assembly line and given the same butch haircut. This would be like giving every woman the same hairdo and outfit to wear!

Once the homeowner becomes knowledgeable about each plant—what it is supposed to look like, how big it should get, its growth habit—he can better judge how to make it look its very best, and not look like every other plant on his property. The homeowner is now correctly pruning and helping each plant show off its best beautifully.

See **Choose Plants for Mature Size** *35*
   Plants for Specific Jobs *64*
   Pruning and Shearing – Two Different Jobs *115*
   Photos *71, 82, 94, 123, 211*

This conifer was left to mature into a naturally beautiful specimen.

This tree needs only a little thinning to correct some inappropriate branches.

These evergreens must be sheared to maintain their formal appearance.

Some shrubs must not be sheared or they will lose their inherent beauty found in their distinctive growth pattern.

These foundation-type shrubs are sheared to keep them tidy, especially important in an institutional site. On a home site, they might be left to grow more naturally with much less attention for a perfect shape.

92 Pruning and shearing are two different ways to trim a plant with totally different results. Pruning entails many different operations and approaches adjusted to each plant. Shearing cuts the outer tips of a plant to establish a definite shape, such as a hedge, ball, cone, or even a rabbit (think Disney World). When used correctly, both pruning and shearing enhance the beauty of the landscape.

Shearing has gotten a bad rap because it is too often used on everything, but in fact shearing certain plants gives a very ordered effect necessary in many landscapes. The key is to select those plants that best respond to this particular method—and there are many on the market. Generally these plants grow into an desired orderly shape already; shearing just makes them neater and perhaps the same size within a group.

The trick is to match the plant to the shape and size desired. If a homeowner wants to "box" a plant when the plant wants to grow into a cone shape (such as a Foster holly), the plant will continually send up shoots for its inherited, tall lean growth pattern no matter how much and how often a homeowner cuts. Yet there are many other plants a homeowner could have chosen that could have been easily sheared to a box shape. Similarly, when the homeowner ignores the genetically coded mature size and wants to maintain a much smaller one (such as keeping a Foster holly at four to five feet, when it's programmed to grow twenty feet or more), it is a losing battle.

Pruning, on the other hand, can require many different operations. Removing dead branches should always be done first. Limbing up could be used to get a tree growing up and over. Sometimes the homeowner can reach in and remove limbs to thin out a plant that has gotten too thick. Crossing branches can also be removed. Sometimes a stray branch will spring out too far; cutting it back to a joint will help the plant to get back into shape—a natural one.

Cutting out old woody parts on shrubs will allow newer growth more space to fill in; even drastic total cut-backs will rejuvenate other shrubs.

In essence, plants can use a little attention with the clippers or loppers. The trick is to use these tools correctly on any given plant to discover its own particular beauty. Pruning can be a lot of different operations; shearing is for forming definite shapes considering the growth habits of the plant being sheared.

Most institutions and many homeowners have turned over their maintenance to professional crews. Unfortunately, in my travels over the United States, over and over again I see many landscape plants sheared into identical "meatballs." In some cases, the landscape maintenance crews inherited a situation not of their doing and must keep the plants under some kind of control. But in too many cases, many plants that were planted for their inherent loveliness have all but been destroyed by this lack of awareness that plants are different and should be treated as such. Why does this continue? Because these crews are not being taught the most basic techniques of pruning. (If they were, it would reduce their maintenance chores even more, thereby reducing costs to the property owners.)

The ramifications of this neglect are far reaching. Because these landscapes are often in public view, many people assume these professionals know what they are doing and go home and do likewise. It is truly an uphill battle to explain to each homeowner what needs to be done. What you as the homeowners are often seeing is not correct. Part of my job is to point out good examples of proper pruning.

These landscape professionals often can produce the most perfect lawn imaginable, edged perfectly and groomed beautifully. But with all the time and money spent on the lawn, very little attention is paid to perhaps the most attractive parts of the landscape. Those continue to be compromised every day by lack of proper training in pruning.

See **Plants – Choose for Mature Size and Shape** *35*
　　　Photo *114*

The Japanese maple at the fence line is limbed up and thinned periodically for a perfect accent tree. The viburnum is groomed to allow its natural growth habit, tipping back an errant branch from time to time.

A little shearing of plants that naturally grow to the desired size and shape makes for a beautiful landscape.

92

It may require a lot more shearing but still the plant choices are in keeping with the size and shape desired. In fact, some are barely sheared because their shape is already quite formal and tailored.

92

These large hollies are kept sheared into a more formal shape. However, their sheared size and shape is nearly their natural mature size and shape, allowing this operation to be quite doable with an experienced maintenance crew. The outcome is lovely in the landscape.

If this same holly were sheared into another shape and to a much reduced size, the outcome would be quite unpleasant and would create a distraction from the landscape.

The mix of textures, plus the formal with the informal style, creates a more pleasing three-dimensional landscape.

92

93 The winter silhouette of any deciduous plant is as important as its bloom or its leaves. Therefore, proper pruning is vitally important.

Most homeowners wish to fill their landscape primarily with evergreens, which are full and rewarding every day. But many desirable plants are deciduous (lose their leaves in winter) from the largest Significant Trees to Ornamental Trees and all of those must-have shrubs. When winter comes, many people think the landscape show is over. They are unaware that winter is just as important as any other season and can reveal great beauty in the landscape. So why has this beauty so often been compromised? Most homeowners are unaware how improper pruning cuts can quickly destroy the beauty and uniqueness of a particular plant. And it is during winter that these improper cuts stand out as sore thumbs to make for a very unappealing winterscape.

Let's discuss how this happens on many landscapes and what a proper cut should have been.

Example: A branch extends out over the driveway and the homeowner makes a stub cut to remove it so the car can get by. He has actually sheared the tree like a shrub. This leaves an unattractive stub to either die back or perhaps sprout multiple unappealing branches the following year.

Better: Instead of the stub cut, he should prune the tree by pruning back to a major joint or even start limbing up the tree to allow it to grow over the drive. The tree will then display its beautiful silhouette all winter instead of displaying a lot of ugly stubby cuts, many with multiple switches growing out at unappealing angles.

Example: A lovely small tree is planted just outside a bay window. It does very well and becomes quite full, perhaps blocking the view more than the homeowner wants. His solution is to shear the plant back, thereby permanently deforming it and destroying any beauty it might have had for winter.

Better: Instead of shearing, pruning this plant will enhance its beauty for both summer and winter.

Selected branches should be removed, making sure to prune back to a joint for a smooth transition. This thinning process continues until the homeowner has the effect he desires. In some cases, the plant is limbed up, which eventually allows it to arch up and over the window.

Example: Still another example is when a homeowner shears a plant because it is getting too tall. I see a plant that was cut at perhaps five feet but it would never have grown much beyond that anyway. The lovely natural effects of the plant are now destroyed, especially when viewed in winter.

Better: The homeowner should ask how big a particular plant might be expected to mature. If it's a plant in the wrong place, then remove it; but if it is in the right place, perhaps just thinning it every few years to remove the old woody parts is all that's necessary.

Example: A last example is about plants that are misunderstood. There was a myth that crape myrtles would not bloom unless they were cut back each year, and shearing their tops was recommended. As the years passed, horrible stubs were created and their winter silhouette was hideous. Slowly this misinformation has been countered and these beautiful trees are being restored back to their year-round beauty, their beautiful silhouettes once again part of the winter landscape.

Better: Plants should be properly *pruned*—not sheared. This means cutting ugly suckers; keeping the main branches and removing spindly ones; removing crossing branches and ones too close together to create a layered look; and always making cuts at a joint, leaving the collar intact for proper healing. Absolutely no stubs should be left to destroy the overall beauty, especially for winter appearance.

When you have loppers or saw in hand, *think* before you cut. Just lopping a limb off to solve your immediate problem can actually create more problems and destroy the beauty of the plant. But with a little thought, that pruning cut can actually solve your problem and put you on the road to enhance the beauty of the plant.

Nature can be very dramatic—but if this plant is stubbed back, its winter beauty will be destroyed. If the homeowner wishes, he might instead remove a limb or two as aesthetics dictate, being careful not to leave any unsightly stubs.

Note the perfectly formed boxwood to the right. Only a periodic light shearing needs to be done to retain this formal shape indefinitely.

93

94 **"Topping" trees for any reason is seldom appropriate. It can cause a hazardous health problem for the tree, and it destroys its beauty, especially the winter silhouette.**

Tree-topping might be done for any number of reasons: Stress might kill outer branches, which are cut back to live wood. The tree might be growing up into a power line or overhanging a house. Sometimes I see trees topped just because the owner wants them reduced in size.

In some cases the cuts can be made judicially, leaving the tree in fairly good shape; but if significant topping—leaving large branches with exposed upward stubs—is in order, the tree needs to be removed instead. Not only is topping detrimental to the overall health of the tree, perhaps causing an even more hazardous situation, but the beauty of the tree is destroyed.

Remember, the roots have established their need for a certain amount of calories. If drastic toppings occur, the tree will recover its calorie loss by throwing out numerous unlovely replacement limbs, multiple suckers, and excessive sprouts everywhere it can. Topping has now created a monster of high maintenance and ugliness.

Cuts should be done to discover the natural beauty of a tree…they should not be the cause of its loss. Remove tree-topping from your list of things to do in your landscape.

See   **Low Maintenance – Picking the Tree for the Right Mature Size** *35*
    Illustration *113*
    Utility – Power Lines *331*

Why would anyone top a tree and destroy its beauty! This sycamore's winter silhouette makes the landscape a magnificent joy.

94

95 Many shrubs have a rather loose growth habit, especially flowering ones (such as spiraea, forsythia, mock orange, and quince). **Instead of shearing these plants to conform to an ideal of a beautiful landscape of neatly clipped round balls, these plants should be replaced with other selections that grow naturally in a formal shape.**

Each of us has a particular personality that sees beauty in many different ways. One can travel to the garden at Versailles, with its endless formal shapes and clipped hedges, and think he is in heaven. Others travel long distances to view famous formal gardens with tulips and hyacinths planted in masses of endless, ordered patterns. Just as many travel to stroll through English gardens filled with countless varieties of plants all mixed together; they come home to their own mix-and-match theme and love it. Others will visit marshes or national forests and find their ideal there.

The problem begins when a homeowner does not identify his personality type. Inadvertently he might have some of these loose, airy type of plants and will try to force them into his acceptable formal shapes. This begins an endless, wearisome chore of shearing these carefree beauties into exact shapes; they respond by poking out branches here and there to mock him; and the end result is a landscape that has been spoiled.

The solution? Once you identify your landscaping personality type, choose only those plants that conform. If a wispy spiraea is bothersome, remove it. If the quince looks too rough, remove it. Do not keep any mispruned plant, trying to force it into an unnatural shape. By making these choices, you'll have your own, very personal beautiful landscape; the neighbor down the street who happens to love all that "messy" stuff will have his.

See **Plants for Specific Jobs** *64*
Use Local Sources *90*

The large arching pyracantha behind these chairs was a favorite choice to espalier on walls (this application has gone out of vogue, fortunately). See how this variety, when pruned upward, allows its natural growth pattern to show itself, creating an incredible massive form that will be nothing short of spectacular when full of berries in winter.

If a formal, neat row of evergreens is more your style, then removing these pyracanthas would be correct. Trying to force this pyracantha into a formal hedge would create a maintenance nightmare and be counterproductive to the inherent beauty of the plant.

96 **Remove limbs at a crotch or juncture, leaving the collar intact for proper healing and for beauty. This means limbs removed from any part of a tree are not cut just anywhere to avoid leaving a most unattractive stub with its inherent problems and ugliness.**

Each juncture of a tree indicates a physical separation to another part of the tree. The swelling—called the collar—at each juncture has special properties that help seal off the wound for proper healing when it's left intact. These junctures are your guide as to where to make a pruning cut.

If you cut too closely to the tree, you will remove the healing properties of the collar. This can damage the tree. If you cut farther out from the collar, leaving a stub, the tree may rejuvenate by sprouting multiple branches (so your cut is to no avail). Or the stub may die back to the collar, thereby introducing the possibility of creating a physical problem for the tree. When properly cut, the tree quickly heals and you are on your way to helping nature create a beautiful specimen for all to enjoy.

Beauty is another important factor. When stubs are carelessly left or even whole branches cut back to stubs to make way for whatever reason, this creates a silhouette that is one of the most unbecoming elements in a landscape. Only in summer, when the plant is covered in foliage, might the silhouette be unnoticed. But a landscape is an all-year project. A properly pruned tree becomes an object of joy and beauty in every landscape every day of the year.

See **Natural Limbing Up** *112*
    Photos *96, 101, 103*

Limbing up is essential in many cases for aesthetics, visibility, and utility elements in the landscape. If these same cuts had been carelessly done with stubs sticking out, many more problems would have occurred.

Note the swelling or collar, then the cut. Proper healing will take place and the beauty of the tree will be intact for a beautiful landscape. Remember, big or small, every plant has this collar at every juncture.

96

Limbing up or removing too many limbs at any one time from a tree can damage, stunt, or kill a tree.

Leaves are the method by which a tree gathers nutrients. Therefore, prune your trees as you would like your own diet to be administered—at a balanced pace in sync with your goals. Any severe reduction of food intake for any living thing can only be bad … starvation is not good for anyone. Temperate cuts every two or three years are more in order. Of course at some stage, the tree will have the branches just where you want them and no more limbing up will be needed. However, aging branches become quite heavy and begin to droop and there you are again, limbing up your tree.

As a tree matures, certain branches will atrophy and need to be removed. This is a natural progression and will usually accelerate as the tree is reaching its natural death.

Necessary thinning creates lovely, healthy growth. A tree or shrub with too many branches encourages insect and disease problems, and makes the plant more susceptible to wind damage.

Limit shearing to those plants that easily conform to a defined shape. Trees such as this one most definitely do not conform. Prune these types to direct all growth into its natural shape.

Every one to three years, as Significant and Ornamental Trees grow upward, remove several lower limbs until the mature canopy height is reached and no further cuts are necessary. It is important not too many cuts are made at one time.

All cuts were made at the collar, which quickly healed, leaving little knobs that will disappear as the tree matures. No stubs were left to grow unsightly sprouts or turn black as they die back to the trunk.

No suckers are allowed to grow.

98 Timing can make a big difference when pruning blooming plants. **Generally, if a shrub or tree needs a full year to set buds, prune only after it blooms, allowing it time to set buds for the next year's bloom. If flowers and berries are produced on new growth, prune in late winter or early spring, because results will appear in a few weeks or months.**

We all know that different plants can be selected to bloom throughout the year in some regions (less so in more severe climates). Here in Atlanta, I can have a winter-blooming daphne and fragrant honeysuckle bush, a cherry tree and azaleas in spring, summer-blooming crape myrtles, and sasanquas that bloom in fall. Perhaps every one of these might need to be pruned at some time for a particular reason. So how do I decide *when* to prune?

Full-year-cycle Plants: Most shrubs and trees begin new growth and set buds for the next year *just after blooming.* It might take the whole year to carry out this process, but some just need a good long time during the growing season to set buds. For instance, the dogwood will bloom in spring and during the summer; and the new buds are grown and become quite prominent just beyond the red berries from last spring's blooms. Other plants such as azaleas do not show off their bloom buds for the next year but they are there; as soon as they quit blooming, new growth produces new buds for the following year.

So what does this mean? It means you should prune *after they bloom,* leaving plenty of growth time to set buds for next year's blooms. For instance, the forsythia might need to be shaped; the spiraea might need to be thinned; the weigela might have become woody and need a full blown cut-back for rejuvenation; the azaleas have gotten too big. But make these cuts either while they are blooming (for flower arrangements!) or soon afterwards.

Flowers and Berries on New Growth: Many plants produce flowers and berries on new growth put forth in a few short weeks and months of spring and summer. There are no sleeping buds waiting to burst open after a long winter's sleep; there is nothing there at all. Therefore, pruning these plants usually takes place just at the end of winter, just before they burst forth in growth.

Take roses, for example. After pruning in late February, the new growth quickly produces a wonderful display. Georgia's crape myrtles and chaste trees usually need some grooming (not shearing) at this time. Nandinas will quickly recover from drastic cuts and produce spring flowers, then fall berries. Every one of these plants produces flowers and berries on new wood. Pruning them at the end of winter and early spring will give them plenty of time to put on their show during the following months.

So how do you know which plant is which? You can either ask or observe. Many homeowners have mentioned to me they do not have any blooms or berries on certain plants. Once they understand this basic principle, pruning is not such a mystery.

This winter-blooming spirea can be cut now for arrangements and, in the coming weeks, thinned and tipped back to remove ungainly growth. New growth will begin in spring, putting on new buds for the following winter display. Remember, many flowering shrubs are very forgiving and can be groomed throughout the year, but if a major cut-back is made too late in the season, there will be no blooms the coming season.

The blue blooms of this vitex tree are set on new wood. This means making major pruning cuts in late winter or early spring, allowing new growth with new buds to flower a few months later in the season.

99 Transplanting can be cost-effective or very expensive. In every case, first evaluate the value of the plant, the time and expense required to move it, and its chances of survival.

Plants installed by the builder at the time of new construction (which may be inappropriate selections due to their mature growth habits) can be properly transplanted, especially large specimens. Since they have not developed extended root systems, moving them as soon as the weather cools off ensures a large survival rate, while labor costs are minimal.

Moving larger established plants can also be done quite satisfactorily. Select only extremely hardy types that have root systems that recover quite well. Replacing mature plants of this type would be costly, so saving them saves you money. On the other hand, there is no savings in transplanting old, large shrubs that are really rather ordinary specimens, just because you could not bear to see them "wasted." These same plants bought new will grow quickly and healthy.

Some plants have such a high mortality rate when moved that it just does not make sense to relocate them. Dogwoods are an example of a plant with a root structure that makes moving them almost impossible (in fact, if taken from the wild, most dogwoods do not survive).

The landscape is quite unattractive as fruitless transplanting plays out, so consider all the factors before moving trees and shrubs.

 100 Transplanting needs to be done in cool weather, accomplished quickly, and plants watered promptly.

Roots live underground where it is dark and usually damp. As soon as the roots are exposed to the bright sunshine and drying winds, bad things start to happen, many times irreversibly. If you cannot have a site ready for immediate planting, wrap the roots in a tarp, cover them with mulch, or temporarily store the plant in a container, adding some water and setting the plants in some shade. In other words, the roots need to feel they have never left their underground home…cool, dark, and damp.

If the transplanting has to be done in the hot months, these operations have little margin for error and the mortality rate will be in question. Also there must be continued daily care (usually monitoring for water needs) until the cooler months set in.

Digging should be done during the coolest part of the day in the coolest times of the year and preferably on a cloudy day. If it turns hot and dry, suspend digging if you can. If you can't, just remember every minute those roots are exposed to this unfriendly environment, they quickly lose their ability to recover and grow.

See **Flowers – When to Move** *154*
Flowers – Their Roots *152*

Transplant or remove.

Transplanting historic and sentimental plants has no monetary value.

Over the years I have seen a plant become a valuable part of a person's life, far beyond its actual monetary value. The cost of transplanting is not even discussed. How hard it will be to dig and haul elsewhere and what its chances of survival are don't matter. Instead, every effort is made to make this operation succeed. I can still remember some of these situations.

"I planted this Japanese maple when we first moved into our old house. I am so glad I found someone to transplant it to our new home." (No mention of the expense of this operation.)

"This camellia has been in our family for three generations. Mama would bring its blooms in every winter and float them in bowls at dinnertime. It has been a real struggle getting it here and keeping it alive but we sure were not going to leave it behind." (No money is mentioned.)

"My daughter planted these irises as a little girl and we have taken some roots to every house we have lived in ever since. They've been all over this country and she has some at her home now that she is married." (No mention of the effort to dig and move these irises.)

Some things do not have a price tag. The landscape is more beautiful because these treasures have been saved and added to the new site with all of their memories intact.

 Transplanting from the wild for your personal enjoyment is usually not the right thing to do and can be illegal. Transplanting as part of a supervised rescue operation is invaluable.

If you want something from the wild that is obviously scarce in that habitat and not easily bought at a nursery, its apparent scarcity should indicate that the plant has a very limited ability to adjust to most situations. Transplanting usually results in failure, and, worse, this plant is no longer in its natural environment where it could have regenerated future plantings. It is important to note that some plants are legally protected from being taken from the wild, to prevent this sort of misguided activity.

On the other hand, organizations have sprung up around the country that rescue plants having intrinsic value if they would otherwise be destroyed by developments. They might be beautiful, grow only in very limited situations (making them quite scarce), or play a valuable role in the ecological whole. Digging and planting them elsewhere might save them. The secondary benefit is that these organizations highlight the value of these plants. When people are willing to give money, go out to dig, and spend time with these endeavors, the public responds by rethinking the value of these plants in their own landscape.

By heightening an awareness of native plants, rescue operations help homeowners better understand these plants' value on their own property; perhaps they will be saved for a more beautiful landscape.

Adding Drama

Flowers and Containers in the Landscape Design

Gardening is a never-ending adventure—Alice's escapades in Wonderland pale in comparison. As the drama unfolds, the homeowner is rewarded by seeing his creation come alive in endless variations.

Containers and raised beds can have a dramatic impact in the landscape. Architectural details of containers themselves create strong focal points, while providing a boon to homeowners with space limitations.

Flower and container gardening are all about planning, but trial and error is all part of the game, leading up to that moment when a combination of plants comes together in just the right way. A gardener can exist without flowers, but he cannot truly live without them.

Any dramatic plan for a flower bed needs to be sited for maximum visibility from the primary living areas.

A seldom-seen bed or one that it is placed completely out of sight, thus making a visit to it one that has to be planned, is guaranteed to fail. (I love reading *The Secret Garden,* but they never mention the secret gardeners!) Unseen gardens can have unseen problems that arise so quietly and so quickly that they overwhelm even the best gardeners. Then after hours of toil to rectify the situation, the gardener turns and walks to the homesite to rest awhile—but gets no reward by looking over the vista because no part of the garden is visible.

On the other hand, if you sit at your breakfast table or lounge on your back porch and can *see* the garden, it will have an immediate and compelling effect. It can be viewed in the morning as you eat a quick breakfast; you'll see the morning dew sparkle and will check out the irises for promising blooms. In the evenings you will find yourself walking out into the garden to pull a few weeds, cut back a plant, or make a decision to move this or that. It is the daily interaction with the garden that is so rewarding. All of the minutiae in a visible garden add so much to your life.

Other easily viewed sites are the Car Area (where many people these days spend a lot of time) and the front yard, especially at the front door (Guest Entrance). These gardens might not be as intimate as your backyard creations, but they are still quite visible and will be enjoyed every day.

It's no secret—"the squeaky wheel gets the oil" holds true with a flower bed. If you don't see it, the flowers will go untended…and their joy will be missed.

See **Indoor Living Space** *46*
  Car Area *167*
  Focal Points *54*

103

This fence is actually for the vegetable garden, which is not always so attractive but still close by for convenience and full enjoyment.

Formal fencing is always level.

This new addition has just the right vantage point to fully enjoy the beauty of this garden.

Full-sun flowers are planted away from large shade trees, which compete for sunlight.

This brick border doubles as an edging for lower maintenance and as a walkway.

Incidental seating provides an inviting respite from working in the garden.

104 **Dream big but start out small.** **The process of creating, expanding, and maintaining a flower garden is probably one of the greatest joys in life, and once a homeowner can reconcile his resources with his dreams, he can better determine the extent to which he wishes to garden. This makes for a successful and beautiful landscape.**

No one can tell another how his time and energy should be spent—and gardening is a passion that really has no common sense to it at all. We will haul manure by the truckloads, spread granite dust until our backs break, till and turn beds until dark, and plant flowers with a vision of fantastic glories ahead while the kids pine for supper. But keep in mind that continually creating and enlarging might eventually lead to overwhelming day-to-day maintenance chores that overshadow your dreams. So figure out your capacity for gardening by going slow.

For example, I had one friend who moved to a large farm in the country, although she and her husband still worked in the city. In my design, I placed a six-by-ten-foot perennial bed at her patio. My friend expressed surprise at the conservative size, but my answer was, "See how this goes, because we can always add to it." Several years later, I ran into her at the nursery. She threw her arms around me and laughed, "How did you know? I can barely keep up with the bed you gave me!" She had the vision of what she wanted, but the truth was that her life allowed her only so much time for gardening.

Another friend moved to a large country estate. She has great strength, many resources, and wonderful talents, and her beds stretch out in all directions. Hers is truly one of the loveliest gardens I have ever visited. But a visit to this garden also includes an introduction to her staff—ladies hired to weed, divide, replant, and do whatever it takes to help her maintain these vast areas of flowers. My friend is willing to accept the maintenance that comes with all of her dreams; the day-to-day process is her joy.

Each one of these people knows who she is and gardens accordingly—and therefore successfully.

See **Low Maintenance – Too Many Projects** *13*

104

The original plan for a flower bed on this historic site was much larger in scale. The caregiver seems to be very happy with this size as the whole property makes many more demands on her time. Of course, expansion is always an option.

The entrance to the toolshed is conveniently located just left of the chimney.

The garden is close by so it will never be ignored.

The natural border—using rocks taken from the nearby woods—adds to the charm.

Notice the mix of edibles and flowers within one setting…herbs, tomatoes, and peppers.

Placing all of these different plants in one setting allows each to take center stage at different seasons.

105 **When planning a flower border, choose plants with these attributes: foliage; long bloom period; noninvasive; seldom needs division to succeed; and disease- and pest-resistant.**

The *foliage* of flowers and complementary shrubs is actually more important than their pretty blooms in the creation of a beautiful garden. Sure, every gardening catalog is full of photos of blooms; in fact, I have often been shown pictures of gardens that customers want to emulate. But once I ask them to cross out everything but the blooms, they become aware that it is the whole picture they want. Blossoms are important but are only part of the whole. The fact that most perennials do not have a long bloom period only adds to the importance of their foliage; it is annuals that create dramatic color in the garden—but many homeowners do not want to replant their entire garden each season!

This pushes the homeowner again to examine his choices on his perennial list. As he considers each one, the image of its foliage begins to take on a bigger and bigger role…as it should. In fact, for some perennials the foliage *is* the reason for its appeal. Has anyone ever cared if a lamb's ear blooms? Some artemisias add color and texture that can truly stand alone. Other plants have so much foliage color that the bloom is only part of the act. For instance, try a 'Bengal Tiger' canna in your garden—what a show-off! And yes, a few hostas have great blooms, but that is not what draws people to the many varieties.

Additionally most annuals and some perennials should be chosen for their *long bloom period.* Most annuals blossom throughout the whole season (but not always). On the other hand, most perennials only bloom for a week or two or three—but again there are some choices out there that go for many weeks and even the whole season. Part of the joy of gardening is tucking in here and there those certain special plants one simply *must* have. But for enjoyment over the long haul, a balance of these plus long-blooming varieties is in order.

The number one functional concern is choosing perennials that are *not invasive.* What begins as a neatly laid out design that looks "oh so pretty" the first year or two can become a nightmare if this negative feature is not noted. A highly invasive flower races over the bed (putting down roots or throwing seeds), swallowing all other beauties in its path; no amount of digging and removal seems to stop its destruction. Use several of these invasive types, and flower gardening will become a never-ending battle. If you must have a particular flower that's known to be invasive, choose its spot well—which means far away from anything else in the garden. My bee balm is down by my streambed. Many unnecessary gardening chores can be eliminated if you are aware of the aggressive habits of a particular plant. Then it's your choice if and where you wish to add it to your garden.

Other flowers are not invasive but *need division every year or two or three* or they die out. This might not seem like such a trial and it is not—until one has purchased too many of this type and the numbers game becomes overwhelming. There is not enough time in the day to keep everything in top shape each Season. I love German iris, fall asters, and other daisy-type flowers but they require maintenance. Sometimes getting everything thinned and divided moves right along, sometimes it doesn't; we'll see how this year goes.

If you must have flowers that you *know* have *disease or pest problems,* keep that list short! You may find yourself spending a lot of time spraying insecticides—and with the need to be ecologically aware, this type gardening shouldn't be encouraged.

So what are the plants that fit this criteria? My list keeps changing a little here and a little there—every year something new will be introduced and I start testing it. Sometimes it is just an old ignored garden plant that has finally been rediscovered. After several years of watchful testing, I add one or two to my list and might shove off others for auxiliary plantings only.

Garden space is valuable. Every square foot takes hard work to prepare and maintain. Putting in the best plants that require the least amount of work for the longest range of effectiveness is just smart gardening.

See **Planting Zone** *28*
Other Factors Besides Planting Zone *29*
Shop All Year *67*
China Cabinet Element of Design *76*

105

The bright-red bee balm is highly invasive under normal situations, but its attractiveness to hummingbirds makes it a must for many gardens. In this location it can spread as it wishes and be enjoyed from a major viewing site above.

Note motion-detector lights, which allow the homeowners to move about easily at night.

This tall, evergreen Ornamental Tree is put to good use as a softening agent at the corner of this rather stark basement area.

To the far right is clethra, another colonizing but quite controllable shrub, which has plenty of room to expand. But there is nowhere in this space that would be appropriate for bamboo, ivy, or other highly invasive plantings because of their overly aggressive and ultimately unmanageable behavior.

106 A perennial can be invasive in one region but not necessarily invasive in another.

One person's plant horror is not necessarily the same for another. In the South, lythrum is a very well-behaved perennial, but move it farther north and it becomes quite invasive in many wetlands. 'Miss Huff' lantana is a welcome addition for the middle South, but in the lower South, many view it as a pest. Recently, I read everything I could get my hands on about Japanese knotweed (not the vine *Polygonum japonicum* but the bush *Fallopia japonica*). I have struggled for years to get mine to grow and I have only seen it twice during all these years, once where I dug my original plant and another in north Georgia. Yet reading about it makes it appear as if it's taking over the world. It probably is, but not in my world.

My advice is to stay informed to be part of the solution, not part of the problem.

See **Low Maintenance – Avoid Invasives** *31*

107 Flowers can be quite tame with their seed dispersal, but others reseed with nightmarish results.

Occasionally zinnias reseed in my vegetable garden or a marigold might sprout up somewhere the following spring. Even several lilies have appeared in my garden from seeds. Most annuals and perennials develop seeds but the seeds usually appear in small numbers if left to disperse naturally. Some gardeners actually collect seeds and store them to plant at the right time. But many seeds are too small or complicated to collect, so most gardeners buy commercially harvested seeds.

Other flowers come back in fantastic numbers due to prolific reseeding. Cleome will seed out like a carpet, and even the tiny seedlings are already sticky, spiny things hard to remove from all the nooks and crannies in any flower bed. My melapodium was finally eradicated using herbicides. One of my favorite annuals, gloriosa daisy, erupts with seedlings coming up all over my wild and woolly natural garden.

Knowing the habits of any flower is knowledge which allows you to garden wisely. It is perfectly alright to ask about the characteristics of every plant you buy or obtain from a friend before you plant it.

This perennial seeds out each spring directly under its broad leathery leaves, giving the homeowner additional plantings without becoming invasive.

These annuals reseed every year to the delight of this homeowner. With no care, this flower acts as a colorful groundcover throughout the summer months. But some homeowners are not always so happy with its freedom in their garden.

108 **The herb garden rates high on everyone's list as a garden essential.** However, herbs should seldom be planted together; instead they should be sited in your garden as individuals, according to their cultural needs and your personal aesthetic desires.

Have you ever visited an herb garden in a botanical or display garden that was just perfect? In fact, the only things in these gardens that usually look great are the tidy fences, smooth paths, and the carefully pruned hedges and edgings. The herbs themselves are often unruly; many are rough, some become invasive, some turn woody, others are only annuals, some are tender and need winter protection—should I say more?

Most homeowners really want only a few herbs to use in their cooking. High on the list are rosemary, parsley, basil, fennel, dill, mint, oregano, and thyme. There are many more herbs and there will always be additions as culinary tastes demand. But where to put them—that is the sixty-four-thousand-dollar question!

The answer is close to the kitchen or where they can be grown successfully. Mint might find a home completely surrounded by concrete next to the back porch steps or in a large urn; thus its invasive qualities are in check but the leaves can still be enjoyed by all. Seeds or plants of basil (oh, the varieties!) can be stuck in anywhere. It's a nice annual for any flower border. The same goes for parsley; just know it's a biennial and will bolt the second year (maybe you'll get lucky and get a good crop of babies). Of course, dill and fennel will give you plenty of babies, maybe too many. Oregano, thyme, and rosemary make great edging or rock garden plants; sages come in many different foliages adding interest to any flower border.

Read about each herb you wish to add to your garden. Their many differences must be accommodated for good results and this might not be in one spot called "the herb garden."

And don't forget containers—most herbs love good drainage. There is a lot of fun to be had planting your herb garden just outside your kitchen door. This might be all the "herb garden" you need.

See **Containers** *156*
 Percolation – Planting Guide *22, 23*

The herb garden is located three steps off the kitchen door and not down the flight of stairs to the main garden. Most herbs love full sun and good air circulation as well as good drainage.

108

109 **Choice of blossom color is a personal matter. From the wild and zany to the most subdued theme, each color is perfect if it pleases the homeowner.**

Watching people at the nursery and enjoying the gardens at many homes over the years, I've seen countless color combinations (both in the flowers and the foliage) that were attractive to various folks. At my nursery a customer might ask for suggestions as he is filling his cart, then as I reach for one color, he reaches over for another. I might select the soft-orange fall aster; he passes that over for a hot-pink rose. One wants a striking yellow-edged yucca, another finds it horrifying. I have come to realize that when putting certain plants together, if the homeowner likes it, it's right!

Colors themselves have their own stories. We often talk about how hard it is to mix reds—they "shout" and most don't complement each other. But men seem to love red and never seem to care how well it all blends with the landscape! Then there are orange and pink tones; usually people love one and will avoid the other accordingly. Whites, blues, and purples are neutral; it doesn't matter how many you have, they go with everything—like your white blouse hanging in the closet. And I always think a spot of yellow here and there is always just right.

The real fun begins trying to time blooms to complement each other—but somehow a late spring changed this and that, and a certain plant did not do well this year, and…well, you get the point. In other words, a beautifully landscaped flower border is a personal endeavor. Trying to get the colors in just the right combinations all through the seasons is really a task for magicians.

P.S. I *love* those weddings planned around a blooming garden. Now that's stress!

The different textures and shades of one color actually create a soothing setting in this landscape.

Bright, bold, and every color in the rainbow make for a splash of excitement.

Wildflower gardening has a wonderful ring to it—but wildflower gardening is neither carefree nor easy. However, if you stick to indigenous wildflowers, you'll have great success.

The word *wildflower* denotes an image of brilliant flowers appearing in far-flung meadows. Surely after driving down the highway and seeing large expanses of poppies and tickweed, we could accomplish the same in our own back yards. But this is another case of not reading the small print.

Wildflower is a term covering hundreds of flowers including perennials, biennials, and annuals. They have many different cultural requirements for certain sites and regions. To establish them on a new homesite, the soil must be rid of weeds (using herbicides) and prepared (but not too deeply or weed seeds will also germinate). For a more perennial-type wildflower, only a lot of maintenance will ensure that new plants are not overwhelmed by weeds, especially in the first years of establishment.

Many of us have been inspired by the roadside plantings by our state transportation departments, but if these plantings are so wild, why have these same plants not seeded other areas? One reason is that the flowers are often chosen for their glorious color (such as poppies), not because they would naturalize on their own in all regions. Even if some escape to other areas, like most wildflowers they do so sporadically and are very site-specific. The intense plantings we see beside the highways were massed together to be viewed by fast-moving traffic. I actually *love* these plantings, but they should be called seeded annuals, not wildflowers.

Large brilliant displays of wildflowers do occur naturally in the wild. Many of us plan trips around these events and pray our timing is right. But most of us also realize that trying to duplicate these unique situations is often virtually impossible back home.

So what is the answer? First, examine your site, because in some cases wildflowers are already present. I had one customer who had a sewer easement and wanted me to design a wildflower garden there. Naturally, she had in mind something like the highway plantings—full and brilliant. But as we walked along, I kept picking a flower here and there and very soon I had a bouquet in my hand. They were the usual wildflowers for her area: none very brilliant but certainly beautiful in every sense of the word. I explained to her that she already had the beginnings of her vision. She just needed to train her eye to enjoy what was endemic to her area and add a few extras as she identified what actually would grow on her site.

On a slope near my home I allow all manner of gloriosa and Stone Mountain daisies, Queen Anne's lace, and goldenrod to race about intermingling with other stuff. Now that's pretty wild and every year is totally different with lots of surprises. We must be on the lookout for unwanted invasives and keep them under control (otherwise we would have only briars, poison ivy, alders, and honeysuckle). This is still not what one imagines as completely wild in the sense that the gardener does nothing.

So am I telling you not to buy the wildflower seeds sold in a can? Actually, no. But be sure to buy seeds for your region. Discovering one, two, or three flowers that love your meadow or that special place in your garden can fulfill your dream of your own wildflower garden.

See **Photo** *52*

There is no end to combinations to get that wildflower look. Every year will be different and full of surprises.

A dramatic iron statue creates a strong focal point in an otherwise unruly setting, which is quite acceptable in a faraway meadow but not so much in a personal landscape garden.

110

A garden of sun-loving perennials seldom succeeds within the root system of large trees, but perennials for shade have adaptive root systems that allow them to compete successfully in this environment.

Everyone seems to be attracted to trees as the focus for a flower bed. We will nestle beds up to a magnificent oak, surround a large maple, or plug away under a massive hickory. But large trees have incredible root systems that spread in all directions, often reaching far beyond their drip lines.

When a sunny perennial border is dug and planted within this area, the tree's roots quickly become quite invasive, at the expense of the permanent root systems of sun-loving perennials. (This is unlike annual plantings where the ground is dug up each season, thus destroying the tree roots that would inhibit good flower growth.)

However, many shade perennials prefer the company of large trees. The spongy leaf matter and intertwining roots make it a little hard to introduce new plants to a forest floor, but shade perennials are in their element there and thrive once established. Mayapples colonize; wood poppies multiply; ferns grace the area naturally; and lady slippers are jewels.

My move to Stone Mountain, Georgia, was my first experience with big trees. I dug, amended, and planted a vision of paradise in a semicircular bed outside my kitchen window. I was horrified to see it deteriorate—quickly! I shifted gears and moved the bed to the side area (but still in view of my kitchen), dug and amended again, and moved all the plants. I still remember the shock of seeing the plants immediately recover. No longer under the influence of the fine old trees, the perennials took off and thrived. As the years progressed, I used the area under the oaks to add wild ginger, columbine, hellebores, and other shade- and root-tolerant plants.

The biggest concern will be whether you have a dry or a moist shade. Before purchasing large quantities of any particular shade plant, make sure your site matches the needs of your plants. (One of the best resource books for the South I have ever encountered is by Lois Trigg Chaplin called *Book of Lists.* Looking at her dry shade list gives a good indication of its difficulties, whereas the moist shade list is quite extensive.) Every region has local gardening experts, and it is wise to follow their advice, especially for any major or prominent situation.

See **Tree Roots** *111*
    Use Local Sources *90*
    Sun, Shade *56*
    Photo *131*

This sunny garden was located in the lawn to eliminate competition from the nearby trees and their roots.

A mortared border of natural rocks creates an attractive, neat edge and a low-maintenance situation.

A path with stepping stones was cut through the bed to give better circulation for a much used lawn.

In and out of shade and sun, plants should be selected to fit the location.

The tidy lawn with neat edges and a few architectural features creates a beautiful landscape. This graceful composition allows the comings and goings of the flowers and shrubs to flow with the seasons.

112 A "cutting garden" is everything on your entire property—and perhaps a snitch or two found in your friend's garden (just be sure to ask first!).

Over the years I have been asked, almost as an aside, to design a "cutting garden." My assumption is the homeowner intends this to be a special place to plant flowers to cut for floral arrangements. Perhaps he is thinking the cuttings will disfigure the plants in the flower border or perhaps she wants flowers that do not necessarily work in the flower border on view. But the reality for most homeowners is that keeping up with one or two beds just outside their patio is all they can handle; remember, an out-of-sight garden is one that easily falls into disrepair.

The real answer to a "cutting garden" is to let go and go cut. Every blade of grass, interesting weed, exotic vine, garish snapdragon, burst of sunflowers, pansy bloom, or willow twig is fair game—every time you step outdoors, the adventure starts. The bloom or evergreen branches you thought you could not bear to cut can—and will—be enjoyed in a totally different dimension. As for disfiguring your plants, so what! By cutting a few peonies, I can enjoy them even more intimately at the dinner table tonight. Fortunately for many flowers, cutting only makes them bloom more; otherwise they might begin to set seed, which signals all blooming to stop.

Plants that don't fit in your landscape are rarely the problem. I have a friend who is a naturally gifted interior designer. Her advice is, "Buy what you like and it will probably all go together." The same is true in the garden: if you like zinnias or white daisies or whatever, these flowers will probably fit in with what else you have in mind for your flower border. You might have a place in your vegetable garden or some out of the way place in your yard for these extras but often they are neglected. It's best to place them where their beauty can be enjoyed daily. And cut away!

113 Annuals are your best choice for all-season bloom. **Few perennials fit this requirement.**

There *are* a few perennials that bloom for a long season—a few. Most have a glorious show, then shut down, perhaps with some good foliage to carry them along. It is annuals that bloom week after week over the long summer season.

The trick is to combine the two—annuals and perennials—to get the best of both worlds. The true fun of gardening is the experimenting with all the combinations of colors and textures, attracting wildlife, adding fragrance, or just being funky. Annuals allow more flexibility in your creation as they are tucked in among your more permanent plantings. Just when you begin to tire of their more garish colors, they are gone, allowing you to visualize next year's adventure.

114 Understanding biennials' two-year life cycle is imperative for landscaping success.

A biennial needs two years to complete its cycle. Seeds dispersed by the mother plant will germinate that same summer. The seedlings remain quite small all winter. When the weather breaks, they quickly grow, bloom, set seeds, and then die—and the process starts all over again.

You can see immediately the problem: in your bed are tiny little plants that need to be weeded around, not accidentally dug up. You can't apply mulch and they might not be where you wanted them anyway (sometimes you can rearrange tiny foxgloves, but forget moving Queen Anne's lace or parsley, with their tap roots).

If left to reseed, biennials are flowers for the very casual garden; it is hard for homeowners to enjoy their unruly, casual ways. (In fact, most people buy foxgloves and parsley every year or two and don't bother with them seeding out.) And if you don't understand the routine, you will forever be baffled by your parsley, foxglove, or whatever that biennial is as it dies just when you thought you got it going.

The biennial Queen Anne's lace is popping up amongst the other flowers. But remember, they must be allowed to die and seed out if the homeowner wants to have a repeat performance next year.

Designing a carport instead of an attached garage gives the homeowner many opportunities to enjoy the natural surroundings upon coming home from work.

This mass of greenery is a fall-blooming biennial daisy. It also must be allowed to seed out for renewal. Just how much a homeowner will accept the down times of dying plants setting seeds is personal.

Flower arranging is one of the easiest and most delightful experiences for a gardener. All that is needed is a selection of "easy" vases and a small, handy clipper. Do not be intimidated by professional florist's arrangements bought for special occasions.

I seldom see fresh arrangements in homes. Why? Perhaps we think we need lots of flowers to make an arrangement. We think we need old-fashioned frogs, wires, putty, or other pieces of equipment to make flowers stand up just so. Worse, we feel we do not know what we are doing because the arrangement doesn't look just like those at the local florist. And maybe we think it takes too much time—a big consideration in our busy lives.

First, a good arrangement will usually need only one, two, or three flowers and some filler for a nice show—not the thirty stems with eight pieces of leathery fern you see at the florist. And where do you get flowers and filler? Everywhere in your garden and perhaps a snip or two elsewhere. Branches off a tree or shrub, tips of grasses, a limb of berries—I mean absolutely everything in your landscape is game.

Flowers and other stuff in the garden come in all sizes, colors, and textures and they will look best with a vase that complements them. Collect vases that fit your taste, in a variety of sizes (but few large ones, since they'll require lots of flowers and filler). The critical feature here is to have vases with a mouth just large enough to accept a complementary number of flowers. For instance, a narrow neck is chosen when only one or two roses were wanted anyway; a little wider neck will take a few more flowers and fillers. (Vases that are too wide require a lot of flowers, and shallow vases present problems supporting the stems, so stay away from these.) What is important is to have a wide variety of useable containers to inspire one to go outside in any season to cut something fresh to display.

Remember that the arrangement is for the personal enjoyment of the family. No one is giving out prizes. A large, formal florist's arrangement doesn't always fit in an everyday situation—but a little personal vase with just a few "weeds" or a branch of whatever with two blooms of this or that can be just the right touch.

Finally, we are all stretched for time. I think you'll find that by using smaller vases and some handy little clippers (mine are a treasured gift from my sister-in-law), one can step outside and in minutes create a vignette of one's choosing. The combinations are endless because nature provides and is just waiting for you to take advantage of its bounty.

The two low, wide bowls on the left are hard to arrange. But the taller vases with smaller openings allow for easy arrangements in minutes.

115

None of these
arrangements took more
than a few minutes but
give great pleasure to
the family.

116 **"Plant perennials, and every year they will just reappear and bloom all summer"—no part of this statement is true!**

Many people believe that perennials are a no-maintenance solution to gardening, when in fact a bed of perennials—with the dividing, replacing, moving, and sharing that come with it—is a never-ending process.

Plants that pop back up every year sounds good, but in reality, some perennials don't survive because of whatever: voles, moles, fungus, insects, too much or too little water, and so on. No one mentions that weeds also come back year after year. Grooming to remove dead and unsightly parts of last year's plants has to be done, not to mention adding a little mulch, fertilizer, and maybe some special attention to certain plants that have to have a spray or two of pesticides. So we do *not* have a situation in which nothing more needs to be done after planting!

And as for blooming all summer, only a few perennials fit this bill. Most have the usual one-, two-, maybe three-week-long show, and then they shut down for the season—so planning a garden with perennials becomes a game of logistics.

In the real world of perennial gardening, it is a process. Think of it like adding a puppy to your family: it's a great joy you'll enjoy over the years, but it comes with certain responsibilities.

117 **Sharing perennials is great fun but beware…weeds, pests, diseases, or just an inferior plant might become your lot. On the other hand, sharing might be the only way a gardener will ever have the chance of owning some precious plant that might never be offered in the commercial world.**

As I write this, I am looking out at a glade of massive lady ferns shared with me by a friend. Nothing could give me more pleasure knowing she had saved them from her property, which was sold for development. There were no lurking blades of Bermuda or nut grass; no signs of any disease. Adding them to my shaded forest was a pleasure because they will remind me of her generosity for years. Fortunately she had warned me of their aggressive nature, and I did not plant them in my more formal garden.

Sharing is actually the keystone to gardening. Steve Bender's book *Passalong Plants* tells numerous stories of how plants remind each one of us of someone or someplace special. "I dug these naked ladies from Mama's place before she moved"…"My friend Holly dug these phlox from her bed over twenty years ago"…"The horticulturist at Stone Mountain Park shared these Stone Mountain daisy seeds and now they adorn my garden over thirty years later." Flowers not only have great beauty, but also hold great memories. But there is a downside.

Some years ago, a tennis partner brought me a can of mums dug from the worst clay imaginable. The roots were so aggressive they looked like a monster—and I was right! This mum took off, spreading in every direction, and it never bloomed. Only after herbicides became available years later was I finally able to rid myself of this "gift." Perhaps you've had someone tell you how he stopped by the roadside and dug daylilies. These old-fashioned varieties arrived in this country several hundred years ago; they are aggressive, tall and ratty, and have few blooms. What a shame to fill a garden with these when the newer hybrids give improved foliage, controlled division, and lots of blooms.

Never look a gift horse in the mouth? Think again. Sharing is one of the greatest joys of gardening but use some common sense.

118 If a mass planting is desired, a trial run with two or three plants in a questionable site can avoid time-consuming, expensive mistakes.

Many times the effectiveness of a planting is determined by its massiveness. A large sweep of ferns, mayapples scattered in large colonies, a whole bank in daylilies, black-eyed Susans along a driveway are examples of what can be a wonderful vision of beauty. Sometimes the choice of plant materials is so hardy that results can be counted on. But…if the envelope is stretched and there are questions of how a certain plant might do, try out a few for a trial run before investing in a wholesale planting.

119 The majority of your perennial choices should be of the "tried and true" variety.

All of us want to have some fabulous plant that no one else has. But there might be a reason for that—it doesn't grow locally! All of us have seen a plant in a book or catalog that compels us to purchase it, only to see it languish in our garden. Experimenting is part of gardening. But when too much of the garden is given over to far-reaching experiments that might have a high mortality or "uglies" rate, then gardening can become more of a hassle than a reward.

Nurseries are always looking out for something new, but when customers ask for help with selections, the first suggestion will be ones that will give maximum success. Over many years, I have ordered, planted, and evaluated many plants. When I started, there were no local nurseries offering perennials or books written for our region; I had only catalogs and generic flower books to excite my interest. Now, with gardening coming to the forefront, we have a cornucopia of nurseries, regional books, and local public gardens to help us make our decisions. Use these resources to choose the best of the tried and true for your region and for your site. Do experiment; but not with your whole garden.

See **Use Local Sources** *90*

Add shrubs and trees to enhance your flower border. Many of these selections should be evergreen.

 Perennials generally need very little fertilizer. Annuals, however, usually love to be fertilized a lot during their short life span.

Successful art is often composed of several elements; landscape art is no different. Flower beds can always be enhanced by adding some shrubs and even trees for visual interest. The number or kinds is personal, but there are many that will extend the value of the border into another realm of beauty.

Think of camellias (sasanqua), fragrant tea olive, aucuba, azaleas, mock orange, forsythia, quince, conifers, or a viburnum or two. The list is endless. Most of these are a constant that need little attention except when cutting blooms and attractive foliage to take into the house for an arrangement. They give dimension, texture, height, and color. Many are sought out for their compelling branch structure and bark as well as their blooms; others for their evergreen leaves or needles. They are a valuable addition to your palette of plants to consider in your perennial garden plan.

Evergreens are even more valuable for those long winter months; they might have been playing second fiddle all summer, but when flowers have died back, the textures, colors, and shapes of evergreens become the main event and can extend the beauty of the garden throughout the entire year. There's nothing like seeing a heavily berried Foster holly or a giant Japanese cedar with tips of all shades of a russet color—these are real show-stoppers. Even a few golden aucuba and winter-blooming camellias provide a necessary dimension when the weather is cold and forbidding.

So no matter how much you just *love* your perennials and annuals, snag a shrub or two and a few evergreens and add them to the mix. If you've had a feeling that something was missing, but couldn't put your finger on just what it was, you may find that shrubs and trees fill the void.

See **Fences and Borders – Accent Bed** *315*
  China Cabinet Element of Design *76*

Perennials will grow leggy, flop over, add too much foliage, and generally perform poorly if they're *over-fertilized*. Annuals will grow poorly, will not bloom well, and generally will not be healthy if they are *not fertilized* well. If annuals and perennials are in separate beds, then the answer is rather easy—give perennials a little fertilizer sidedressing in early spring but feed annuals constantly throughout the growing season. When they're mixed together, well, you will have to parcel out the fertilizer accordingly.

The worst scenario that I see, because many gardeners don't know quite what to do, is doing *nothing*! The plants literally starve. Manufacturers have taken three basic components—nitrogen, phosphorous, and potassium—and have packaged them in such various forms as to make the cereal market look tame in comparison.

Keep it simple. Buy something that is for flowers, (it should say so on the package). Use a slow-release type such as the man-made pellets or an organic combination. These release nutrients over a long period with less chance of burning your plants from excessive zeal. If you see your perennials zooming all over the place with markedly fewer blooms, then you know you have overdone it. Next year you will hopefully become more restrained. Use all your zealous attention on your annuals; they love being fed all season.

Increasingly, research shows that organic fertilizers have additive characteristics. As they are used, soil condition is *improved* as well as fed. Don't be thrown off by the low numbers on the fertilizer ratio that indicate the relative percentages of nitrogen, phosphorous, and potassium. Research shows that organic products do have an edge to being a better choice for your fertilizing needs over the years. It's not just the ratio numbers on the bag but all the ingredients combining to make a better product overall. But remember that using the ordinary stuff found in a cheap bag of 10-10-10 is better than using *no* fertilizer (essentially starving your plants). Hot dogs might not be high on anyone's nutritional list, but it beats starving.

The root systems of perennials are extremely variable. Getting to know the roots will be your best guide as to how to grow them and move them.

Whenever you acquire a plant, look at its roots. The tough roots of a daylily or hosta should tell you that these will take a lot of abuse. Other plant roots are light hairy filaments that seem to fill a little spot. Or another has a long taproot that will cause the plant to die if it's cut. Another is a giant tuber that has little eyes where the plant will reemerge each year. When you have this knowledge, you will know how to dig to share or move it.

The most surprising root I have encountered was of *Amsonia heubrectii*. Before it became available through growers, I wanted to offer it to my customers. I had a very mature one in my garden that became a knock-out every fall with its vivid yellow foliage that lasted for weeks. These roots were new to me since I had never moved it. Out first came my spading fork, then a shovel, then a mattock, and lastly an ax. The roots were virtually rock-solid; only with great effort was I able to extricate it from the ground and then chop it into pieces to pot up for customers!

I even transplanted a piece to our farm, only to run a ditch witch straight through it, cutting it up into even smaller pieces. These bits lay around in some debris for many months until I discovered them. I planted them, up they came, and now I know that this is probably one of the toughest perennials I have *ever* encountered.

Look at the many types of bulbs sold dried in a package. From this one might surmise that plunging them into a wet, soggy environment will bring their life to a sudden end as you'd expect them to rot. Or have you seen a container with the plant's roots crawling over the sides and through the drainage hole? Guess how this plant will behave in your garden? You might want this, you might not. I'm always amazed at the roots of a clematis vine. The top is so delicate, but even the smallest plants will have strong full roots that tell you that the clematis will be a tough cookie when it's established.

So don't be afraid to handle your plants when you purchase them, or share with a friend, or just when you're moving them around in your garden. Pay attention to those roots because they give out a lot of information.

Getting to know you.

Jumping the gun on grooming can add unnecessary labor to your gardening.

Picture this: A mass of daylilies, ferns, or asters has finished its seasonal show. Your reaction might be to get in there and remove all the dead foliage and perhaps spread a little mulch over the bed to give it a fresh clean appearance. But is this debris all that unattractive? More important, have the plants truly dried and become brittle? If not, then you must manually cut each stalk to remove it. If you wait until the perennials dry completely, the stalks will often just break away for easy disposal.

I have in mind a garden bed that had a lovely stand of fall asters. As soon as they quit blooming, in I went to clean up. As the years progressed (and as my chores increased around my home), I'd delay this task longer and longer. I began to see the winter foliage had a nice soft brown color; in fact it was very pleasing. Still later I found myself cleaning up the bed just before new growth emerged. By that time, the stems were quite brittle and removing them became a simple and quick task. It didn't take being a rocket scientist to start looking around at other flowers; I decided that unless they were terrible unsightly, they were best left to become quite dead and brittle late in the season if not just before spring. My time and labor were greatly reduced by being a little patient and learning to enjoy another aspect of perennial gardening—winter beauty.

 Grooming the perennial bed is necessary to maintaining the joy and beauty of your garden. It is a never-ending process throughout the year.

One customer called me back to look at the perennial garden I had designed for her. You could see the disappointment in her eyes as she looked down at her garden. I asked her for some clippers; they were in such poor shape that I knew immediately they were never used. I began grooming, cutting off dead leaves or ugly spent blooms, and pulled some weeds. In just a few short minutes, she was astonished at how pretty her garden now looked! Here again was the misconception that one needs only to plant perennials to have a permanent solution! Grooming is an important part of the whole process.

My second example concerns a young lady who had me back to see her garden in late summer. She stood over a number of tall, dramatic seedpods of some lilies that had bloomed dramatically earlier that season. Now what to do? Do you cut them down or leave them? My response was to ask, do you regard them as beautiful? I laughingly told her that at her age, the blooms were the important thing, but at my advanced age, the pods were becoming prettier and prettier. So it was her personal choice if she wanted them in the garden for a time, or to cut some for a dried arrangement, or take them all out.

So when should one groom? Anytime a plant looks withered, spent, ugly, dead, or diseased is the time to clip away. Some plants continue to display graceful color and texture throughout fall and winter. Their foliage and pods need to be left until their beauty has faded. In late summer, some of my veronicas just look ratty. I clip their foliage and throw it away. Just down the way are my sedum 'Autumn Joy'. Fall is their favorite season. They will continue to display their dried form until new growth appears in spring. But if something happens to spoil their beauty, I would groom (clip!) them too.

Often I have seen beautiful gardens fall into ruins because basic grooming has not been done. In our hectic lives, the process of pulling weeds and cutting out dead debris is probably one of the best exercises to connect with the outdoors and yourself.

Mulching is not a big factor for perennial beds. A light covering is all that is usually needed.

I have often read articles stating mulch should be applied to perennial beds to inhibit weeds and conserve moisture. In principle that sounds pretty reasonable. However, except when one is putting in new plants, an excess of mulch just gets in the way. A little scattering of your preferred mulch keeps dirt from splattering and washing away, but soon the plants start growing, spreading, flopping, and generally throwing themselves all over the place. A heavy layer of mulch is just an annoyance. In fact too much mulch will keep the soil too moist and most perennials don't care to have wet "feet."

Some perennials do have root systems that tolerate increasing moisture due to heavier layers of mulch. For certain plants such as daylilies and similar flowers that are set in rows, maintenance is important, which means pulling weeds. For this situation, a heavier mulch layer is helpful. For those who have decided to grow marginal specimens, piling on the mulch for winter is also important. But in general, perennial beds usually need only a light covering.

See **Proper and Improper Mulches** *24*

 The overriding rule to the timing of moving perennials is when you can or need to.

Yes, there are definitely better times of the year to move certain perennials. But when a friend offers a prize specimen and you know you will probably not be able to come back later to dig, grab it then! Wrap it up well, keep the roots moist, and plant it as soon as possible. Trying to design flower bed colors is just impossible when the plants are not blooming. In fact designing flower beds always has an element of the unknown since one plant might grow twice as big as expected, and another remains so puny that the space is wasted. Waiting until fall just so you can watch one plant overtake another or a neighboring plant languish in a location it does not like is just not right. Move plants whenever they need to be in a better location. Fall or spring might be the best time by the books, but perennials are not very orderly.

Some of the best trips I have made over the years were with the Daylily Society traveling to wonderful gardens whose daylilies were for sale. Oh, the choices! Finally you pointed out your heart's desire and the owner came over with his spading fork and dig out your favorites. Bag after bag would be dug until the bus was bursting. Each person knew when they returned home, they would plant them immediately. There was no waiting for fall for these buyers!

Of course we all know that daylilies are tough plants, but so are most perennials. Poke around them to see how the root systems work so you'll know how to dig accordingly. Plants with big tough roots can have their dirt knocked off, the tops cut back, and the whole plant can be stuffed into a paper bag and taken home for planting. Other perennials have tiny fibrous roots that seem to have a hard time staying together; they will need to be carefully dug up so that the whole root area stays together and gently moved to the next site. Others might have a taproot; only the most careful digging will be successful.

Just remember, there is always an optimum time to move any perennial. However, in the real world, the optimum time is when the situation demands action.

See **Moving Plants – Quick and in Cool Weather** *126*
Beware Sharing with Others *149*

127 Gardening is art, and the land is your canvas.

In all my years of visiting gardens and helping others with garden design, I can only marvel at the limitless creativity I observe. I come away inspired at the various ways people see beauty and how they enjoy outdoor space. My only goal is not to indoctrinate so the garden becomes a "paint-by-number" product. Rather, I want to introduce people to the joys of gardening and inspire them to carry forth and do their thing.

As in painting, everyone can purchase tubes of paint and a blank canvas. What comes next is the artist. No one can tell the artist how he will create. He has studied the masters; taken classes to understand the basics; practices techniques; uses various materials…but in the final analysis, he paints from the heart. So must you garden.

128 **Consider your lifestyle before making any container planting a cornerstone of your landscape plan. Planted containers dry out very quickly and need attention, usually daily.**

Why would anyone want containers in their landscape if they are so demanding? Because they are fun, very showy, and an extremely effective way to create dramatic interest in very special spots—if the homeowner has the time to maintain them. If the landscape plan is centered around the use of containers, problems can arise when their absence causes an obvious void in the overall beauty of the site.

I had just such a job where the hardscape had been planned with numerous containers strategically placed for a very dramatic effect. Planting beds were drastically reduced. I asked the couple if they were prepared to plant and maintain so many of these urns daily, since both worked full-time jobs and traveled extensively showing dogs on the weekends. After discussion, it was decided they couldn't manage. So we changed the design to create and enlarge the planting beds, and built a small pond and a beautiful outdoor fireplace. Now they had strong visual elements in the landscape that weren't demanding on a daily basis.

See **Photos** *71, 158, 316, 321, 323*

This homeowner could just as easily have planted flowers in the ground. The containers are not a critical element in this landscape.

This homeowner is having great fun with a difficult spot. She is an avid gardener and loves the creativity of arranging her containers and flowers each year with several on permanent display for winter. Their daily maintenance is part of her love of being outdoors.

Window containers add so much but if this homeowner has other plans for a busy summer, the landscape would not fall apart with their absence.

Notice the color is from the foliage, not the flowers, and also how beautifully they complement the surroundings.

129 **When the use of a planted container for dramatic effect fails for whatever reason, consider presenting it unplanted or substitute a statue appropriate for your landscape.**

Many times I've come onto a landscape and noted that there are certain spots that would be greatly enhanced if some element such as a planted container was introduced. It might be at the front entrance, a corner of the swimming pool, or on top of a dramatic brick column. But for whatever reason—the homeowner travels, the exposure is too harsh, the care of the container keeps being forgotten—the container is always a failure.

Two solutions come to mind. If the urn is decorative in its own right, allow it to stand alone, unplanted. Just because a former owner filled a yard with planted containers doesn't mean you have to, if your lifestyle does not accommodate their care. Another solution is to replace it with an object that architecturally enhances the landscape. This might be concrete pineapples on top of that brick pillar, two bronze dogs greeting visitors at the front door, a reclining lion stationed somewhere in your garden, or a beautiful heron near your swimming pool. None of these are planted or need any care, but still provide a dramatic element that the homeowner thought only a planted container could give.

See **Creatures in the Landscape** *376*

This home has wonderful wide, easy steps for numerous grandchildren to sit and play just outside the kitchen. There are even several seats for the adults to sit and join the fun.

Notice the contrasting paint on the backing of the steps creates a visual break and a safer situation.

Pineapples are a symbol of hospitality and for this busy homemaker, much easier to take care of than a big urn filled with flowers needing daily care.

The landing is generously proportioned, providing a wonderful space for everyone to venture into the landscape.

129

Even in the cold winter months, this handsome dog greets visitors at the door. The plant can be replaced as the homeowner wishes.

129

This scene shows many interesting objects that can be arranged at any time and for any season with just a hint of a plant for accent.

130 **Raised beds out in the landscape can be quite effective.** However, carefully consider any plans for raised beds to adjoin the structure of your home.

Raised beds out in the landscape can be quite beautiful. They can be part of an enclosure element, can define space, and can help create special garden effects. Their use can also be quite helpful when good drainage is needed.

Occasionally, I find a raised bed adjoining the main structure—and in too many instances, some construction detail was not noticed and long-term damage occurred. Consider that the outlying bed wall acts like a dam for any water coming in, and since it is a planting bed, water is actually added to this space right next to the building! To make this work, the building must be completely secured against *any* water getting inside the structure and proper, fail-safe drains must be installed to remove excess water.

I suggest that no beautiful architectural effect created by a raised bed attached to the house is worth taking the chance of structural damage—especially when they could be used quite effectively in the landscape.

See **Proper Grading – Drainage** *17*

Higher mounding in the center of this raised bed promotes good drainage and creates a dramatic effect in the landscape. The addition of the solid border helps direct traffic as well as contains debris.

CHAPTER 4

Creating Rooms in the Landscape

Beds and Paths

Most people know how to approach interior decorating—the function of a room determines where it is placed and how it is decorated. But step outside and homeowners don't know where to start.

However, exterior space is really no different from indoor space. Humans relate to defined spaces that have discernible functions, so the goal is to recognize the four distinct "rooms" and plan for each space. Divisions usually include planting beds, a fence, or maybe a cluster of trees. The other major consideration is creating the necessary passageways connecting these rooms for proper circulation.

Once these spaces are defined, the homeowner has a landscaping plan: first, creating the space and, second, adding additional elements to decorate the rooms.

131 Your property has four different and distinct rooms defined by their use. **Their identification is a major step toward a functional—and beautiful—landscape.**

The outdoors has four "rooms," each with its own distinct function. Additionally, each room might have several locations, which can be the beginnings of a confusing landscape or the beginnings of finding some answers.

Guest Entrance: The Guest Entrance includes the entire front landscape, the front door, the walk to the door, and parking for visitors, giving guests easy access to the front entrance.

Car Area: The function of the family car (or cars) has grown so much that the space required is often about the size of the house itself! However, the Car Area should be seen as a semiprivate area used by the family; its function is utilitarian.

Utility Area: The Utility Area is where the homeowner keeps all tools, machines, and any messy stuff pertaining to jobs around the house or hobbies.

Outdoor Living Space: The Outdoor Living Space can be quite simple but it can also become quite complex when more and more divisions are made. The homeowner might add a pool here, a patio there, a series of small gardens, a play area for the kids, and a retreat in the woods. Outdoor Living Spaces can truly explode with myriad design features when creative juices get to flowing!

Planning your house and its surrounding land with these four rooms (or functions) in mind will give greater enjoyment and create more beauty than any other factor.

 132 The Guest Entrance should provide a continuous, direct line from the street to the front door for guests coming to your home.

When the various facets of the front entrance are not solved for the visitor, he must figure them out as best he can: Should I park here, maybe there? Am I blocking someone? How am I going to back out of this driveway without hurting my car or their landscape or the mailbox? What a narrow sidewalk; should I walk in front of my aunt or should she go first? These concerns send a strong message; is it the message you want to send to your visitors?

Actually, attention paid to the front entrance has declined at the expense of the Car Area: the need for so much more space to accommodate modern cars has superseded the need for visitor space. But no matter how casually you entertain, don't neglect the Guest Entrance.

See **Mailbox** *202*

Level Parking *215*

Visible Front Entrance *205*

Five Foot Wide Walk *226*

No One-Step *274*

Illustration *271*

Landing – Adequate Size *238*

Covering for Landing *234*

Photos *200, 205*

133 **The Car Area is a semiprivate space for the homeowner to park his vehicles and enter the house.** But this space has evolved into much more: storage for tools and trash receptacles, a major athletic arena, and the entrance for most guests. Recognizing these additional uses helps you design good solutions.

The location of the Car Area is found just about everywhere—in front, on the side, around back, under the house, and detached from the home. Some homesites have multiple Car Areas. The love of vehicles seems to know no bounds.

The interesting thing about this area is that it has expanded to serve more functions than the original use for the car, including storage, a tool shed, a coat room, garden paraphernalia storage—whatever. In fact, many garages no longer have room for the cars! The parking pad of the Car Area also doubles as a sports arena for basketball, skateboards, bikes, and every other wheeled contraption. Storage for most of this equipment is usually found inside the Car Area.

Additionally, this space is seen as extra parking for guests and the place where they are expected to enter the home.

My opinion is that all of these activities are probably warranted. Yes, you need space for tools and miscellaneous stuff. Yes, sports equipment needs to be stored somewhere. Yes, there does need to be parking space for guests. And yes, you and your guests might need a convenient entrance to your house. However, consider organizational solutions—built-in cabinets for tools, perhaps a separate shed for gardening, a niche for sports equipment—as well as architectural ones—designing a gracious secondary entrance, planning in advance for visitor parking—which will make the final landscaping step an easy one.

See **Level Parking** *215*

Dimensions for Parking and Exiting *216, 217*

Structures *292, 294, 298*

View from Indoor Living Space *46*

Flower Bed *130*

Photo *17*

This open carport has no room for storage or hiding one's stuff. Be sure Utility Areas are designed close by for these essential needs.

The division between the Guest Entrance and Car Area can be subtle and also interesting. Notice the different plantings and architectural elements such as the bench and support posts.

133

133

This detached garage can store all manner of stuff away from the living space of the house; additionally, its architecture makes for a complementary whole.

Older homes and many newer homes have a separate garage for their Car Area. This creates an opportunity for more windowspace (light) for the home.

This large, old ornamental shrub is a perfect room divider between the Guest Entrance and the Car Area.

The addition of a brick parking area for guests at the front entrance created a definite division between the Guest Entrance and the family Car Area. The dimensions necessary for parking and exiting were checked before the project began.

134 Utility Areas can have several different locations. **Carefully consider them in your overall design or their inherent mess will intrude into other areas.**

Utility areas can be found in your garage, in your basement, or perhaps in a separate storage building. By their very nature, they are messy. So what is the problem? Perhaps no separate entrance was planned to the basement utility area, or perhaps no interior space was set aside for messy situations.

Ask yourself these questions: Is a garden shed planned? Where will it be located, either for convenience or aesthetics? Is a workshop needed? Where will all the sports equipment go?

It's best to plan ahead for these situations. By doing so, you will locate these essential items into a spot that's convenient yet out of sight so that your beautiful landscape will remain beautiful.

See **Structures** *292, 294, 298*

Power of the Sun *242*

Architectural Complement *42*

Steep Roof Line *302*

Separate Entrances of Utility *233*

135 Outdoor Living Space can be one room or many different rooms, depending on your space and needs, coupled with your desires.

The Outdoor Living Space can be a simple, "plain Jane" backyard or it can extend to the most flamboyant, outrageous proliferation of rooms that anyone could ever imagine. It is just a matter of your lifestyle and what you can do, manage, and pay for. Many people will make a list: I want the pool over here, a small vegetable garden there, the kids play area in that direction, a small putting green, and a small pond with flowers.

Half the battle is making a list of these desires. However, the rest of the battle can be won only if the homeowner is armed with sound principles of design: circulation, dimensions, how people react to space, how the sun influences the site, and on and on. None of these considerations are complicated; they just need to be understood and addressed.

The Outdoor Living Space, Car Area, and Utility Area converge in this space but because the carport and garden shop were built to complement the main structure and are beautifully maintained, the combination works beautifully.

The screening between the Car Area and the Outdoor Living Space takes on a whole new meaning with these exciting plantings. No monotonous row of overpowering shrubs here.

Plenty of space and nice wide doors make this garden shed a wonderful workstation.

136 Bed lines, plant groupings, and structures define rooms in your landscape.

Because of their flexibility, these elements can move in and out, creating definition, entrances, exits, and directing flow. A few trees planted between the carport and the neighbor's home creates an agreeable room; bed lines in the backyard contour around a lovely patio, sweeping along the back edges to create another space for a small back lawn, while revealing an opening to an even larger space for a children's play area.

In your home, you might be able to see into another room but the home's architectural features (an arched doorway, perhaps) define the move from one room to another. The same lovely effect is produced in the landscape when a bed line or plant grouping is used as a visual clue to move from one defined area to another. Whether the space is reduced to attract a more intimate gathering or is opened up for a grand scale adventure is personal preference.

See **Symmetry** *92, 94*
    Ornamental Trees *99*
    Attributes of Fence *306*
    Photos *44, 162*

137 Use your bed lines for problem solving.

Every site has a list of problems or situations that must be dealt with. Often they can be addressed by marking off a bed or a grouping of plant materials. For instance, trees are needed to shade a western exposure…plan a grouping of canopy trees. Your neighbor's carport is in full view…mark off a bed and plant a wonderful shrub border. A steep slope needs controlling…set it aside and cover with forsythia. A storage shed is not so attractive…plant a bed of evergreens. Grass no longer grows in a particular location…expand your bed to take in this now bare area and plant shade plants such as Lenten roses. Your back yard is too big and imposing…allow the bed lines to create smaller spaces for more intimate enjoyment. Your front yard is long and narrow…draw bed lines to alleviate this unappealing alley look.

See **Plan to Hide Utility Items** *60*
    Too Much Concrete *218*
    Slopes *32*
    Needs for Circulation *186*
    Where Does Grass Grow *355*

Invitation to play!

If the home sits low on its foundation, the bed lines used to separate the house from the lawn need to be held fairly close to the structure.

If a homeowner has a structure that sits low to the ground whose windows are only a few inches or feet from the ground, his choices are limited to the few plants that remain low enough to avoid growing over the structure in the coming years. If the planting bed is drawn too large, the problem becomes how to incorporate plants effectively.

Groundcovers can be used effectively but tend to have weed problems and need a good maintenance program to stay neat. A better solution would be to reduce the size of the planting bed and use an appropriate groundcover sparingly with some low accent shrubs and Ornamental Trees.

See **Use Few Plants Under 2 Feet for Low Maintenance** *20*

Special Interrupted View *74*

Check Plants for Mature Size *35*

Inversion of Planting *176*

No Shrubs, Show Foundation *176*

 Bed lines are used to frame your trees, so never crowd the bed line close to their trunks. Grass will not grow there anyway.

Aesthetically, trees and lawns are a beautiful combination. Functionally, however, the lawn will not be doing so well when planted too near a Significant Tree. This is the time to pay attention to Mother Nature. When she speaks; you should listen. Pull the bed line back until you find growing grass and you'll be pleased at how much better your landscaping looks. Not only will you no longer be fighting the grass battle, but your tree will look better in this larger space.

The lawn and the planting beds should act together to frame your trees. When the lawn comes too close to the edge of the forest or too close to any one large tree, the proportions are out of kilter—like a large oil painting with a tiny mat and frame. Instead, pull the lawn back and away from these trees so they are in a space large enough to accommodate their magnificent presence.

See **Significant Trees** *96*

Where Does Grass Grow *355*

140 Bed lines should be drawn in large, broad strokes both for beauty and ease of maintenance. **This is another case of form and function going hand in hand.**

Bed lines should sweep, taking the eye around and about for a graceful adventure. Think in long, broad strokes. Forget quick, jutting turns and angles. In fact, when laying out your beds, try to imagine cutting your lawn along these edges. If it looks like a hassle, it probably will be. Smooth out the bed lines for beauty…and mowing ease.

See **Keep Items Out of Lawn for Low Maintenance** *34*
   **Front Walk Designed with Smooth, Broad Lines –
      No Wiggles** *228*
   Photos *69, 87, 229, 258, 318*

141 Planting beds and plant groupings are the major elements that create mystery, depth, and adventure in your outdoor rooms.

Have you ever noticed how people love to look around a bend in a river, a road, or a trail? Have you ever been in a garden that meandered here and there, and you felt you were going on a wonderful adventure? Taking a space—no matter how large or small—and cutting off some vistas while opening up others, to expose different pieces of the landscape, adds depth as well as interest.

See **Pond – Natural Setting** *360*
   Pond – Meandering Shoreline *364*
   Placement of Patio *266*

Large broad curves that stay far from these magnificent trees give plenty of room for plantings. There are no chopped up spaces with little paths wandering in and out.

Mystery, depth, and adventure are created by these bed lines.

Several seating choices are scattered about.

Bed lines should frame trees, not squeeze them into an unnatural space.

A dramatic focal point with the moon gate adds a destination to the journey.

These bold bed lines are the definition of this wonderful room. The tightening of space creates a portal before expanding outward for a visit to this inviting fountain.

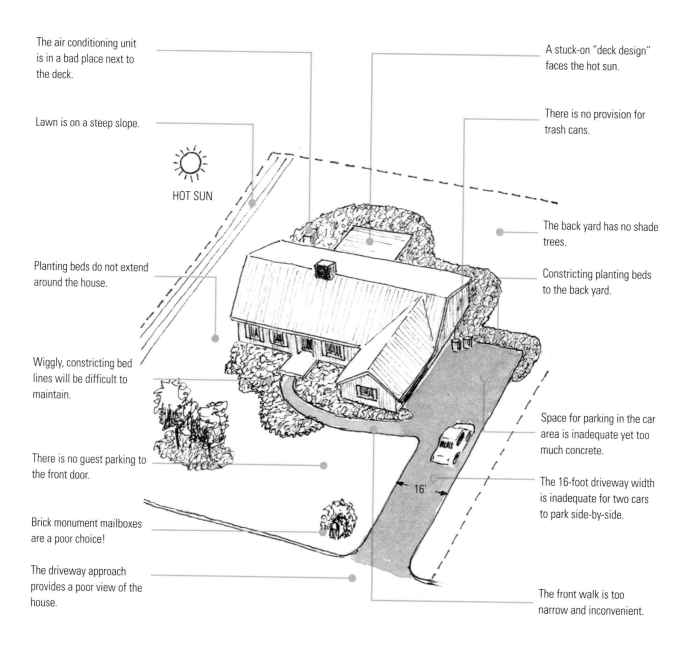

The air conditioning unit is in a bad place next to the deck.

Lawn is on a steep slope.

HOT SUN

Planting beds do not extend around the house.

Wiggly, constricting bed lines will be difficult to maintain.

There is no guest parking to the front door.

Brick monument mailboxes are a poor choice!

The driveway approach provides a poor view of the house.

A stuck-on "deck design" faces the hot sun.

There is no provision for trash cans.

The back yard has no shade trees.

Constricting planting beds to the back yard.

Space for parking in the car area is inadequate yet too much concrete.

16'

The 16-foot driveway width is inadequate for two cars to park side-by-side.

The front walk is too narrow and inconvenient.

Better Choices
Laying out good bed lines does matter!

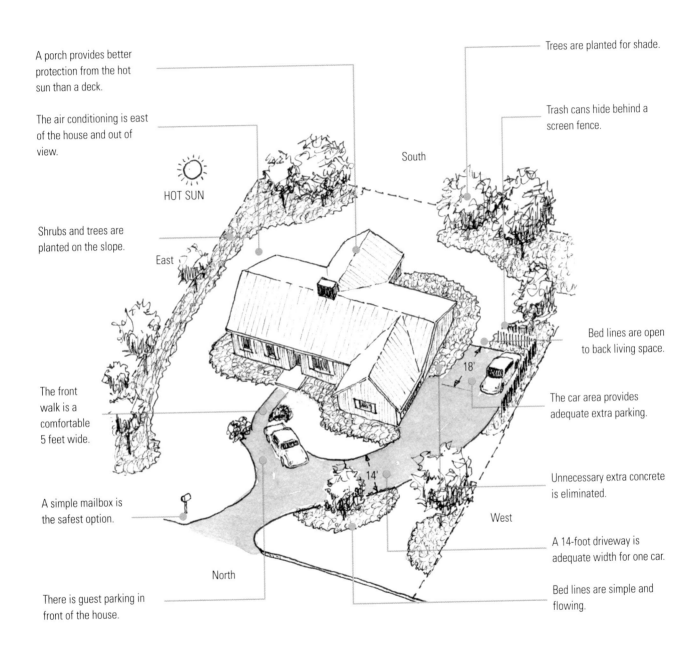

A porch provides better protection from the hot sun than a deck.

The air conditioning is east of the house and out of view.

Shrubs and trees are planted on the slope.

The front walk is a comfortable 5 feet wide.

A simple mailbox is the safest option.

There is guest parking in front of the house.

Trees are planted for shade.

Trash cans hide behind a screen fence.

Bed lines are open to back living space.

The car area provides adequate extra parking.

Unnecessary extra concrete is eliminated.

A 14-foot driveway is adequate width for one car.

Bed lines are simple and flowing.

HOT SUN

South

East

West

North

18'

14'

144 **Allow the lawn to directly connect with the home if the foundation is aesthetically pleasing.**

Foundation plantings came into vogue because the foundations themselves were unattractive. Over time, the plants were seen as attractive additions to the overall setting. But some foundations are actually quite attractive and are designed to be part of the whole architectural picture. I sometimes cringe as I approach a beautiful home with an expensively applied foundation of some rock or fancy brickwork and I am expected to "landscape"—which means designing a plan so that shrubs cover this beautiful feature.

If you have a beautiful foundation, consider allowing the lawn to connect with it; shrubs or a tree can be added at strategic areas to create some depth and interest. If beds must be added, plan a design that will leave open areas to show off this beautiful architectural interest.

See **Special Interrupted View** *74*

Grass, Best Type for This Idea to Work *354*

Photo *62*

 145 **If large plantings are needed for a home that has a low profile, invert the normal planting scheme: plant groundcovers next to the structure and use larger plants farther away.**

I remember one job where the contractor felt I had mixed up the plants: to him the large gardenias should be sited closest to the house, and the ajuga and other small plants would be next. But there was a problem: a small sitting area with windows very near the ground was quite exposed to public traffic. By expanding the bed, placing the larger gardenia hedge on the outside edge, and leaving the immediate space for low, small flowers below, the problem was solved. In fact, the area was enhanced by this three-dimensional solution—and the homeowner enjoyed the creation of a small intimate garden out her window.

This theory also works for a low-slung home that needs some aesthetic "weight," or some larger plantings so the house does not seem so tight in appearance.

See **Plants for a Low Foundation** *171*

This foundation actually plays a dominant role in the architectural beauty of this house. What a shame it would be if it were covered!

The porch is less than 2 feet above the ground. The larger plants at the beginning of the walk add dimension and interest to the landscape, while smaller plantings are located next to the porch.

This large circular drive and wide front walk give all visitors perfect access to the front door.

To the right is a traditional planting bed with larger shrubs next to the house, where there is room, and smaller groundcovers reaching out for a lovely settled, landscaped look.

A 3-foot wide bed created for shrubs is too narrow; 5 to 8 feet (or more) is more realistic, considering the growth patterns of most plant materials. Know the mature sizes of the shrubs you intend to plant and use a measuring tape; it is a wonderful reality check.

Anticipating plants' growth is one of the hardest landscaping concepts for most homeowners to grasp. When a little plant in a plastic container is bought at the local nursery, it just does not seem realistic to think that it might mature to a size that takes over! (Usually taking over a spot right next to the house, shutters, gutters, and siding!)

Outdoor space is actually quite overwhelming for most people. The anxiety of designing large beds located away from the primary structure is quite intense when the size necessary for success is hard to accept.

However, if the planting beds are initially drawn in large bold strokes with adequate depth, the homeowner can make better decisions for correct placement. That Foster holly sited ten feet from the corner can now grow to its normal height of twenty or so feet tall and ten feet wide without affecting the structure of the home.

See **Check Plants for Mature Size** *35*
      Prune for Natural Beauty *114*
      Pruning and Shearing *115*
      Photo *87*

146

Notice how the mowing lawn edge is located away from the large trees, making it easier to mow.

The bird feeder is out of the lawn area, keeping it from becoming another lawn-mowing obstacle.

The open, friendly fence along the property lines creates a sense of enclosure but not entrapment.

Most shrubs need bed width of 6 to 8 feet or more. Look at the growth habit of each plant and give it space to grow naturally to its genetically coded size…not the size you see it growing in the can when it is brought home from the store.

These hydrangeas love to flop out. How nice to see space given to them!

147 Borders outlining a bed line that will be visible should use the most aesthetic materials that are available and affordable. **Borders and walls that will not be seen, but which are needed for structural reasons, require materials only of the quality necessary to perform the job.**

Spend money where it is important for the end game. Any wall or border that is in constant view and is visually part of the landscape should use materials that complement the intended vision for the garden. This is the time to stretch the budget and buy that beautiful stone or hire a good brick mason; it is no time to scrimp buying rigid wood edgings, colored commercial concrete blocks, or plastic edging.

Conversely, I have often seen incredible sums spent on walls that absolutely no one will ever see; all the work of the stonemason or bricklayers will go unnoticed and unappreciated. Poured concrete, commercial building blocks, or railroad ties would have been better choices!

See **Use Only Natural Materials** *48*
Mortared Bed Barrier *182*

148 A slope or bank does not necessarily need a retaining wall. **The cost of building retaining walls should cause you to look at your options closely.**

The destructive nature of new construction causes many homeowners to believe a retaining wall is necessary. All existing plant material has been removed, leaving the land bare; with the first rain, erosion becomes a major problem. As the construction progresses, the erosion problem only accelerates. The homeowner is horrified by these steep rutted slopes and thinks that only monumental terracing with expensive walls will solve the problem.

Obviously, in some cases the slope can be so steep and in such a vulnerable spot that a wall is the only solution. But in many cases, the only need is to reintroduce shrubs and trees, mulch to help absorb rain, and maybe add some temporary silt screens to control heavy runoffs until the plants mature. Proper grading is also a critical element to divert water from washing directly over a vulnerable slope. Getting the land back to a natural state will take care of almost any slope unless there are special circumstances.

See **Job Description of Trees and Shrubs** *64*
Set Wall Back at Driving, Parking Areas *214*
Slopes, Problems *32*
Erosion Control, Use of Plants *108*

These beautiful brick steps will be seen both from the house and the pool/patio; but the small retaining walls in the side yard will never be visible and are there for functional use only. Therefore, the materials used for the retaining walls are a not-as-attractive but cheaper material.

Notice the same measurement for each riser and tread ensures a graceful, safe walk down this side yard.

This retaining wall was recommended because a slope would have killed the on-site grove of some much-desired native trees.

Any constructed border must be solidly mortared if it is to be an effective barrier against invasive plants.

A loosely constructed border will not keep unwanted invasive weeds and grasses out. In fact, the tiny crevices, nooks, and crannies create the perfect environment for the very same plants you are trying desperately to keep out of your planting beds, such as bermudagrass. It will become impossible to keep them out. If you must have a loosely constructed border or low wall, adjacent plants must be noninvasive, such as fescue grass, or inert materials such as those used for a path or patio.

See **Kinds of Grasses** *354*
      Perennials – Non-Invasive *134*
      Borders Used as Paths *197*

A country lawn always has invasive lawn plants ready to take over any planting bed. But with a mortared border, this problem is solved.

The total of different plant materials is over 60 and growing. Putting them all in one "China cabinet" makes it work.

A little open fence gives added separation from this backyard Outdoor Living Space and the Car Area on the other side.

149

These loose rocks are only a decorative edging. A solid border is not necessary because the grass in this lawn is a type that grows individually from seed and has no invasive underground runners.

This 6-foot high fence creates a neat, crisp enclosure separating the lawn from a very close neighbor. Its height provides plenty of security for this homeowner.

Fences give instant privacy yet leave plenty of room to include interesting plant materials in the garden.

This delicate Ornamental Tree has been carefully limbed up and thinned to create a lovely accent along the edge of this border.

150 **Do not cover beautiful walls or borders with plantings.** **If any are needed in front of a wall, plants should be chosen only as enhancements. If appropriate, plantings can be on the upper side with some cascading over.**

I have often seen perfectly beautiful retaining walls masked by shrubs planted at the base that quickly covered the entire facade. Even the wrong choice of plants cascading over the wall can soon mask what was a perfect beauty. By poking through the tangle of plants, I've sometimes rediscovered a wonderfully weathered rock or brick wall.

Think carefully before you plant in front of your beautiful wall. If it is quite low, no plantings should be installed (except possibly a small item here and there for interest). If the wall is of substantial size, a few judicious choices to break up the monotony of such a huge mass would be in order. In no case should an invasive plant such as ivy or a large shrub border be planted; the wall will be obliterated. Use a light touch when choosing plantings for that lovely cascading effect; walls and borders should be softened, accented, and caressed, but not covered up. They constitute major architectural features that enhance your landscape as few other elements can.

This incredibly dramatic, old granite wall is only enhanced by the interplay of plants; this homeowner wisely chose plants with loose habits, allowing this drama to unfold.

A welcoming bench acts as a strong focal point; notice the large stone at its base for feet to rest off any moist ground.

150

Only a cascading evergreen has been allowed to cover any part of this owner-built wall. Otherwise, it is left uncluttered for ease of maintenance and for its inherent beauty.

No plantings at the base of this wall mean low maintenance and a beautiful landscape.

150

Walk out every door and all around the home landscape to determine natural paths and walks; the most successful ones are circular, with no dead ends.

As soon as I start working on landscaping a home-site, I start walking. I imagine how I would drive up, get out of a car, walk to the front door, walk around to the back, walk out from exit doors, and so forth. I also ask questions such as: "Do you plan to use this door or that one?", "Is this utility door for big items or just a small work entrance?", or "Do you envision walking out into your woods?"

Problems arise when walkways are laid out with no consideration to this very basic element of design. One sees visitors cutting across lawns because the front walk is inconveniently placed; dogs and kids create unsightly shortcuts because they refuse to go the longer way; and other walks are never used because no one ever comes out a particular door or goes where the walkway goes.

To avoid this costly mistake—because walkways are expensive to install!—walk out every door and all around the property. Imagine how visitors will approach the house, how you will use your patio, or where the kids will play. Remember that going in circles is a good thing—install gates in fences and use other remedies to prevent dead ends.

As soon as you are comfortable with where you want to walk, get out the spray paint and mark it. Now you are ready to pour concrete, set in stepping-stones, or just open up lawn space for walking.

See **Kids Love Circles** *344*
Junctures *219*
Front Walks, 5 Feet Minimum Width *226*
Photos *47, 191, 193, 199, 211, 245*

Even in more informal sites, paths belong where people will naturally walk. The main walk leads to a two-car parking area but, when party time begins, the second walk brings in many more who may have parked on the field beyond. The circular nature of this layout is very inviting, especially since the primary walk is rather enclosed for a definite in-out walk.

One can just imagine people standing about talking and enjoying the outdoors in this functional layout.

Many circular paths make this entertainment area quite agreeable.

The sunroom has two doors: one to the grill and the other to a small patio, which steps down to the pool.

The summerhouse has two doors: one to the sunroom and the other leading to the pool.

To the right of the summerhouse is the path to the play area, which leads one back to the open area and the kitchen.

The pool curves around the house with a path through a gate leading to the front door.

151

Steppingstones are landscape magic! If used correctly, they play an important part both aesthetically and functionally; if used incorrectly, they create a hazardous, detracting element.

There is a dreamlike quality to the notion of using steppingstones in the landscape. One can just point here or there and out comes, "Oh, we'll put some steppingstones there. That will be just perfect." And it certainly might.

Steppingstones used on a fairly routine basis must be large, thick, solid, closely spaced, and placed in the ground just low enough to avoid the lawn mower (if laid in the lawn) and just high enough to be in sight. (As time goes by, some readjustment will be necessary, especially if the soil moves from freezing and heaving.)

A good local stone company will be invaluable, as each stone might need to be hand picked. They will be expensive—and the number needed could be rather disquieting if a good solid path is desired.

Take care at installation to prevent the path from becoming a hazard; if a homeowner finds himself walking *beside* steppingstones instead of on them, something is wrong. Then it's time for a correction or removal, as they will have lost their magic. And you know, designing the landscape is all about magic.

See **Grass as Paths** *192*

    Choose Material for Safety and Endurance *196*

The magic of these steppingstones does the trick as they create a more casual feel to this landscape. Yet they are laid for a safe, firm footing.

This path connects the homeowner's Guest Entrance room (front yard) to the back to enjoy his Outdoor Living Space (a patio with a fireplace and a pond).

These two urns and the texture change of the brick indicate the presence of steps.

153 Use steppingstones as directional tools in the landscape—especially through gardens, to show shortcuts, and to show how to move through landscape rooms.

In the Garden: One of the more beautiful sights in the landscaping world is the use of artfully placed steppingstones through a garden. The stones often become part of the overall art created in the garden—and they also keep everyone out of the mud, and from stepping on the flowers!

Shortcuts: There are always landscapes that must adjust as people naturally take the shortest route from Point A to Point B. Providing steppingstones will at least get everyone using the same shortcut, and prevent degradation of the landscape.

Movement from One Room to Another: Major transitional spaces should be treated with great respect. Steppingstones should be large, attractive, and give people signals of where they should be going and invite them to go a certain way. There might be other items to note this transitional space, perhaps dramatic urns, an arbor, or a special planting.

154 Small decorative steppingstones are just that; use them only as decorations in the garden.

Many decorative steppingstones are quite charming and add some personality to the garden. However, most are small and often not very sturdy; any real walking on them is at best a hit-or-miss situation. Siting them as art to be appreciated is their best use.

The Ornamental Trees have been limbed up, allowing anyone to walk casually about the garden without ducking. After a few more years, a few more limbs will be removed.

Without these steppingstones, the opening to the garden beyond would not be noticed, leaving the most thoughtful guests in a quandary as to where to enter. The urns give additional clues.

153

155 **Paths of gravel or crushed brick, or solid brick and stone set in porous sand or concrete all provide a solid, dry surface for good walking. Maintenance issues should be your only consideration.**

All paths located in shade can become mossy, sometimes dangerously so. This is true even if this surface is mulched naturally by trees or by a commercial product. Solid brick and stone often develop that Old World look but they can be rather treacherous; it is necessary to clean them from time to time, even if it means removing some of their mossy charm. More porous materials such as crushed gravel and brick are less likely to become slippery because water drains away more rapidly and they provide good traction. All paths in shade also have the problem of debris, which collects and then decays; paths are often lost under years of accumulated debris.

Paths made of gravel, crushed brick, or similar porous materials may have weed problems when they're located in sunlight. Debris breaks down into their small crevices, which certain weeds just love. Paths made of solid brick and stone set in sand also face issues of freezing and thawing, which causes heaving, creating very uneven and dangerous surfaces. If these same materials are set in concrete or asphalt, many of these problems are eliminated. It is an expensive alternative but a much more permanent solution to many maintenance problems.

Are paths made of these materials worth it? You bet. They make for wonderful walking on a solid, dry surface, allowing accessibility in all kinds of weather for all kinds of people. Plus, they are beautiful. Beautiful paths beautifully done are one of the most important keys to a treasured landscape.

See **Use of Pea Gravel** *192*
Photos *81, 338*

The edging of choice is found right off the site—as natural as it can get.

This woodland walk will always be accessible in any weather because of its solid surface. Maintenance will also be at a minimum. Weeding the flower beds is one thing but weeding a walk is just not inspiring.

Everyone will accept a walk going up or down or around a curve but never tilting to one side. If necessary, cut into the slope as shown here to get a nice level surface for good walking.

155

Connecting the Guest Entrance to the Car Area was important for good circulation. Just as important was setting these bricks in concrete for virtually no maintenance. The homeowner chose to keep the original brick walkway, which has some problems, but its historic value outweighed removing them.

Notice the path has been allowed to remain on an incline instead of adding a dangerous "one step."

The modest width was chosen to identify it as a secondary pathway, but the nice flanges allow for a comfortable walk in any direction.

155

156 Grass is an excellent path material except in very high-traffic situations.

A path or a walk can also just be a pathway. When laying out any landscape design, delineating all circulation pathways is critical; an arrow on any plan will show the homeowner where he could expect to use his space to move easily from one area to another. In other words, all pathways should be laid out from the beginning.

Often, on seeing the circulation arrows, the homeowner will ask, "What is the path made of?" The answer is grass! Grass is an excellent pathway. I only suggest installing a hard surface path if it had been determined that a heavy traffic area would quickly wear out a grass path. Bottom line, grass is an excellent and cost-effective surface for pathways.

157 Pea gravel should be used as a path only if one has a full-time gardener—or if you decide to become the full-time gardener! In addition to its high maintenance, it is often quite loose and difficult for many to walk on.

Pea gravel is beautiful, but its maintenance makes it suitable only for very few situations. It does best in very controlled areas where the least amount of debris will collect and a routine weed herbicide spraying program is maintained. Extra gravel must also be added to from time to time as the stones "disappear."

Using pea gravel is actually accepting a lifestyle: some people love to work in their garden and the artistic effect is so important that any maintenance chores are actually part of the enjoyment of the garden itself. So the decision to use pea gravel should be made on the reality of your personal willingness to take care of this high-maintenance item.

See **Loose Stones in Concrete** *36*

The path between these two rooms could have been a solid surface of brick or stone or perhaps steppingstones in mulch—or it can be just grass. Any of these options would show someone where to walk.

Some neat elements such as these lawn edges and the surface of the grass are important elements in a landscape. They counterbalance the exuberant but often untidy nature of plants.

The original pea gravel is now set in concrete. The nostalgic effect is still there but not its maintenance and its difficult walking surface.

The path is laid out to circulate throughout the garden, inviting visitors to come in and walk about with no feeling of entrapment.

The low wall and the few Ornamental Trees give just the right amount of enclosure to create a relaxed feeling for this space.

157

Commercial pavers should stay at commercial sites.

 Any pavement or permanent materials chosen for walkways should aesthetically enhance your home. Simplicity is truly a virtue here.

I may have stepped on some toes in the past; I am sorry. Commercial pavers are wonderful when used in the front of a hotel or a "Grand Municipal Building", but in front of your beautiful home, they look commercial. Their more standardized configurations and great durability make them appealing to use, but refrain—please.

Thankfully, newer selections that have a more natural look appropriate for the homeowner are becoming available. Plus, newer techniques combining other materials are available for all those hardscape applications that are so essential for a beautiful landscape. Just remember, keep it simple. Pavement should seldom be a major attractive item in the landscape.

See **Visual Statics – Use Natural Materials** *81*
Photo *148*

Walks are usually seen as gracious but utilitarian means for traffic flow. Any medium chosen for its construction should become part of the architectural whole, as well as add to the garden effect. Very seldom is a walk seen as a separate entity or an art object with special accents or treatments to make it stand alone in the garden.

The problem begins when homeowners are presented with endless—and I mean endless—choices with portfolios full of pictures to choose from. They all seem so exciting that anyone could be drawn into a choice that does not blend with the landscape, the house architecture, or anything. This is the time to pull back and think of the whole picture. Do you really need certain motifs? Is the color of the concrete, brick, or stone going to enhance your existing structures? Will it blend with the landscape?

If at all in doubt, keep it simple. Remember, when all other elements of your site come into play, your walks should not be a focus. Elegant: yes. Ease of walking: yes. An attention-grabber: only for limited exceptions.

See **Architectural Elements Complement** *42*
Photos *85, 166, 243, 299, 347*

159

The adjoining Guest Entrance and Car Area create a large area of hard surfaces. Adding distinctive surfacing materials can break up the monotony. But the choices are often overbearing and detract from the architecture of the home. In this example, the surfacing is a perfect complement, with a subtle gray color and a design motif that blends with the architecture.

This design has three components: First, the motif guides any visitor to the front door. Second, the design creates a patio effect by not extending outward into the driving lane. Third, the overall design was kept simple to avoid detracting from the lovely architecture of the home.

This stamped concrete pattern was chosen because of the safety factor—flat surfaces with small seams.

The choice of surfacing materials is very important for safety, endurance, and to fulfill its job description.

Not all surfacing materials such as stone, brick, and tile are alike. Several job sites I've visited have demonstrated this problem to the owner's chagrin. One person chose stone so brittle it quickly broke into pieces—yes, it was laid in concrete! At another site, the stone become as slick as glass when it became wet. I have also seen this problem with some tile choices. Another homeowner had laid a beautiful brick front walk but the bricks were low fired. After only a few freezes, most of them were torn into small chunks; the whole project had to be replaced with appropriate high-fired bricks. It's difficult to use unwieldy surfacing materials for patio surfaces as the furniture will not stay steady.

The second problem I often see is the application of concrete in forms that are not acceptable for everyday human use. Stamping is one example; when the pattern chosen is flat and the seams are very small, this motif can enhance any patio or walk. But when the stamping motif mimics cobblestone (with round-ed surfaces and deep seams), the surface is impossible to manage and even quite dangerous to walk upon. I hope some of these offerings with ankle-turning designs will go the way of the bouffant hair-do.

So, what is the sixty-four-thousand-dollar question? Ask yourself, "How will the materials I choose stand up to traffic and the elements to be the right choice for my uses?" It might not cost sixty-four thousand dollars, but surfacing materials can be a big-ticket item to correct. This is the time to ask questions of merchants selling the product and the artisans doing the installing. I also think actually running some tests yourself might be in order. Throw some water on it and start walking and then pull furniture across it to see what happens.

Hard surfaces are a major element in any landscape. No plantings can overcome if this is a major negative force. But when the surfacing is attractive and comfortable to walk on, few elements can match its positive effect on the surroundings. Its beauty is displayed every day despite the comings and goings of the plants around it.

See **Photos** *227, 303*

This surface is safe for walking in rain or shine and will stand up to freezing. These points were checked out *before* installation.

The color choice of the tile is aesthetically pleasing to the architecture as a whole.

This fence, and especially the gate, set this landscape apart from the ordinary. Any plants will only enhance its already compelling setting.

Paths can double as an edging.

Many ideas can serve double duty as answers to other problems in the landscape. With an invasive grass lawn that continually needs edging, a homeowner who likes to get out in the early morning when the grass is quite wet might install a narrow solid edge just wide enough to use as a pathway, solving both problems.

See **Grading at Construction Time for Level Surfaces** *17*
Need for Level Surfaces *53*

A gardener adds another Low-Maintenance element by bricking a small path around the edges of her tough-but-invasive lawn. Another reason for this path was the multitude of small grandchildren, who love to travel around in circles and love to follow paths.

A steep roofline always makes any structure more appealing in the landscape.

The detached garage gives this homeowner a chance to visit the outdoors even briefly before entering her home.

Note the two doors leading into the garage. One goes to the cars but the other leads to the utility space—how nice to have planned to have them in separate spaces.

161

Walks or any space to be used as a pathway are expected to go up and down but should never tilt to one side.

Walks laid out in the landscape naturally often go up a slope and perhaps down to another area. Walking up and down is expected if the land is not flat.

What is not expected or acceptable are walks that tilt to the side. No one will find them comfortable to walk upon or will feel safe as each stride must adjust to accommodate the angle of the path. Additional problems face anyone with limited mobility.

There is an old saying, "Haste makes waste." Whether the path is going to be poured concrete, steppingstones, or just grass, if the land slopes sideways, it *must be cut out* to create a level surface to walk on. This requires an extra step, usually with large equipment to obtain the proper grade. The problem lies with not identifying this as a problem until the end. Correcting this situation later becomes problematic and very expensive.

In my work, I've found there are times that I'm never on one level piece of ground. A homeowner will soon tire of adjusting for this tilt when he walks his property, and will use the landscape less and less. But if paths are cut so they are level, his enjoyment will increase tenfold.

Up and down, of course, . . . but never tilt sideways.

 Paths through natural areas such as woods are determined by taking a walk— just a few trips will quickly indicate a way. Additional delineations should be kept low key and natural.

Many homeowners ask for a path through their woods (or I might suggest one to be established in future plans). Most think this is supposed to be a formal path; maybe it's even been graded and perhaps has a good hard surface.

Woods are different. Paths are to help the homeowner know his property by directing traffic through the trees in a manner that does little damage to the environment and gives the homeowner a sense of direction when he is walking. Strolling willy-nilly through the woods is not always fun for people.

So how does one go about creating a walking path through the woods?

The first step is to start walking. Your property has its own character. Taking only a few trips through the woods—usually about five or six will do—results in a discreet but easily identifiable path. (Have you ever seen a deer trail?) You will be surprised how easy it is to find the way you like to go and how quickly a path is made just by walking over the same trail several times. If you want to mark the path, do so with natural materials, especially ones that are visible all year— rocks, evergreen plants, old logs. Never use railroad ties, landscape timbers, or other materials that look angular, coarse, and in every way…unnatural.

Sometimes homeowners use materials such as shredded cedar, pine straw, or some other material to mark the path initially. Even a crushed gravel or brick base can be used for those needing a more stable but porous surface; after a few fall leaves, these materials become muted. (Your concern is that they don't become buried.)

Nothing is more enjoyable than a walk in the woods. Settling on your best pathway should be as easy as just making the trip several times…and *voilà!* there is your path—it's that simple.

See **Use Only Natural Materials, Especially in Natural Settings** *48*

163

After several months of walking through the woods, this path and others beyond became the ones of choice. No path was created traveling straight down into the on-site ravine, which would create an impossible, erosion-prone mess.

Notice the circular route, which is always more inviting than a dead end that requires one to turn around and walk back.

Even in the dead of winter, these rocks taken from the site help tell visitors, especially the young grandchildren, where the path is, protecting some of the more delicate plantings off to the side.

CHAPTER 5

First Impressions

The Front of the House

The front of the house is the first sight guests will have—and the homeowners will see it every day! It encompasses the two most ignored rooms in the landscape: the Guest Entrance and the Car Area.

Social trends have dramatically enlarged Car Areas, but often at the expense of a beautiful approach to the home. Guest parking has been eliminated, walks to the front door are awkward, and ways to exit the property are a puzzle.

Landscaping is a way to deal with all Outdoor Living Space, but these two important rooms set the tone, and no plantings can overcome bad decisions here. When ignored, corrections are nearly impossible; when identified and acted upon, the solutions set the stage for a beautiful landscape.

164 **The numbers of a mailbox are the first impression of the landscape. To create a good impression, three elements are essential: numbers should appear on both sides (never on the front); they should be large enough to read from a distance; and numbers should be reflective for night visitors' ease.**

Don't assume you know the direction your visitors will approach; placing numbers on both sides of the mailbox ensures that even if a guest overshoots the drive, he'll be able to identify your home when he turns back. Numbers located on the front of a mailbox cannot easily be read and are hazardous, whether street traffic is heavy or not. Large, contrasting, reflective numbers make it easy for approaching guests to know they've arrived, without causing any traffic backups.

 165 **Keep the mailbox simple. Building a monument for a mailbox can be a high-maintenance and sometimes dangerous affair.**

Large mailboxes constructed of brick, stone, and stucco can be quite attractive, but consider that the ground may shift, bricks may become dislodged, and hinged doors may become difficult to close. And can anyone see past a three-foot by three-foot block? It's very expensive to repair vehicles and mailboxes when collisions occur.

Keep it simple so when time takes its toll or a disaster happens, a replacement mailbox can be put in with a minimum of effort and expense. No landscape is enhanced by a mailbox in bad repair.

See **Photos** *165, 213*

A disastrous meeting with a big mailbox.

164

Both sides of mailboxes should be numbered, big enough to read, and bright for night visibility. Any plantings should be postman-friendly.

If your mailbox is close to your home, plantings might be appropriate, but a distant mailbox should be left as is.

Most homeowners will walk only a short distance to maintain a flower bed; one located at the end of a long driveway often becomes an unnecessary burden and will be neglected. Distance is the key: after about thirty to forty paces, the rate for maintaining successful plantings declines. So if the mailbox bed is close to the home, keeping the bed looking attractive is easy. When planning your landscape around your mailbox, think about getting in a car or walking down a long driveway to weed, water, fertilize, and mulch a bed you view for only a short time as you get your mail.

In most cases, just keeping the area neatly mowed and edged is really all that is necessary for a well-landscaped entrance.

See **Low Maintenance** *13*

 No vine or heavy, prickly shrubbery should be used at the mailbox unless it is definitely not blocking visibility of the numbers or access to the mailbox.

A mailbox nestled in a lovely bed of flowers and shrubs is very inviting; in nearly every job I do, the homeowner asks me for something at their mailbox, usually a vine. But any plant that ends up hiding the number or making access to the mailbox difficult is a problem—for guests who don't know where they are and for the mailman who might be confronted with bees or other pests.

So choose your plants wisely. Think ahead to how they will affect your mailbox for the sake of your visitors and your friendly mailman.

See **Check Habits of Plants for Problems** *30*

If your home is on a large enough lot, make every effort to direct guests toward the beautiful Guest Entrance (at the front door), not to the Car Area.

Siting a house has many components, and often the driveway element is ignored until construction is nearly over. Before deciding to wrap up the Car Area as quickly (and cheaply) as possible, I recommend that you walk over the property and note if there are locations where the driveway could actually enter better. Wow! Doesn't the house look beautiful from this direction!

Adding parking space for guests to access the front door (not the family's Car Area) adds to the pleasure of the visit and the graceful landscape.

See **Contractor** *37, 61*

Significant Trees *96*

Power of the Sun *57*

Interrupted View *72*

Natural Litter, Importance *106*

 Planning for guest parking is vital, and it's equally important to allow for a proper exit.

Most driveways are laid out with only the homeowner in mind, but a little forethought will eliminate years of bottleneck traffic and inconvenient situations for guests and deliveries. If visitors are expected to back out—even if the driveway is short and straight—exiting into a heavily traveled street becomes problematic, even dangerous. In most cases, visitors are also expected to park on the driveway but usually block everyone else's way. Then, they're expected to drive to the Car Area, turn around there, and exit. All of this is very awkward for everyone.

However, the expense of pouring extra concrete—and the idea of covering up some of that spacious yard—often stops some homeowners from solving this landscaping problem. At the very least, consider a double-width area on the driveway to allow one car to drive by another. If possible, a pull-through drive, or one that allows a turn-out or turn-around, is best, and if there is space to do it without using the homeowner's Car Area, that's even better.

See **Avoid Hard Structures Next to Drives and**

Parking Spaces *214*

Parking Dimensions *216, 217*

No question here of one's destination. And how inviting!

See page 211 for a photo of this home's guest parking in front of the carport, away from the Car Area.

The construction manager saved many Significant Trees and consequently their natural litter (nourishment).

Trees have been limbed up over the years for good visibility of the home.

A wide front walk allows for a comfortable entry.

This contractor provided a parking area convenient to the Guest Entrance. The shared turn-out space for both homeowner and guests eliminates potential problems.

The area for Guest Parking was filled in to guarantee it was conveniently level.

Even this little space—enough for one plant—between the Car Area and the Guest Entrance creates an important division.

169

Even spacious farm settings need to provide visitors a convenient place to park. This young couple created a welcoming approach to their home.

The homeowner's driveway moves around to the right to his private Car Area.

169

A few shrubs and trees and a bumper made from an old cedar tree alert guests to stop before going over a bank.

Guest parking spaces were filled in to make sure the area was level.

Guest parking is to the left and the Car Area is to the right. Both have plenty of back-up space for easy exits.

This example shows a nice balance of Significant Trees and open space for the warming rays of the sun.

169

Circular drives provide easy front-door access.

Lots of evergreens and bold textures enhance this setting.

This drive has space for two cars to pass side-by-side easily.

169

A new Significant Tree was planted in anticipation of the probable death of an old oak on the corner.

No steps except the one expected at the front door landing.

A brick layout creates a front walk, a landing for a comfortable bench, and a sense of enclosure for such a large space.

Area dimensions were measured to guarantee the right amount of space needed for parking.

This landscape makeover included a main level parking area, necessitating a turn-out for exiting the new garage. Extra parking space was added for many visiting friends and family.

Guest parking is located right at the front door and out of the way of the homeowner's drive to the Car Area.

Note the use of posts and soft shrubs to separate the visitor parking from the Guest Entrance.

The homeowners removed many large shrubs for this front makeover. However, this holly was put to good use by limbing it up.

This space is open to the lawn for good circulation.

Short driveways where a car must exit into the street must be absolutely straight for backing out; there must be no obstacles or curves to maneuver for an exit.

 Several approaches to a homesite can be confusing. Be sure to provide visual clues to direct visitors to the front entrance.

You'd be surprised at some of the strange and interesting situations I have seen over the years: culverts that were just off-center enough to fall into; trees that were "saved" but which then had to be maneuvered around; curves added for interest—but the really interesting things were the tire marks all over the lawn (by the homeowners who backed out every day!).

Keep this simple advice in mind. As an additional note, this design element is *especially* important when the driveway slopes downward, as mirrors can be deceiving in this situation. So keep it straight, and always make sure you have a good angle at the end for turning out.

As land is developed, the homeowner adjusts to the different approaches to his home and to other destinations such as a barn, lakesite, or other destinations. But the visitor's only clues may be a more-traveled gravel driveway or simply intuition. For the person delivering a package or arriving for an appointment, this puzzling juncture causes a great deal of anxiety and concern. Can I turn around? Can I back up? Will I get lost? With my four-wheel drive vehicle, discovering I have arrived at a mucky barn instead is okay, but for most people, getting "lost" is not a pleasant experience.

So give some clues at important junctures. A lovely fence, a post light, or plantings can direct traffic. Even placing a sign or arrow with your house number on it might be in order. The job of every host is to make the visit as pleasant as possible for the guests. This means telling each visitor how to get to your house in a gracious way and allowing them to enjoy the true beauty of the surroundings.

This couple and their guests never have any problems backing out this straight drive. There is nothing planted at the street, nor is there a big mailbox blocking your vision of oncoming traffic. A beautiful landscape softens any hardness a straight driveway may give. A small turn-out is for special situations only.

Street landings are an option when visitors park on the street. **When possible, give visitors a firm landing for their comfort and safety.**

Many homes, especially those sited on small lots in town, only have street parking available. Often this space is quite confusing and difficult to access due to street trees and their roots, odd plantings to trip over, fire hydrants, street signs, and other obstructions. If local codes permit, take this otherwise forbidding space and construct a level, comfortable landing. This helps visitors direct their parking and access the property. It also creates an additional element for a beautiful Front Entrance.

Steps to the front walk are accented with bed lines and shrubs for beauty and safety.

Note the lights on both sides of the street steps and the post light at the front door steps.

Comfortable and inviting landings for street parking add to any landscape.

A simple mailbox with numbers posted on both sides gives good confirmation of the address.

173 Any parking pad that ends at an abrupt drop-off should have some vertical elements (trees, large evergreen shrubs, lamppost, fence) installed about 3 feet back from the end of the pad to help the driver know where to stop. **An additional bumper guard for the tires is also very important, but it must be kept low.**

It's hard not to be anxious about the possibility of rolling off into the ravine when all the land falls away in front of the car and there are no visual clues. Vertical landscape elements—as well as a low bumper—take care of most of the stress when parking in these situations

Remember that a car can overhang the pad by two to four feet, so make sure these elements are back far enough to avoid being hit. Also note that any installed tire guard should be low enough not to destroy anyone's bumper if the driver happens to move up too far.

See **Plants for Erosion Control** *108*
    Level Parking Spaces *215*
    Choose Plants for Job Descriptions *64*
    Photo *208*

174 Avoid building confining, hard structural elements (of brick, stone, etc.) adjoining locations where people are expected to drive or park. **If there is no alternative to a wall or a fence, set these hard elements several feet away from the edge of the paved surface. Constructing them tall enough to be easily visible by drivers is very important. A wonderful alternative is to eliminate any structure by grading a slope and planting shrubs.**

Many people have homesites that are very confining. The driveway and parking areas are next to a building or a retaining wall, or maybe a fence. Due to space, there are no alternatives. As the years progress, a little nudge here and whack there take their toll.

But in many situations, there are options. If the structure is a retaining wall, then the wall needs to be pushed back several feet to permit space between the hard surface and the wall. Another alternative is to eliminate the wall but to grade the bank so it's sloping and plant heavily; in this case, only a small curb is needed. Once the plants have established, vehicles can nudge and even whack them with much less damage to both the plants and the vehicle.

See **Slopes – Maintenance** *32*
    Use Natural Materials *48, 180*
    Photo *85*

Come on back!

A set back wall or a slope are options.

175 If the driveway is steep, extremely curved, or has any characteristic that reduces visibility, plant large trees or a fence along one side as a visual guide. **Add post lights where needed to improve lighting. Everything must be visible from the driver's point of view.**

If you've driven in the mountains, you know the ravine on the side can be a little unnerving because all visual clues are missing. Private roads (usually very narrow) with special driving conditions should be enhanced with visual clues such as tall trees, high fences, and post lights to aid the driver as he maneuvers the unfamiliar terrain.

All visual clues must be chosen with the driver in mind—not a person walking up the drive—so they must be visible from a car. Small shrubs and low lighting are no help; in fact, they add an element of stress since the driver must concentrate on not running over them! I have even seen curbing added—but one mistake has the driver changing a tire.

Instead, tall trees, large shrubs, tall post lights, and substantial fencing are all good choices to give visual guides. The sense of security is immeasurable to any newcomer or even the homeowner driving home on a dark, rainy night.

See **Fences** *307*
Significant Trees *96*

Trees and fences lead the way.

176 Any area where a vehicle is expected to park must be as level as possible.

When one parks, the car should be on level ground. Otherwise one person may hold the door open with his foot, hoping it does not get away and smash him on the head or take a few fingers, while another person spills out in a most indecorous manner. If the ground is sloping forward, engaging the emergency brake is essential for fear of losing one's car to a far ravine.

The result of unlevel spaces is their markedly diminished usefulness. No one can work on or wash the car…no basketball…no using the space as a good flat area in the sun for any number of things…and the visitor parking space looks more like an obstacle course than a lovely landing for getting in and out of the car.

Talk with your builder and with your grader. If they tell you these landing pads need to slope wildly to one side because it must drain water, tell them that "level" does not mean "perfectly level." A small grade outward is all that is necessary for drainage. A typical car pad is about twenty-four by thirty-five feet, or eight hundred forty square feet of solid surface. That is a lot of wasted space if it is not level. Like landings, porches, decks, and patios, the Car Area is a people space that should be level for human use.

See **Kids** *348*
Construction – Finish Grade for Level Spaces *17*

Can you get the door open, Ethel?

These measurements are used in every parking lot across the country. They will also work for you, ensuring a driveway that is both functional and attractive. Extending any of these measurements is usually confusing and wasteful. Reducing them creates inadequate space for parking and maneuvering.

Parking and exiting is unique to each site. Measurements must allow for a rational starting point. It is important to test-drive each design to check for hidden errors (such as driving over areas slated for growing grass or shrubs), and to identify spaces marked for surfacing that may prove unnecessary.

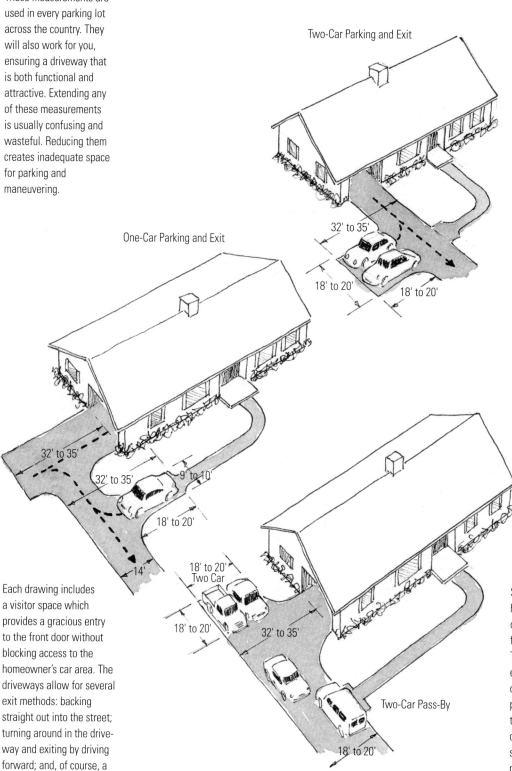

Two-Car Parking and Exit

32' to 35'

18' to 20'

18' to 20'

One-Car Parking and Exit

32' to 35'

32' to 35'

9' to 10'

18' to 20'

14'

18' to 20'
Two Car

18' to 20'

32' to 35'

Two-Car Pass-By

18' to 20'

Each drawing includes a visitor space which provides a gracious entry to the front door without blocking access to the homeowner's car area. The driveways allow for several exit methods: backing straight out into the street; turning around in the driveway and exiting by driving forward; and, of course, a circular drive that keeps visitors moving forward.

Square footage for outdoor hard surfacing is often close to the total square footage of the home itself. These projects are expensive and their impact on your home's value is permanent. The conscientious homeowner will design his home's outdoor surroundings with careful planning and forethought.

If you look at all of these illustrations, you will notice that the dimensions are the same for each situation. This is because standard dimensions apply for driveway widths and parking spaces and other dimensions are standard to allow adequate space to back up and pull out for exit. Another minimum (but not maximum) dimension is necessary to construct a circular drive. Once these standard measurements are accepted, most driveways and parking spaces can be correctly laid out without pouring too much concrete. Having too much ambiguous space is confusing; no one knows what it is for or how to use it.

Circular drives must have a *minimum* diameter to accommodate most cars. However on many sites, a circular drive can become quite large and its exact layout will be dictated by the landscape features of the site.

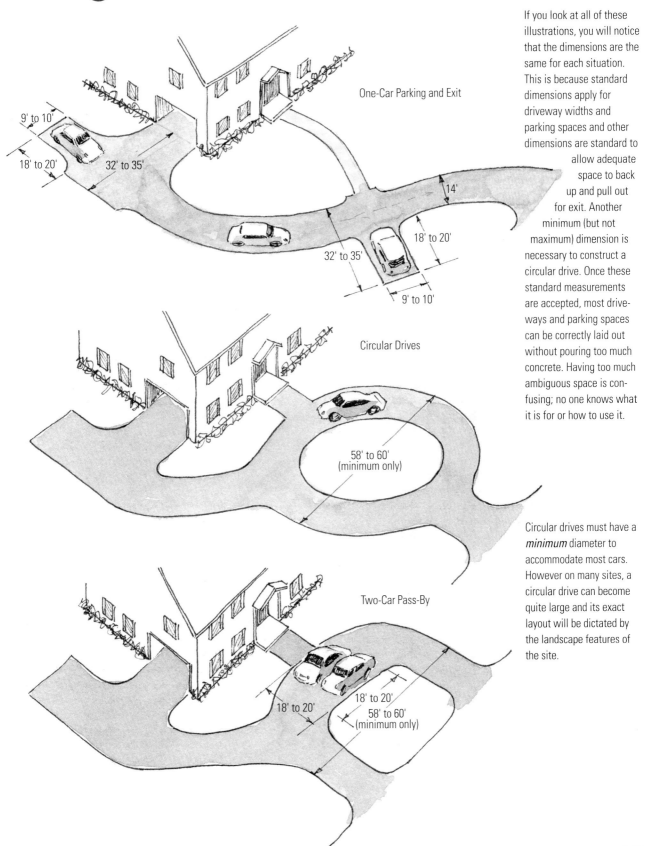

One-Car Parking and Exit

9' to 10'

18' to 20'

32' to 35'

14'

32' to 35'

18' to 20'

9' to 10'

Circular Drives

58' to 60'
(minimum only)

Two-Car Pass-By

18' to 20'

18' to 20'

58' to 60'
(minimum only)

179 **Don't depend on standard guidelines when laying out the area for carports, visitor parking, or any other projects concerning vehicles.** **This is particularly true of turn junctures. Test-drive these spaces before a permanent surface is applied.**

Hard surfaces are expensive and permanent, and cover large areas with a compelling presence. By using some basic, easy-to-use measurements, the homeowner can get a workable outline for his hard surfaces. But it is only when he physically drives the layout that he can be reassured he's poured enough—but not too much—concrete.

This is especially important when determining a turning radius: when the angle and width are not correctly anticipated, grass is run over, mud holes develop, and everyone is unhappy. Any additional concrete always looks like an unattractive patch job.

Performing an on-site test-drive is the best way to determine where to pave, and where not to pave, potentially avoiding additional expense and an unattractive, unnecessary, and confusing surplus of hard surfacing.

See **Plan Utility Systems** *60*
Provide Guest Parking *205*
Planting Spaces Between Hard Surfaces and Large Structures *265*
Consider View From Major Living Spaces *46*
Front Walk, Minimum 5 Feet *226*

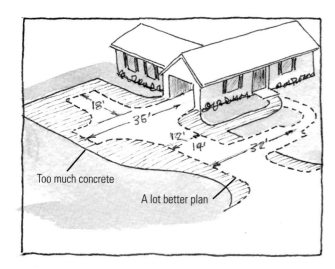

Enough is enough!

Pour it, boys!

Asphalt guest parking meets the front walk of colored concrete. A bonus is the extension of the walk for an even more comfortable entrance— and a big welcome.

This juncture off the Car Area is inviting.

An open iron fence with a gate for easy access, Significant Trees, Ornamental Trees, walks open to the lawn, and flower and shrub areas congregated into agreeable spaces…mystery found around each corner!

181 **Consider these three important elements when planning the back door: provide some kind of cover and a generous landing; design an architecturally appealing facade (but secondary in design to the front door); and be sure it opens into an attractive space.**

Many homes are designed so that the back door will be the one used most, not only by the homeowner, but also by many close friends and relatives. Function and beauty are the twins in all design—so if this is a major entry used daily by family and friends, a great deal of attention should be given to essential elements of design that address both issues.

All entryways should have a cover and a generous landing, especially this one. Functionally, it will protect the homeowner and any guests from driving rainstorms or searing sun. This cover and landing also add a three-dimensional element to the architecture of the house, making a big contribution to the aesthetic value of this space. A cover could be a projection, an alcove, or a porch.

The back door should be attractive. If it is too plain, the element of its being a proper entryway is diminished. I have seen too many back doors with just the minimum of trim work so that its plainness does not give it the visual dominance it should command. Functionally, this leads to confusion for people deciding where to enter. Aesthetically, everyone should want this major entryway to be attractive. (However, no matter what, its attractiveness should not outshine the front entrance; there should be no confusion that the "back door" is what it is and the front entrance is what it is.)

Where this entry lands inside the house is also of paramount importance. The best design would provide an alcove or hall. All utility elements such as the laundry and storage areas should be off in their own space, with everyday junk confined behind doors. Even coming directly into the kitchen or breakfast room would be lovely and certainly preferable to coming through a mass of stuff that can never be made attractive.

See **Porches as Transitional Spaces** *252*
Main Door is Dominant *231*
Steps *270-283*

Low evergreen plantings, a medium-sized shrub to visually balance the large wall, and an Ornamental Tree accenting the corner makes a safe, effective low-maintenance landscape.

All essential elements have come together to create these successful back doors. They all have a covering that protects the door itself as well as anyone entering. Each has a generous landing to accommodate the homeowner as well as visitors. Each opening is also architecturally attractive to create a visual connection to the landscape. And one can safely assume the space immediately inside is inviting, attractive, and not a mess.

The placement of several Ornamental Trees creates a visual break from the Car Area. Just a little limbing up and thinning will maintain them as attractive specimens in the landscape. Improper blunt cuts would destroy their beauty.

Lovely back doors make great foils for small landscape elements added as the homeowner wishes. Within this alcove, we can see a small basket of flowers and a small windowbox.

Entering the home through the back door leads to a pretty, inviting kitchen. The walk-in pantry is located behind closed doors and the out-of-sight laundry is conveniently located near the bedrooms.

This back door opens to a porch where there is plenty of room for congregating and enjoying the outdoors before entering the home.

These rooms face a southern exposure, which supplies inviting warmth, but the sun's power is buffeted by the shade of various cooling trees.

Front walks situated on hilly terrain should have an extended shoulder or level area on both sides of the walk. In the absence of sufficient space for shoulders, additional low plantings along the edge and even handrails will create a comfort zone for visitors.

Even a generous five-foot-wide walk cannot compete with a landscape immediately falling away to one side. Beautiful vistas are missed because any person walking on this surface will be worried that one mis-step will send him tumbling down the hill. However, a generous shoulder will alleviate this problem, and if shoulders aren't possible, adding some soft shrubs of about two- or three-foot height will "hold him up" but not block the view. If the situation is particularly treacherous, a set of handrails will assure anyone that everything is under control.

See **Choose Plants for Job Descriptions** *64*
3 Foot Fence, Architectural Interest *310*
Use of Iron *310*
Avoid Sticky, Abrasive Plants Next to Walks *91*

This front walk has a dangerous drop-off, but a tidy, open 3-foot fence solves the problem beautifully. Other options would be a handrail or some low plantings.

Note the limbing up of this important Significant Tree as it matures in height.

The front door walkway should begin where you want visitors to park. If the site allows, the front door should be in view when the car comes to a stop. The front walk should also be an agreeable distance from the Car Area, which helps separate these two rooms from each other.

First impressions are always lasting ones. A good design for the front walk should eliminate any confusion about where to park and how to enter a home. Sometimes factors about the site can force visitor parking quite close to the carport area. In these cases, it is even more important to include design features that dramatically emphasize where the visitor is to park and in every way encourage him to walk to the front door (rather than use a side entrance). The most obvious and easiest method is to dramatically widen the beginning of the walk, even continuing the walk down the driveway, creating a "landing pad." This and a few more accents create a welcoming entrance that few visitors will ignore.

See **Junctures** *230*
Lighting *334, 336*

184 The walk to the front door should be approximately 5 feet wide or wider so that two people may walk comfortably side by side.

A five-foot width will comfortably accommodate two people walking shoulder to shoulder. If you want your visitors to see your outdoors as an extension of your home, this gracious front walk allows them to travel comfortably to their car with conversations uninterrupted, no decision as to who goes first, and adequate space to negotiate their exit.

Remember, the front walk is an extremely important extension of the home. A narrow front walk is not only out of proportion to the architectural whole, it also diminishes the value placed on a friend's visit! The extra money spent on this one element will do more for the visual beauty and practical application than any you might spend elsewhere.

See **Walks in Broad, Easy Strokes, No Wiggles** *228*
No Single Steps, Few Exceptions *274*
Guest Parking *205*
Photos *62, 200, 239, 330*

The extended walk down the drive directs visitors where to park. A walk running close to the house is awkward.

A large, comfortable landing was added.

The parking area gives the best view of home.

Two major Trash Trees (sweet gums) were removed for safety and better balance of light. Many other Significant Trees remain.

184

An enlarged landing at the base of the steps creates a small room, inviting visitors to stop and enjoy the surroundings.

A wide walk is essential for two people to comfortably walk side by side. Five feet is the minimum.

The stone selection complements the home.

The flange at the drive creates a visual and physical connection for guest parking.

This new construction began with a temporary narrow, loose, pea gravel walk. A solid walking surface is safer; the pea gravel was later used to texture the concrete turnaround.

Do not line the entire length of your walk with plants. Instead, plan areas that open to the lawn or other paths to invite a gracious exit to other parts of the landscape. (The only exception is a very short walk or one that is only decorative.)

The old-fashioned practice of lining walkways actually traps visitors, as there is no comfortable way to exit. It removes the rest of the landscape from access, and becomes a high-maintenance element for the homeowner, as plantings often overhang the walkway, further reducing the width available for anyone to use. Instead, have areas of lawn or other openings that abut the walk. At these places, anyone is free to move into other areas of interest, adding a greatly needed element of circulation.

Sometimes front walks are quite short, or the purpose of the front walk is for decoration only. When no one is actually expected to enter the home via this route, the drama of beautiful, colorful plantings lining the unused walk adds immeasurably to the landscape.

See **Low Maintenance, Avoid Plantings Under 2 Feet** *20*
  Grass, Invasive Types *354*

 Broad, easy curves are used on a front walk when necessary. Otherwise the walk should be straight.

Use broad strokes when deciding placement of the front walk. Decide where you want your visitors to park and imagine them getting out of the car and walking at a comfortable angle to the front door—that is your path. Visitors want to walk gracefully. They do not want to be looking down, so do not add unnecessary bends, wiggles, and curves that only complicate the walk.

See **Photo** *221*

The traditional plant edging is not found here. Instead, this gardener wishes everyone to feel free to explore her landscape.

An extended bed adds dramatic interest, creating an oasis of beauty.

Plenty of soft plantings enhance all entrances.

186

A post light is excellent for safety and to designate the space for guest parking.

A visitor welcomes his own parking space, out of the way of the homeowner.

Note the angle at guest parking for easy access to the walkway.

No wiggles here; only a broad easy curve will do.

The bed line directs your eye to the front door.

187 Added features indicating the beginning of a front walk are essential to aid the visitor making parking decisions. **These features create an oasis of beauty to send a strong message of "Welcome."**

Just like the front door, which is usually very dramatic and has many embellishments, the juncture of the front walk to the driveway should also have its own embellishments. This tells the visitor in no uncertain terms that he is a very important person, you want him to park in a specific spot, and he is welcomed into your home.

One of the most important features is to create a landing by widening the paved surface. Depending on the usable space, this flare could be an additional two or three feet, or even as long as a full parking space length of eighteen to twenty feet. Sometimes this expanded space can be a different texture or even incorporate a decorative motif that coordinates with the home's architecture. Adding shrubs helps soften the look and also designates this area as a separate space just for parking. A light post is certainly a clear symbol to anyone to indicate where to park (besides the light it casts at night). A tree could provide much wanted shade for parked cars. Other options are a small fence or perhaps a statue to welcome guests. Even a small flower bed would add loveliness to any situation.

What is created is a small oasis that allows visitors to feel they have been given their own parking space and have been graciously invited into the home through the front door.

See **Lighting** *334, 336*
Surfacing Material *194, 196*
Significant Trees, Climate Control *109*
Ornamental Trees, Interest *99*
Three Foot Fences *310*
Photo *228*

The inviting circular walk indicates to each visitor to park his car at the curb and where to enter the home.

This Ornamental Tree is a perfect focal point in this outdoor entrance room.

The stone walk adds a textural change to help create a room in the landscape.

The low, mostly evergreen plantings and comfortable chairs on the porch add another strong welcoming note.

A 5-foot-wide walk ensures a comfortable space for people to walk side-by-side.

188 **The main entrance to your home should stand out as the primary door for entering. All other doors must be secondary. Similarly, secondary entrance doors should be identified as such, to differentiate them from closets, utility rooms, garage access, and other nonentrance doors.**

Generally, it's not hard to recognize the front door (Guest Entrance), especially in more formal architectural designs. However, homes of a more rambling, casual nature often have various doors scattered along the front, with no particular outstanding feature that directs anyone where to enter. To correct this situation, additional features need to be added to the main entrance to tell visitors just where to enter without any ambiguity.

The solution to this problem is to visually set the front door apart from all other doors. Adding more pronounced architectural features such as trim work or painting the door a different color often does the trick. Simpler solutions include a special doormat, a small bench, or perhaps some urns and other decorations. Even a little welcome sign or a posted house number will direct anyone to the front door if there are any unmarked doors elsewhere.

Additionally, side or back doors intended as entrances should be identified to spare visitors expected to use them the aggravation or embarrassment of knocking on the broom closet door in error. Again, you might add extra trim, a prominent doorbell, a welcome sign, a nice doormat, or some container plantings and other objects of interest.

The main idea is that there should never, ever be any ambiguity on the part of any guest as to which door should be used.

See **Utility Areas Planned** *169*
Guest Parking Direct to Front Door *205*
Utility Doors Separate from Living Spaces *233*

Which door?

Two doors…which to choose? It's easy because the one on the left has a more dramatic architectural façade and planted urns on each side of the door.

An Ornamental Tree softens the exterior and creates a divide between the two doors.

Plenty of space for plantings softens the effects of an expansive hard surface.

Notice the stone landing separating the space from the Car Area.

188

This gentle message says: Don't knock or leave messages or packages here. Go around to the front door.

188

189 **All doors leading to utility or workshop areas need to be separated from entrances to living spaces. Utility areas are nearly always messy while living areas should be maintained for everyday living.**

I often see doors to a living space and the utility area located very near each other along the back exterior of houses; some even share the same hard surface. Perhaps the homeowner sees himself working on a project or believes getting his stuff in and out easily is important. However, not only are most projects messy, but they do not finish on schedule. The dilemma comes when someone wants to straighten up but the ongoing project prevents this. The result is that no one can be happy with project debris spilling out onto the nice back porch meant for relaxing.

The answer: separate the two areas. Locate the utility door to the side, away from the living space doors. If possible, set it back out of line from the living space. Even better, locate the utility entrance around the corner totally out of view.

Also never join the utility area to the living area by sharing a hard surface. Even a small planting bed will soften and separate the two areas. Planting a small tree creates an umbrella effect so the view from the upper stories is shielded from the sight of the lawnmower and gas cans spilling out of the utility door just below.

Just as you would not allow your washer and dryer to intrude into your living room, why allow your utility space to detract from your beautiful outdoor patio?

Two different uses require two separate entrances, which will never share the same hard surfaces. For even more separation, consider recessing the utility space or even moving it to the side or to a separate structure.

190 **All doors should have a covering over the landing for functional reasons; more important, these coverings are a major transitional element to integrate the home with the outdoors.**

Every door exposed to the elements will deteriorate much more rapidly than one that is covered. Unlike a window, doors must open and close continuously and they are much more vulnerable to the elements: a pounding rain or searing sun can ruin the best of doors over a short time.

Additionally, anyone coming to a door appreciates the protection covering provides. Fumbling for keys, trying to handle packages, perhaps watching a kid or two, and dealing with the dog—all are accomplished with more grace when one is out of the elements.

Even more important, these coverings provide an essential transitional space with the outdoors becoming a part of the home's interior. Coverings come in all styles and sizes, from a minimal canvas awning to a roofed landing to a full, covered porch with chairs and rockers. Regardless of size or dramatic impact, coverings are vital elements in any landscape design, providing the necessary transition from the indoors to the outside garden. The architectural projection itself reaches out to create a visual dimension that an otherwise stark, flat surface does not provide, while the overall dominance of the home is reduced to more human terms as these covered spaces embrace the outdoors.

See **Photos** *62, 243, 299*

A welcoming bench invites everyone to sit and enjoy the surroundings.

A generous landing with a welcomed cover keeps any visitor out of the elements while waiting for someone to answer the door. This quiet oasis invites visitors to enjoy the surroundings in total comfort.

This door has a 4-inch riser height because rain could reach this space, harming the home's interior.

190

191 A landing should be provided for every door to the outside.

The action of opening a door always has its problems. Keys, groceries, dogs, kids, even managing one's coat can create all kinds of hazards. With a generous landing, at least the person is entering or exiting on the same level. After regrouping on this stable area, the steps can now be managed.

Unfortunately, these landings are often left off, meaning one immediately steps out onto the top row of steps. This creates an awkward situation—if not a terrible hazard. Additionally this situation causes an incredibly abrupt division of the house to the outside. One might do without a covering…but never without a landing from an exit door.

See **Steps** *270-283, 287*
Photo *65*

Constructing steps without a landing is hazardous and creates an abrupt division between the interior space and the outdoors.

This generous landing creates a direct connection between the interior space and the outdoors. It is that very important space where one pauses before entering or exiting, perhaps looking around to feel the wholeness of the surroundings.

Gently curving steps accent the placement of the patio space.

This generous landing provides a convenient place to pause.

The wide wrap-around step gives easy access to several directions of interest.

A 6-inch riser and a 14-inch tread create a perfect step for gliding up and down off this landing.

Every door leading to the outside must have a generous landing before steps are added. A covering can be optional, but landings are not.

Note the step at the front door. When there is no covering, the elements can compromise the situation; this is a very important detail.

Two ornamental dogs tell any visitor, "Watch out, there is a step."

192 **All landings should be adequate for two people to stand comfortably upon before exiting or entering.**

 193 **Railings at landings and stair steps are always welcomed, for both safety and aesthetics.**

Remember, five feet is a two-person width. Much less than that and people will have a hard time to maneuver. This dimension should expand for the front door.

In all cases, these landings should be in proportion to the homesite. I have often walked up to a beautiful home to find myself staring in disbelief at a front door landing absolutely too small for anyone to stand on, compounded by an outward-opening screen door. This is no place to chop off a foot or two because the long-term effects can rarely be remedied. This area sets the tone for first impressions of hospitality, so be generous when planning the landing.

See **Front Walk is Minimum 5 Feet Wide** *226*

Photos *62, 65, 226, 243*

Railings are usually governed by code regulations. But sometimes codes do not specify railings; the homeowner then has the option to do as he wishes. Obviously, if the landing is hazardous, a rail must be installed.

Stair steps are particularly hazardous, and rails are often not provided. But anyone who has vision or physical problems appreciates these aids. If possible, be sure these are added to your plans. Your grandmother will thank you.

Rails add a touch of aesthetics to your landscape by adding a sense of enclosure, creating a special space. Even if the drop-off is minimal with only two or three steps, a light iron rail with a lovely curve and finial can contribute to quite a lovely setting. In other cases, the choice of railing can be a dramatic architectural statement at the entrance. Instead of the landing seeming to float out in space, rails create a lovely and safe outdoor room, which increases the beauty of your landscape.

See **Iron** *310*

5 feet x 5 feet is the *minimum* landing size!

All landings should be constructed in a way so they will never sag or pull away from the home's structure.

Contractors use many methods to skin this cat. Increasingly, I see a genuine awareness of this problem. It is critically important to address it to prevent bad results coming back to haunt the builder and the homeowner. Many old homes have been ruined by large, old steps tilting here and there; not only are they ugly, but they become a real hazard. It's quite expensive to correct the situation and very difficult to match materials.

Discuss this problem with your builder during planning. Any concrete, brick, or stone structure has enormous weight, plus the ground below has its own dynamics. If allowed over time, this mass will settle where it wants. I often see the top steps pulled away and skewed from the landing or the house entrance, and the bottom steps no longer level with the walk. Taking strong preventive measures during construction will save you money and avoid a safety hazard later.

See **Selection of Contractor Equals Low Maintenance** *37*

Sagging, narrow, and dangerous old steps were removed. The new steps accommodated the new, large landing and were constructed of even, proportioned dimensions.

The light post is in position for beauty and safety.

Light iron rails provide security with the unnecessary visual weight of wood.

Special attention was paid to ensure the correct riser and tread dimensions were incorporated, making the steps comfortable for walking.

CHAPTER **6**

Indoor and Outdoor Transitions

Steps, Porches, and Decks

Outdoor sitting spaces are major features that integrate the home with the outdoors. They provide vantage points to enjoy a vista—which then propel everyone to venture into the landscape.

No matter whether you choose to install a porch, deck, or patio, each requires careful consideration about how it is placed in relationship to the home, how it will be constructed, and how it will be protected from the elements—particularly the sun—if it is ever to be the destination spot you want it to be.

Furthermore, the transitioning steps—from home to patio, from deck or porch to garden—is a vital element that determines the ultimate enjoyment of these very important home features.

195 **The power of the sun will have a major impact on any open deck or patio. The choice of a porch will ameliorate some of this power but the sun will still need to be considered for comfortable living space.**

We all know that too much sun can make any space unbearable for comfortable living. We also know that the absence of any sun will make for a dank, dreary, mossy no-go zone. So what's the answer? Avoid extremely costly mistakes when adding decks, porches, or patios by looking at the power of the sun or its absence and making adjustments—because the sun will not!

If a deck or porch is close to ground level, the homeowner can anticipate adding trees and shrubs for shade if they are not already in place. If more immediate and complete shade is desired, plan for the deck to become a porch; if that is not possible or desired, adding an arbor might be just the thing.

But consider what happens to a high deck that receives lots of sun—getting anything planted, especially on a sloping lot, that will reach a necessary height to provide shade (and getting it done within

an agreeable time frame) will be quite a challenge. Thus, enjoyment of the deck will be diminished. Instead, reduce the high deck to just an attractive, complementary landing that will accommodate a few necessary items—a grill, potted plant, and maybe one or two small seats—and then get on down to a lower level where cooling shade can be more easily sited.

Conversely, watch out for plans that place a patio or deck entirely in the shade. If this space gets *no sun,* the space will go unused; plans for a large, comfortable let's-sit-outside-for-a-relaxed-evening will not happen. Why? Because this space will grow mold, it will be uncomfortably chilly, and so forth. Again, downsize the space for your immediate needs—a nice landing with a cover for a lovely entrance to your home, a place for the grill and maybe space for some decorative item for interest—then position your major Outdoor Living Space to receive some sun.

Remember: plants can help, adding a porch roof can help, changing your design can help.

See **Power of the Sun** *57, 58*
Significant Trees *96*
Plants with Job Descriptions *64*

The flexibility of a plan that combines both deck and porch allows anyone to adjust to the power of the sun.

Significant Trees offer shade and cooling breezes.

The 10- to 12-foot width of this patio space allows plenty of room for a table.

Flooring is laid in a traditional design.

195

196 The design for the primary Outdoor Living Space should accommodate all anticipated guests in one place and on one level.

I call this the "rubber band element" of design: People will move out only so far before they snap back to a congenial mass to join other people at an occasion.

When homeowners are planning construction of Outdoor Living Spaces, the creative juices begin to flow: Let's put a little space over here and then step down over there and wind about until the space is filled with adventurous nooks and crannies. These artistic endeavors are quite charming and make great photo ops…but where will people actually congregate when they show up for a party? The answer: all in one space—probably the kitchen. Gatherings generally do not break up into twosomes and threesomes and space out over any real distance. Those distant nooks and crannies will be briefly visited but soon that invisible rubber band snaps them back!

Besides the fact that these smaller spaces now make placement of furniture problematic, there are hazards associated with maneuvering steps to different levels while carrying plates of food, paying attention to a conversation…the list goes on. Plan for your lifestyle, plan for the number of people you routinely entertain, and then plan a functional Outdoor Living Space that will accommodate everyone in one place, and on one level.

See **Steps – Different Outdoors** *272*

Single Steps, Avoid or Give Plenty of Clues *272*

No Built-In Seating *261*

Comfortable Seating *322*

Enclosure *50*

Photos *51, 246*

This sun porch addition allowed a formerly inadequate outdoor patio to be reworked into something fully functional for family gatherings.

The furniture to be used was noted, allowing the design to accommodate its use. Exact measurements, not wishful thinking, guarantee a happy result.

The exit door has all the attributes to make it work: a cover, a large landing, and wide, comfortable steps.

A Significant Tree was added after a mature specimen had died. This one was chosen because of its good habits, a necessary consideration so near an entertainment space.

196

Simple, curved steps lead to one main patio centered around a pond and an outdoor fireplace.

The colors of the stone and furniture are coordinated for a unified, comfortable arrangement, which complements the architecture of the home.

A low wall was built on the outer edge of the patio to create a small degree of enclosure for the immediate space. Ten feet farther back on the property line, a 6-foot pierced brick wall encloses the entire back garden.

Two steps lead up to a side garden used as a passageway, which is not part of the patio space.

The patio was designed with exact measurements to ensure correct placement of furniture and good circulation.

196

This former courtyard had multiple spaces with steps appearing here and there. The site was leveled and expanded into one area using the original bricks. Now there is great flexibility for furniture arrangement and for people to move about comfortably.

Plenty of planting areas, most using evergreens, were planned to soften the large amount of brick.

Paths on each side and another in the middle provide access to the surrounding garden.

The exit (with steps) is identified by tightening the space and plantings.

The addition of a low wall on the outer two corners creates a cozy feeling.

197 **Decks or porches that are designed so they are too long and perhaps too narrow are not appealing. The space can be modified to solve this problem.**

Any room (for example a hall, living room, bedroom) that is long in relationship to the width is unappealing. A natural reaction is always negative, like entering a dead-end street. If the design of your deck or porch looks like an alleyway on the plan, it will feel like that when it's built. Plan to break up the length with a screened porch, an arbor, or an architectural break in the line.

Additional exits should be provided to eliminate that dead-end feeling. Otherwise, no one will venture to that dead space, leaving it unused. But if it's opened up, the space will become true living space.

See **Photos** *237, 317*

 198 **When planning Outdoor Living Spaces, think big—leave plenty of space for furniture. A chair needs a minimum width of 6 feet and a table with chairs to seat four to six needs a minimum of 10 feet square (12 feet square is even better).**

Sometimes a homeowner wants to include a few chairs on his front porch, a porch that was intended only for decorative items. Plan ahead before you find out too late your space is too small; one or two feet often makes all the difference.

Dimensions for all outdoor features should be more expansive beyond the exact measurements to accommodate specific chairs and tables. The reason is simple: Indoor space is restrained with walls and ceilings, but outdoor space has only tall trees and sky. Drag some furniture onto this imaginary space and see what you are comfortable with. Then build it.

See **Circulation** *186*
Comfortable Seating *322*
Photos *242, 243, 244*

Six feet is adequate but an 8-foot-wide porch gives this homeowner a few more options. Be sure to check your house plans for this important measurement.

This wonderful porch measures 12 feet across. The furniture fits perfectly for easy living, with plenty of room to move around gracefully.

This furniture was chosen for its comfort and movability for relaxed social gatherings.

The view from all windows is open to the grand vista beyond, not blocked by heavy furniture.

199 A grill is not art, and no matter how magnificent, it should not be seen as a major focal point in your landscape. **Place its location carefully for maximum safety because it is hazardous.**

Of all the items desired for an Outdoor Living Space, the grill is perhaps the most awkward and obtrusive. It is quite large, it must be close by in order to watch the cooking process, and it must be away from combustible things. The goal is to find that perfect spot—which means removing it as a major focal point both from the outdoor space and from the visual field inside your home, while maintaining safety.

Is there a blank wall, available but out of the way? Does the Outdoor Space need to be extended somewhere to accommodate this need? Could the grill be moved off the deck or porch to a few steps lower, somewhere on the ground level? Just a little planning here will ensure that the grill becomes what it needs to be—a wonderful tool near which everyone can gather to enjoy the cooking and conversation.

See **Design for All Your Needs** *250*
View from Major Sitting Areas *46, 253, 266*
Outdoor Fire *368*
Photo *85*

The addition of this sunroom and pool area included a design for the placement of the grill in a spot that is safe and unobtrusive, yet convenient.

Architectural elements and plantings indicate to everyone this is a secondary door.

Large landings and walkways make for easy comings and goings.

A porch gives protection from the elements; a deck would be too exposed.

Wide steps with rails, even risers, treads for the steps, and a comfortable large landing are part of this good design.

This side kitchen porch was specifically designed to project out to hold the grill. Its position does not block the outdoor vista from either of the major inside viewing areas.

199

200 Adding porches can be tricky. **A project like this could require expensive structural changes and might not be doable at all.**

Many homeowners either expect to add a porch at some later date as part of their overall plan or—when faced with the broiling sun—decide they would like one now. They belatedly realize the architecture of their home does not support an addition at all, or only at great additional expense.

It's very difficult to try to predict the future when building or buying a house because one has so many things to consider. But if you *know* adding a porch is in your plan, check with someone in construction to get some good advice as to how it can be done now or in the future. You definitely want to know what the major hurdles for a project of this size will be.

See **Summerhouses, Alternative** *253*

201 When designing your outdoor entertainment space, consider whether it will comfortably accommodate all your needs. **Will your outdoor furniture fit? How does it relate to your traffic flow? How does it relate to indoor spaces—is anything blocking your view? You may find a scale drawing useful.**

All kinds of things go onto outdoor spaces—tables, chairs, urns, water fountains, swings, grills, even pretty shelving and buffet tables. With just a little planning, maybe an hour or so with a piece of grid paper and some cutouts representing your equipment and furniture, the deck, porch, or patio could be adjusted a little here or there for great results. Now the steps to the outside are moved for a better exit, the deck is extended a few more feet over one side to make room for a buffet, or the grill is moved out of the way. Remember, adjustments made on a piece of paper are quite cheap. The same adjustments after the project is over or even during it are quite expensive.

See **Architectural Details, Complement** *42*
     Circulation *186*
     One Place, One Level *243*
     Dimensions for Furniture *246*
     Photo *246*

201

Hardscapes should be designed from exact measurement to ensure that the permanent, expensive results fit the needs of the situation. Moving plants around is one thing—moving solid concrete, stone, or wood is another!

Steps lead from the main floor to a small area of decking just outside the kitchen door devoted to the grill. This couple did not wish to have a major grilling area in this patio space.

Behind the steps is a secondary passageway to the Utility Area, convenient but out of the way.

An arbor with swing is sited so it overlooks the garden.

The main entrance passes by another table and chairs for anyone choosing a sunny time together.

A summerhouse invites everyone to come out of the elements. These ample dimensions allow for a table, chairs, and a serving table.

Steps provide an easy access to the garden below.

202 Porches are a major transitional element in the landscape. **They have more impact for the quality of life than any other room in the house. Porches connect the inside to the outdoors, enhancing the full appreciation of both.**

Porches can soften the passage between the great outdoors and the air-conditioned, controlled interior of the home. The homeowner can be outside and yet still be close to the home's amenities. Hot sun and dousing rains can be alleviated, and if the porch is also screened, bugs are no longer a nuisance.

There seems to be no room in the house more enjoyed than a porch with comfortable chairs and rockers scattered about and a table for a casual meal. Anytime of the day and for many months of a year, one can sit, hear the rain and wind, smell the flowers, listen to frogs and crickets, watch children playing—and yet, the floor is dry, the seats are clean and comfortable, and any hot sun has been tempered. What joy!

Recently, I was working at a magnificent brick home that has many beautiful architectural features. But every window and door opened directly to the outside. The owner visited her neighbor's newly constructed home with its lovely front porch and another along the back. She remarked that this was what she would have liked instead. The porches invited one to come in, and made visiting much more relaxed. Porches provide a space to pause between the harsh outdoors and the insular interior. Unfortunately this homeowner missed including this very important feature to her own home.

If there is space for one porch, even a small one, it might bring more joy than any other space in your house.

This porch overlooks a garden below. The homeowner can hear sounds from the pond and wildlife and feel the breezes without being exposed to outside elements.

The added garage brings a beautiful dimension to the landscape besides its obvious functional use.

Arbors or summerhouses added to decks or patio areas can give protection from the sun and add architectural beauty. They are important alternate choices when a porch cannot be built.

In some situations, adding a porch is just not feasible, but the homeowner must still have protection from the weather. An arbor will give some protection but mainly provides shade. Only a summerhouse gives the most complete protection from the elements.

Structurally, arbors are easier to add to decks than covered porches. They don't keep out the rain, but the dappled shade and the sense of enclosure add an interesting dimension that makes the whole much greater than the sum of its parts. Planting a vine to climb upon the arbor brings the outdoors even closer.

With a solid roof—and perhaps screens—a summerhouse offers even more protection from the elements and is a delight at all hours.

See **Structures** *292*
    Photo *47*

 If you paid a significant amount of money for a view, make sure your outside porch or deck—or its accoutrements—doesn't obstruct this all-important inside view.

Many house designs focus on spectacular views, and the home has beautiful windows overlooking these impressive vistas. If a wide deck or porch is constructed along the side of the view, the view from the inside could be marred—with a view instead of porch rails or furniture.

Remember that views from inside should be enjoyed from a seated position, and plan accordingly, by simplifying porches or moving them.

See **Choice of Rails** *260*
    Better Option – Patio *264*
    Photos *47, 247*

This summerhouse was added to give the homeowner much needed shade to enjoy her surrounding sunny garden.

A berry-bearing Ornamental Tree was planted outside the window as an interrupted view, giving great interest and depth to the landscape. Watching the dynamics of living trees and their many winged visitors far outweighs seeing everything in the distance.

Keeping the suckers cut and a little thinning over the years will keep this tree open and attractive.

The warming morning sun is always welcomed.

Everyone wanted a clear view of the lake; therefore the porch was not extended.

This deck was purposely designed to be located at the side because of the downward distant views of the river below.

The most durable and attractive materials should be chosen for your deck. Expect your contractor to use them with the same respect that's given to interior spaces.

A deck (as well as the roof) is the most exposed and vulnerable area of the home. Investigate all new products for durability as well as aesthetic qualities to prevent or alleviate many down-the-road problems. You could be saving yourself great expense to correct these problems, if not preventing a complete deck makeover. Decks often seem to be built as an afterthought to otherwise lovely homes. Marginal materials, often rough and twisted, are haphazardly pieced together in such a manner that no one can enjoy the space. The flooring warps and often rots in an untimely manner; the rails are so splintery no one would dare lay a hand on them; and the pickets are so thick and clumsy, the landscape beyond is marred just looking past the poor carpentry.

But a well-built deck extends the beauty of the home as a wonderful transitional space into the landscape. The flooring is even and strong and will endure many years; the rails are crafted to support anyone leaning over to observe a distant vista or to stabilize someone descending the steps; and the posts and pickets are designed and constructed to enhance the entire outdoor living space.

Maybe that "last project" in the whole building cycle finds everyone exhausted and over budget. But a deck is often allowed to be the runt of the litter, leaving the homeowner to deal with the multiple problems of a poorly built deck—often sooner than should be expected.

See **Choice of Rails** *260*
Contractor for Low Maintenance *37*
Photos *237, 249, 251, 286*

 Most decks should be seen more as transitional spaces and less as active living spaces, unless perfectly sited and covered—possibly even screened—for protection from the outdoor elements (sun, rain, cold, heat).

It's all in the percentages: Unless a deck has the right amount of shade and breeze, it is often neglected because of mosquitoes, wet furniture, glaring sun, and so forth. The area becomes a collecting place for unused pots or it might be perfectly decorated but rarely used. I suggest that most homeowners would be better served with decks designed as beautiful *transitional spaces* from the home or the porch before descending to perhaps another Outdoor Living Space such as a patio or a swimming pool.

The implication here is that a deck design might be minimized in size to more of a landing, and all money put into a more agreeable Outdoor Living Space.

See **Power of the Sun** *57, 58*
Significant Trees *96*
Landings *236*
Photos *242, 258*

With three choices for relaxation—the porch, the stone patio, and alongside the pool—most people choose the porch and the pool. The stone patio is quite beautiful but its main function is to be a lovely transitional space.

The pool house, which is sitting in a major viewing space, was painted and trimmed to complement the architecture of the house.

Note the steps are accented by contrasting materials, urns, and a planting bed.

A low evergreen hedge creates a necessary enclosure from an unused, downward-sloping space in the landscape. A tall screen would have given a trapped feeling.

The choice of flower colors complements the stone on the patio.

Note the bed lines pull the eye around to the main event—the house.

The treatment of the support posts and screening add drama to the landscape.

The porch on the right is recessed, giving it a decidedly cozy feeling.

The extra-wide steps create a wonderful open view to the lake beyond. The steps are backed and painted with a contrasting color.

This backyard walkway is still 5 feet wide, plenty of room for two people to stroll.

The porch on the right is the primary place for relaxing. The porch on the left is really a covered landing for a beautiful entry to the interior. The remaining open decking is a transitional space connecting all exits and leading down to the landscape. It will only be used for relaxing if more sun is desired or on special evenings.

207 **Decks and even porches accomplish more if they are recessed, even slightly, into the structure of the house, as the subtle feeling of being embraced by the home adds comfort, while the architectural angles add visual interest.**

Structurally, decks tend to be very open with only flooring and perhaps a rail; the higher the deck, the more vacuous the space surrounding it becomes, creating a feeling of being out of control as people lose visual contact with the ground.

To alleviate the sense of a deck floating in space, the homeowner should plan on recessing the struc-

ture into the house. It provides actual extra structural strength, of course, but also provides psychological strength with a feeling of being enclosed and embraced by the house.

Even if the deck or porch is close to the ground, recessing still holds great value. The added angles are admired for their architectural interest, and the recessed nooks provide a space to retreat from wind or sun.

See **Enclosure** *50*
Circulation *186*
Choice of Rails *260*
Photos *247, 258*

This porch is recessed even further past the entryway to create the perfect dimensions for a comfortable table and chairs.

Notice the details for the steps: backing to the steps as well as a screening from the underside. This allows the landscape plantings to be more decorative and less about trying to cover up an unpleasant view.

207

The choice of rails, pickets, or even privacy screening will have a major impact on the enjoyment of your deck or porch. Decide on your intended goal and take it from there.

A "room with a view" overlooking a lake or beautiful woods needs to be as open as possible. In a densely populated area, however, a homeowner might want privacy to enjoy the outdoors quietly. The choice of rail and picket design— should they be lightweight iron? heavier wooden banisters? closed off completely?—should address this by deciding the style that suits your goal.

See **Architectural Complement** *42*

    View from Inside *253*

    Photos *10, 42, 59*

 Decks and porches are part of the architectural whole. They should never bisect or crowd architectural features on the house, but should enhance them.

The design of Outdoor Living Spaces should frame features on the home; they should *never*, ever bisect any feature on the house or even crowd them. Why would anyone want a deck that bisects two beautifully paired windows, for example? A rail just a few inches away from a door or any major feature leaves us with a squeezed-in impression. Whether a deck is planned at the beginning of the architectural design process or added after the home is built, note these architectural features and adjust.

The initial deck design cuts the window feature and crowds the sliding door. A better deck design frames the architectural features of the house.

Solid panels

Lots of privacy.

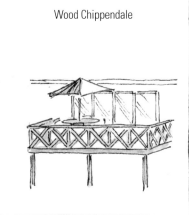

Wood Chippendale

How pretty!

Iron rails

What a view!

210 Do not construct built-in seats with backs on a deck. **A flat bench with no back might be acceptable, but individual seating is a much better choice.**

Here are five reasons built-in seats should not be constructed on your deck—and I mean *never. One:* they block the view with their heavy construction. *Two:* they make a person face toward the house—not to the garden. *Three:* they force people to sit shoulder-to-shoulder to converse, not at the more agreeable 45-degree angle that individual chairs allow. *Four:* they are often coarse and dirty because wood will splinter and become rough with age. *Five:* they are never comfortable because most carpenters are not chair-builders.

I have more reasons, but you get the point. Flexibility and congeniality are key. Individual chairs can be moved about for the needs of every guest. They can be chosen for the conditions of your region. They can even be changed out as the situation changes.

A flat, wide *backless* bench is usually used on a low deck to add seating and control traffic in place of a rail. Use materials that weather well and stay smooth; swimsuits and nice clothing do not go well with materials that snag. This long flat surface can also become an unfortunate collection site but at least obstruction of a view is minimized.

See **Seats, Benches** *322*
   Design for View *46*

 211 The flooring of a wood deck should be kept simple, usually at right angles. **Do not allow anyone to use a chevron (V-shape) design on an otherwise simple, straightforward deck.**

Architectural elements play a dominant role for the beauty of your home. The flooring of a deck, however, is not where any attention needs to be drawn. The interest should be the details on the house structure, the rails and pickets, and your furnishings…not the flooring.

Occasionally, carpenters like to use angled or chevron decking; remember, they have built a lot of decks and want to do something different. However, this is not where the "different" should be.

Do use angled flooring where the house angles and the flooring follows the angle; visually it is expected and runs with the natural flow. But say no to angles for the sake of angles.

See **Photo** *242*

The Two No's.

212 Before paving extra parking or utility space at the back of a daylight basement, remember that paving a driveway to adjoin this secondary, lower-level space will be expensive, and you'll be looking at concrete from your primary viewing space.

Many homeowners regret paving the back of a daylight basement. Every day they must look out from their primary viewing space and what they see is concrete. Then there is the stuff that accumulates. If the space faces the hot sun, heat radiates off the surface and rises to the house.

Additionally, this area may not have the space to actually serve as a utility area—I've seen many homes with access doors but vehicles couldn't get in and out because they had no room to turn around. Consider moving the vehicle entrance to the side, or recessing it, so it's hidden from view. Consider adding a third or even fourth parking space to your present garage on the main level. If the basement utility area will be used rarely, drive on the grass!

Consider a separate carriage house or workshop close by. Nothing is more elegant than these stand-alone additions to the landscape; often they can share the existing parking pad and driveway.

Cars are a very important part of our society, but their presence should not supersede the importance of the landscape, which is our major connection with the natural world.

Avoid back yard parking.

213 Don't be tempted to use space under the deck as storage, unless there is added construction in place to keep the area dry. **If it is waterproofed to create a dry space for good storage, have plans for camouflaging.**

Decks weep water. If you have a high, open deck that has not been waterproofed underneath, you have two options.

From a maintenance standpoint, the easiest solution is to put down a layer of rocks. This will absorb any splashing drips from above and will not collect water, with all of the problems that causes. Many plants can also survive in this mostly sunless place, so it is just a matter of aesthetics whether this is the second option. If the deck is high and open and the area below it is quite visible, a gardener type will want to install plants. Some homeowners prefer to just put down mulch, but the right kind should be chosen to avoid attracting termites. (Note: mulch does deteriorate and will need periodic replacement.) What should *not* be an option is the storage of stuff unless this space has been waterproofed; wood attracts termites, equipment rusts, and other items collect water that provides a breeding ground for mosquitoes.

If it's waterproofed, this space is wonderful for storing all kinds of utilitarian items—but be prepared to screen the area with plants, hardscape, or both. This space is the petticoat of your home. If it can be seen, make it pretty; if it's for utility, close it off. Wet or dry, plants or storage—this space should be seen as a major feature of your landscape.

See **Support Posts** *263*
    Trim Underneath *276*
    Structures *292*

Our perception of structural strength is often dictated by what we see. Steel posts might well be strong enough to support the deck, but their visual weight is not in proportion to their structural strength—they look skinny. Building a wood structure or a brick, stone, or stucco surround for these support pieces will do wonders for the beauty of this area.

Additionally this is also a critical visual space. Looking back from the garden, if the undersides of these outdoors spaces are parsimonious, the whole effect can become compromised. This is just another detail that should never be overlooked when finishing out your home.

See **Photos** *66, 258, 259, 283, 329*

The distance between the main living spaces and the outdoors should be minimal, just a few steps. This means a homeowner can get up from his breakfast table, open the door to the outside and quickly step into his garden to pick some basil, pull a few weeds, or just take a stroll. Likewise, the kids can jump up from the table, grab some stuff, and off they go.

When the home has a daylight basement, the main living quarters are off the ground at least twelve to fifteen feet—a distance that must be accounted for with long runs of steps both inside and outside the house. If lengthy stairways are the only way to get outside, the family finds itself enjoying the outside landscape less.

Solving the problem is not very hard. The real problem is not knowing there is a problem until the home is completed. *If only* they had pushed some dirt over to create an on-grade exit; *if only* they had designed the basement at the end of the house leaving most of the backyard level with the house; *if only* they had added a door exiting out the back to allow access to the outside…*if only*.

The placement of a daylight basement will have a major impact on this very important element in your landscape—make sure you plan for it!

Trapped!

An exit door plus a better grading plan equals connecting with the outdoors!

216 **If a deck is planned that will be situated close to ground level (by just a few steps), a better option is replace the deck with a ground-level patio.**

The positive attributes of a ground level patio greatly outweigh those of a deck just a few feet off the ground. For example, a patio can be moved away from the house structure, allowing planting spaces between its hard surfaces and the "hardscape" of the house. A patio's outline is more flexible, allowing it to fit the needs of the situation. It is made of durable materials such as concrete, brick, or stone. Even more important, no constricting rails and steps are needed, which allows everyone to move about freely into the landscape. The trapped feeling a deck might impart is gone, and only a gracious feeling and closer connection to the outdoors remain.

Decks are hard to construct for lasting beauty and durability. Most deck rails are heavy and block views, and if there are no deck rails, accidentally stepping off the deck is always a problem. The aboveground space is also confining for seating and traffic flow.

Obviously, there are factors that will make a deck preferable. The land might have a drainage problem, the terrain may not support a ground level patio, or maybe the architectural design of the home makes a deck a better choice. But if there is a choice, building a landing and steps and moving activity to the ground level is preferable.

See **Enclosure** *50*
Plan all Essential Space *40*

This couple originally wanted a deck, but a ground-level patio made more sense once the need for circulation was identified. A deck would have cut the garden into two parts and severely limited use of the backyard. Constructing a patio also allowed the furniture to become less obtrusive by moving it out of eye level (lower and to the side).

The low wall creates a small enclosed space and helps direct traffic onto a woodland trail.

217 **Leave planting spaces between the patio or any large hard surfaces and the house (or other structure).** **Otherwise, a very harsh environment can result due to too much hardscape (concrete, brick, wood) without the softening effects of plant materials.**

Too much brick, stone, or concrete can develop into an oppressive situation: the sun's heat is absorbed and radiates back, creating an ovenlike effect. I've heard a variety of excuses why this mistake is made, but none are valid. Often I see this harsh environment at the Car Area. Concrete is poured even where no hard surface is needed. Lovely plants that could have softened the home's exterior (and perhaps hidden some utility elements) are eliminated. Patios are sometimes sited right up to a home's outside; again, there's no good use for this hard surface but the com-bined hard surfacing traps heat and creates a sterile environment. Even swimming pools often have solid fences or walls with no plant relief in sight. Container plants are often employed to relieve the situation, but they need constant maintenance and still often cannot add the softness a planting bed could have achieved.

Plants are essential to bring their cooling properties to an environment. Plant choices are endless and exciting while any hardscape is permanent and hard. Achieving the balance between these two landscape elements should be the goal of every homeowner.

See **Containers** *156*
Fences *309*
Enclosure *50*
Too Much Concrete *218*
Photos *101, 195, 223, 232, 245*

Swimming pools located in constricted spaces are particularly notorious for excluding any plans for planting beds. Containers seem to be the expected alternative, but their maintenance is unrelenting. Plants in the ground—even in small spaces—are much easier and more forgiving as one can see at this pool.

This 12-foot-wide deck provides plenty of space for tables and chairs and a passageway for swimmers. The back walk needs only a 4- to 5-foot width.

Placement of any patio area should take into consideration two things: whether the patio will obstruct a view from inside the house, and the view from the patio itself.

Occasionally, a patio might become an obstruction to a more important view. A homeowner might sit in his main living area and find he is looking straight at patio furniture and not the lake he centered the whole house around. The patio could easily have been sited elsewhere and still have been convenient for use, but it was placed where patios are usually placed without consideration of the inside view from the house.

Sometimes there are options when siting a patio. Step around the corner, and see what happens if you place the patio in a less obvious location. Or take a walk and find a place away from the house—who says it has to be right next to the door? Take a lawn chair and sit in the space for a while to see if it "feels" right.

A special view, a delicious breeze, a warming sun through the trees…all kinds of magical moments are waiting to be found. This is now your patio—the one away from the house, down by the lake, or out in the garden.

See **Level Spaces** 53

   Structures, Arbors, and Summerhouses 292, 304

   Comfortable Seating 322

   Formal, Informal Seating 325

   Fire 368

   Lighting – Cafeteria and Italian 336

   Photo 264

The vista from inside is of a lovely formal archway and garden. The patio was designed to accommodate the furniture and for the grill to be close by, but also to avoid blocking this view.

218

The beauty of a ground-level patio is the homeowner's option to place it wherever he has the best sensational view, breeze, shade—or whatever suits his needs. The short distance from the home, with its cooking supplies and restroom facilities, makes this a wonderful spot for entertaining.

A cozy feeling is created by the arbor, small wall, large fireplace, and comforting trees, making this spot one to visit over and over.

219 To create a feeling of enclosure and to help control traffic, add a low wall to one edge of a patio. **If the wall is approximately 17 inches high, extra seating is provided along its length. Do not encircle more than a quarter or third of the circumference of the patio.**

Patios are created for entertainment, but people can be unpredictable. Without thinking, a visitor might exit through the beautiful flower and shrub border and not via the gracious exit that was provided. Children in their exuberance will spill out beyond the patio space and go in all directions with no thought to your lovely plantings. Who wants to be admonishing kids and guests to watch out, or stand silently gulping air as someone accidentally steps on your favorite plant? A low wall is a great way to protect your plants and direct traffic, while adding visual interest and a congenial feeling of enclosure.

See **Circulation** *186*
Enclosure *50*
No Built-in Benches *261*
Photos *51, 244*

This 17-inch wall has doubled for years as extra seating for this family's children and their friends visiting while also helping direct their playful traffic. But its main purpose is as a pleasant enclosure for intimate outside gatherings.

220 **All outdoor sitting areas should have a firm base of concrete, brick, stone, or packed gravel—not soft, damp lawn or earth.**

Why is a firm base of some type of *dry* surface so important? People like to sit knowing their feet will stay dry and bugs will not be crawling up their legs, and be confident the outdoor furniture will not slowly sink into soft ground. If the opposite happens (shoes get wet, bugs are slapped, or someone repeatedly tries to find proper footing for their tilting chair), the visit inevitably will be cut short.

We think we can entice someone to sit here or there because the furniture is just *so* inviting. Many catalogs artfully portray them casually located about the lawn or along a path, so who could resist? But *if* you wish sitting areas to be truly enjoyed, a firm base for them is essential. Whether it is under an arbor, along a wooded path, or simply some chairs positioned under shady trees, the ground must always be firm.

See **Photos** *82, 367*

This beautiful natural litter is what Mother Nature wants and this homeowner lets it happen.

A nice picnic can be spoiled by soggy surfaces. Using some on-site historic hexagonal paving stones, this problem was permanently solved for fun times with grandchildren.

221 Steps—from the deck to the lawn, from the patio to the pool, from the parking area below to the front door, and so forth—must be consistent in size (both riser and tread) for safety and aesthetics. **Don't wing it! Take measurements and do the math.**

Steps are inherently dangerous. Constructing them only after repeated measurements enhances safety. After the first step, we mentally calculate how much lift or drop to expect for subsequent steps. When there are surprises, we stumble. No homeowner wants to create this situation.

Here's how to avoid surprising your guests (or yourself). You'll need a measuring tape, and you may want to sketch it too. Take the vertical measurement to know how many feet there are from the bottom to the top and divide that number by what you think you would like to use as a riser height. For rather long runs of six, seven, or more steps, a riser of around six or seven inches is about right. If there is a short run or the slope is very gentle, a smaller riser of four to five inches is used. After the riser measurement is settled on, just plug the figure into the following formula, and out pops the tread measurement. When you have a very specific beginning and ending point, you'll need both the vertical and horizontal distance to scale out the descent since you must end up at a certain point. Use graph paper to help come up with the answer.

The measurements for the riser and tread dimensions are based on a tried-and-true formula: double the riser measurement (which you've already determined) and add a number to equal 26 to 28. For example, for a 4-inch riser, you'd double 4 to get 8, and add 18 to 20 to arrive at 26 to 28. So the tread for a 4-inch riser should be 18 to 20 inches. The formula might also be shown as $28 - (\text{riser} \times 2) = \text{tread}$.

Examples

- 4-inch riser
  $28 - (4 \times 2) = 20$
  meaning that the tread should be 18 to 20 inches

- 5-inch riser
  $28 - (5 \times 2) = 18$
  meaning that the tread should be 16 to 18 inches

- 6-inch riser
  $28 - (6 \times 2) = 16$
  meaning that the tread should be 14 to 16 inches

- 7-inch riser
  $28 - (7 \times 2) = 14$
  meaning that the tread should be 12 to 14 inches

Every once in a while someone will half-listen to these measurements and think the magic is in using one or the other. They might like the nice wide tread or they want a certain riser, but they do not see the whole picture. These measurements are interrelated. Deciding on one measurement necessitates using the correct measurement for the other part of the step. Just take the time to scale these measurements out so you will have a wonderful result.

See **Provide Landing for All Doors before Steps Begin** *236*
Photos *62, 181, 196, 239*

These steps were carefully measured and laid out for an even, comfortable walk (6-inch riser and 16-inch tread).

Steps were added to give good circulation from the main entrance to the back garden and parking.

Easy tread and riser dimensions were chosen for this outdoor space.

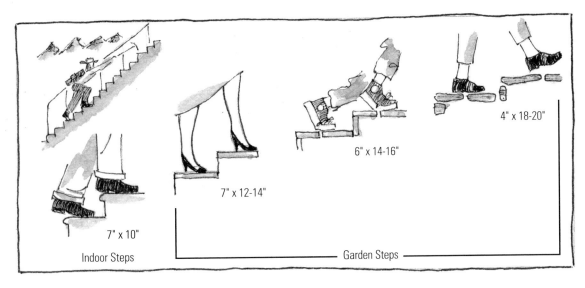

7" x 10"

Indoor Steps

7" x 12-14"

6" x 14-16"

4" x 18-20"

Garden Steps

Climb or Glide

222 **Steps for the outdoors are different than ones found in the house. Even though the riser/tread equation must be used, the grade should be more gracious, the width of the steps should be expanded, intermittent landings can be added, and if possible, the steps should meander along with the natural terrain.**

Indoor steps are actually regulated in many areas by building codes because there is a very real need to eliminate odd steps that cause falls. Outdoor dimensions are not constrained by the rigid dimensions of the indoors. Steps should be more gracious, broader, gentler, and in every way much easier to walk. If there are more than five or six steps, add a landing to catch your breath and take a look too.

Therefore, use your step equation to come up with the correct dimensions, reduce your riser wherever possible, and make those steps wider than you ever thought likely. It is amazing how often I've seen a lovely garden ruined by a narrow set of steps with a riser designed for mountain climbers!

See **Natural Use of Materials** *48*
Slopes *32*
Lining Walkways with Plants *228*
Photos *237, 240, 249*

This rather steep, very long stairway down to the lake has many elements to enhance the journey: a 7-inch riser was needed but a generous 14-inch tread allows for an easier climb. Plenty of landings were constructed, giving needed breaks along the way. Wide steps allow two to enjoy the garden journey together. Also several places open up to walk out across the expansive lawn.

222

Some steps have expected variables for their riser and tread dimensions.

222

223 **A single step in a walkway is never acceptable, unless it occurs where it is architecturally expected and is marked as such. However, it must be a real step and not a toe-stumper.**

The one-step problem usually arises when there is a slope and somehow the person forming the walk says to himself, "Well, let's see, how about a little step here to make up the difference." Unfortunately, a solitary step placed with no apparent logical reason goes unnoticed until someone breaks his ankle.

However, the exception to the one-step rule occurs at junctures: going from the parking area to the walk, for example, or the walk to the front door landing. The difference is there are architectural changes, plantings, maybe a post light, or just a widening of the walk—all features to let the visitor know that there is something to note...and it is a step...and only one.

Most important, these one-step situations should be a definite step, not a little toe-stumper, which is perhaps the most dangerous of all situations. These should be avoided.

See **Junctures** *219, 317*
Lighting *334*
4 Inch Step to Inside *279*
Photos *210, 211*

Joel, watch the step!

Plants are chosen to do a job. Some are in strategic places to screen. Others are needed for shade. Still others are chosen for their beauty and fragrance, like this one chosen to enhance the pierced brick wall—not cover it up.

No one will miss seeing this one step. The textures of the parking area and the patio differ, plus an additional accent edging creates a definite division of space. There is plenty of lighting and the bed lines tighten up to dramatically indicate an entrance as well.

223

With the walk opening up to the patio, this step will not be missed thanks to the light at the juncture.

223

224 Steps and porches made of wood can often have an unappealing backside; consider adding architectural details to make it more attractive if this space is part of the landscape that's on display. **If steps are out in the open, another option is to encase the whole column with hard materials or shrubs.**

In most cases the undersides of stairs are exposed; this is true as well for the undersides of porches and decks. This space is unattractive and detracts from the landscape, but there are three options to remedy it. If there is room for shrubs, they can do a wonderful job of camouflaging this tangle of wood supports. If there's not enough room or the use of plants is not desired, a surround can be built around the whole structure giving a necessary visual weight. A third option is to add trim to the underside, giving it a beauty of its own.

I visit many construction sites and see the different stages of building a home. Inside, every stud is covered and decorative trim applied, often in great detail, but somehow the outdoor staircase and the undersides of decks and porches with unattractive beams and supports posts are left visible. Yet every day they are seen as part of the whole when the homeowner is outside. I suggest giving them a dressing just as important as any that are given to those same spaces found inside.

See **Support Posts** *263*
   Photos *259, 286*

The addition of these 2-by-2-inch cedar strips under these steps creates its own beauty in the landscape for anyone walking down to this garden space.

224

There was no room for plants next to this staircase, so this builder built a beautiful screen and trimmed out the underside of his porch.

225 Mark the edges of steps or the presence of steps to provide a visible warning, particularly when the materials used seem to blend and blur the edges.

We have all encountered steps that are just not easily seen, especially when going down. "Oh my! Where did that come from?"

One method to help identify these steps is to paint the edge of each step, or choose a different material to use along each edge. This might be done with brick, wood edging, or any textural change that gives a good contrast. Install small lights at strategic spots, or mark each step in a long walk punctuated with these intermittent steps by using accent plants. A rock outcropping could be installed to draw attention to a change in grade using steps. No matter how perfectly spaced with the correct tread/riser dimensions, stairs can still be a hazard. Providing visual clues is a big help; they often become part of the beautiful landscape.

The summerhouse had one odd step all around of various dimensions, causing a major step-up and step-down problem. Once painted with this dramatic shade of red, the owner has had no problem.

Many urns were removed, leaving only a few left to plant—and take care of.

225

If the steps are made of wood, always make sure there is a backing to each step. If the steps are brick, the end piece should be solid (not ones with little holes leftover from construction).

Often the backings of wood steps are left off. This diminishes the sense of security and stability because the openness of the steps makes one feel uneasy. Additionally, the area behind the steps is often dark, unappealing, and hard to landscape and maintain. But when the backings of steps are in place and are painted or stained—sometimes with contrasting colors—the effect on the landscape is dramatic.

Sometimes, brick steps have a problem because the same bricks used during construction are then used to finish out the ends of the steps. Unfortunately, those bricks have unappealing little holes in them and it's impossible to improve their appearance. To prevent this, special order solid bricks for the step ends and for any other projects you may have where the sides of the bricks will be visible. Otherwise, landscaping will be necessary to hide this flaw, which sometimes only creates more problems.

See **Photos** *158, 282, 283*

 If exposed to the elements especially rain, exterior doors must have a step-up to the inside of the home, usually about four inches high, just at the threshold. If the exterior door is completely protected from any rain, this step-up can be eliminated, and the inside and outside flooring can be level with each other.

The four-inch step just at the threshold is a protective measure to prevent any moisture from getting inside during a rainstorm. Anywhere else, a step of this kind would be a "toe stumper" but here it is expected. Obviously, if the exterior door leads out to a large covered porch, this step-up is not necessary since no rain can reach inside anyway.

What is *not* expected is an actual extra step located at any exterior door, then a landing, then perhaps "real" steps to the walk. If this happens, the builder has made a mistake in setting his beginning elevations, and is trying to correct the error by adding a miscellaneous step (or two). This is hazardous and often protrudes onto the landing. This awkward, out-of-blue step diminishes the transitional effect the homeowner wants for his landscape by creating a disruptive element just as one is exiting. Let your builder know a 4-inch riser is expected, but not a miscellaneous step especially at your front door.

See **Contractors, Architect** *37*
Photos *62, 210, 211, 234, 325*

228 A landing and stairs set in a semicircular motif is beautiful, but certain considerations—space being chief among them—dictate that this is rarely suitable for the front landing. **On the other hand, it works beautifully in a garden setting.**

When you remember that a front landing should be at least five feet square, adding a curved dimension to this means taking up a lot of space in hardscape (doing the math, you end up with a roughly twelve-foot landing). Since every layer of steps requires another two feet or so of more surface area, a circular front landing grows in size exponentially. (Reducing the size of the landing increases the potential for accidents, as curved lines are the most difficult to manage.) Furthermore, an outward-curved landing presents confusing choices: Should guests exit at any point? Why would they want to? How does the sidewalk join up? Does it encompass the complete diameter? Or does the walk shift inward, leaving some steps ending at the landscape? With some steps ending up at the planting bed, how should this be landscaped? Certainly people are not expected to walk into shrubs!

Simply put: Stay away from semicircular landings. Instead, look for other designs that give that desired curved look without the problems.

On the other hand, moving people onto a lawn from another level of the garden via a circle of wide, low steps is a message as lovely as any poet's words. The semicircular motif could be quite effective as people would be encouraged to venture out in any direction to explore the rest of the garden.

See **Photos** *236, 240*

This semicircular landing works because several elements are all present. The landing is part of the larger patio, there are only two steps, the bottom landing is completely bricked, and no constricting sidewalk (with landscaping) obstructs the exit. But these combined requirements are rarely found to allow this motif to work in most home exits, especially at the front door.

Notice the steps have been painted to accent their presence leading off the patio. This is especially important to prevent a problem with a toe-stumping bottom step.

Another example of a beautiful curved step without the problems of using a half-circle motif.

Note the wonderful wide treads and small riser with lights at each set of steps.

The steps curve gently, allowing the land to dictate the natural flow of the walkway.

228

229 **The width of steps is vitally important—anything much less than 5 feet is too narrow.** Width can increase to fulfill the demands of specific situations and provide dramatic impact too.

From the largest to the smallest decks, even one that is no more than a landing, the width of the steps should accommodate two people. When folks encounter something less than five feet, they line up to ascend or descend and all social conviviality is lost. Wide steps offer the perception of a gracious welcome!

See **Illustration** *271*

Front Walk Minimum 5 Feet Wide *226*

Photos *59, 249, 258, 347*

230 **Sometimes a basement is too important to be blocked by a staircase from the deck or porch above.** If possible, move the staircase to the end of the deck or porch. Plan generous dimensions and a bit of drama; in fact, overemphasizing its presence is better.

A large deck or a gracious porch demands an equally large and gracious exit, but sometimes this exit cannot be front and center because of the basement below. Once this exit is situated off to one side, it will lose much of its prominence. This is certainly the time when the dimensions of this exit should be generous and inviting and its architectural features should also be accentuated. No one should have any doubt that this staircase is intended to welcome visitors out into the garden below.

See **Plan All Essential Uses of Space** *40*

Consider View *46*

These magnificent steps are in complete balance with the architecture of this home. Even though most homes will not have such dramatic dimensions, few situations arise that do not need a 5-foot width to establish a true connection with the outdoors.

Backed steps and screening of the undersides make landscaping choices simple and easy.

229

230

A lot of talking and walking helped the homeowners finally come up with the solution of building the steps off the end of the porch because every window downstairs was visually very important. But notice the dramatic architectural elements used on the staircase—there is no question it has the same value as the rest of the home, or what it is intended to do: encourage guests to go out into the garden beyond.

231 Steps from a porch or a deck should lead one out to the garden—not back to the house or to the Car Area. **Once the position of the bottom landing has been established, auxiliary paths leading back to the basement or to the Car Area can be determined.**

New construction often distorts thinking in this instance; with the backyard a mess, the exit from the porch or deck generally leads straight to the Car Area to get everyone out of this mess. But once construction is over, the backyard starts becoming the garden—and if the steps from the porch lead only away from the yard, you end up with a landscape that's not quite connected with the house…and rarely used.

Instead, situate steps to reach out to the garden beyond, no matter how imaginary it is at first. This allows the deck or porch to become the major transitional element it's intended to be, with everyone invited to move on out and enjoy what is beyond—a garden, swimming pool, patio, the kids' play set, and a lovely lawn.

If there is a need to plan walks to the basement or the Car Area at the juncture of the bottom landing, then do so. A nice walkway is always appreciated, but these areas should not be the destination of steps leading from a porch or deck.

See **Break Up Long Staircases** *288*

Four Rooms in Your Landscape *164*

Outdoor Living Space *169*

Photo *59*

There is still a walkway up to the Car Area but it's certainly not the focus of this design.

The challenge to this new homeowner was how to access the space below from the main floor. The idea was to build steps off the upper deck, descending across the sunroom windows and the downstairs office. The end of the steps would lead back up to the Car Area. The idea of a garden below was not in the plan.

With this revised design extending the deck far to the right, the steps are now directed to a wonderful patio area, freeing up the entire downstairs space for a beautiful view out to a lake.

Steps off porches, decks, and landings should not run along the side of the house unless there is no other choice.

Space considerations will often determine this design; some steps must be aligned next to the house because there is nowhere else to put them. But when the porch or deck is expansive and there is plenty of room for an alternative positioning, do it. Your builder might suggest that running steps along the side of the house is cheaper, but of course that is exactly what it looks like—cheap.

When rebuilding this deck and staircase, the suggestion was to redesign the steps away from the brick wall and make sure the steps were 5 feet wide.

The addition of a landing plays a critical role in creating this simple but effective staircase.

With the space now available between the staircase and the brick wall, evergreens can be planted to soften this overwhelming hard surface.

232

Sometimes steps must be built next to a structure. On this site, the land slopes downward, making any more projections outward unfeasible. With the steps kept wide and a generous landing below, the results are quite acceptable.

Note the "borrowed view" beyond.

Because of the home's architecture, the steps from the landing had to abut the house, but when the steps were extended, they were turned away from the house, creating a lovelier sense of space and allowing for additional plantings to soften the otherwise hard corner.

If the staircase is fairly long, break it up with landings and possibly turns.

Descending or climbing stairs that are more than eight to ten steps becomes arduous for many. Inserting a landing breaks the journey and adds an element of safety too.

Another way to alleviate the "fire escape" feel of a long staircase is to expand the width of the last three to five steps (including the adjoining landing). This can be particularly effective when the staircase projects directly out from the house. Here children love to sit and play and a beautiful urn or small bench could be an attractive addition.

The staircase becomes even more interesting when it takes a turn at a landing. Of course, in many situations, a turn is essential for the steps to work, but sometimes it can be added just because it adds interest to the overall design. So look carefully at this architectural element—a little more expense might add a knockout element of design to the landscape.

See **Dress Up Supports and Under Steps** *263, 276*
   Photos *41, 282, 285, 286*

 Porches, decks, or patios that are only a step or two from the ground often benefit from having these steps run the entire width of the structure. Consider allowing them to wrap around a corner for a beautiful directional traffic flow. The tread and riser dimensions can be exaggerated for a comfortable glide to and fro.

Porches and decks can seem confining. So if they are already very close to the ground, why not open up the side that leads to the garden with a step that runs the entire length of the structure? This encourages traffic flow outward and enlarges the Outdoor Living Space encompassed by the patio and the lawn area.

See **Outside Steps Different from Inside Steps** *272*
   Photo *237*

This arbor is strongly built to support a beautiful but heavy vine.

Rails—even for these few steps—are quite handy, especially for those with elderly relatives.

This deck is actually a passageway. These open, wide, generous steps lead out to the main garden—and away from the Car Area. No constricting steps here trap the homeowner on his beautiful porch.

The two dogs are given shade and access to a fenced-in yard but the clever design of the porch gives the homeowners their own space too. Planning for your doggie needs is very important if the landscape is to succeed.

CHAPTER **7**

Form and Function

Structures in the Landscape

Whether intended for aesthetics—a cherished gate from the old homestead, an arbor under a shady tree—or strictly utilitarian—a shed to store landscaping equipment, a detached garage—outlying buildings should enhance the landscape and the homeowner's enjoyment of it.

Every structure in the landscape has a major impact. Books have been written solely about the form/function dichotomy, but the important point is that every homeowner must take a positive role in addressing these issues. Construction workers often think more about utility than aesthetics, leaving the homeowner to camouflage what he can later, but it's far better to plan ahead.

235 **Outbuildings are fun and invaluable. They add visual and emotional interest to any landscape, while moving some activities from the home to outbuildings adds immeasurably to the quality of the home-owners' lives. Careful planning ensures they'll enhance—rather than detract from—the landscape.**

People love outbuildings. They love detached car-ports and garages, sheds, workshops, arbors, swim-ming pool pavilions, cabins…you name it, they love to look out and see other structures. Some might be explored; others suggest fun entertainment; still oth-ers tell of activities going on.

So why do modern families (and their home builders) try to squeeze everything into one facility? Why is the lawnmower stored in the carport? Why is someone hammering downstairs? Do all carports and garages have to be attached to the house? Is all enter-tainment just in the basement?

Consider your activities, consider alternatives for using all of your landscape, and plan for one or more outbuildings (which is actually often more cost-effec-tive than centering all activities in the main home)—not only for efficiency and accessibility, but their visual beauty as well.

Did I hear you say "visual beauty"? Yes! These structures must be first considered for their practical use, but if the aesthetics are not also addressed, the results will forever stare everyone in the face. The right pitch of the workshop roof, a nice-looking siding, a sturdily constructed shed, and a freshly painted pavil-ion will work together to make a beautiful setting.

See **How Your Home Relates to the Outdoors** *39*
Plan All Essential Uses of Land *40*
Architectural Complement *42*
Placement of Work Doors *334*
Maintenance or Lack of – Profound Effect on a Landscape *38*
Photos *12, 79, 145, 167, 168, 197*

A combination garage and bonus room set apart from the main house enhances the possibilities of enjoying the outdoors. No one will ever miss the blooming hydrangeas or the scent of gardenias as they walk out to the garage!

More light is available to all living spaces in the home when a garage is built apart.

A landing midway on the bonus room steps adds immeasurably to their attractiveness.

Wide front steps and front walk is a wonderful welcome to all visitors.

235

These restored buildings dating to the early 1800s create a vista of great beauty. Personally I do not miss these "good old days," but their presence is a valid reminder of our place in history.

If there is junk, it is stored inside. If there are unsightly weeds, they are cut. In all landscapes, a good maintenance program will be all that is necessary for a beautiful outcome.

This young couple knew how important it was for their outbuildings to be attractive. Just by duplicating the same tin used on their home's roof, their collection of structures is quite effective.

Notice the steep roof line of the main house. The open carport and the shed also have an appealing roof line, not one that's laid too low.

Except for the vegetable garden, there is little need for expansive flower and shrubs beds unless their maintenance is addressed.

236 A garden shed can be the most dramatic outbuilding in your landscape.

One doesn't have to look at very many garden magazines before coming to the conclusion that garden sheds have a huge appeal. In fact many gardens are built around these enticing structures, which become the major focal point of the garden.

Once you decide you need (or want) a garden shed, consider how it will be used. If it is to be totally utilitarian with no redeeming aesthetic qualities, its placement must be out of view. It can be camouflaged by a screen or situated around the corner. (There is nothing wrong with a big, hulking piece of plastic, but it doesn't need to be in the middle of your garden for all to see!) If it is to be a garden focal point, have fun with it! From window boxes to gingerbread trim, plan a structure you'll love to look at.

As the human eye glides over a landscape, it actually moves from one point to another—the good and the bad. With some creativity and paint, a garden shed can be a beautiful addition to your garden.

See **Roofline Steepness** *302*

237 Utilitarian concerns for your garden shed include having a water supply and some hard surfaces, especially outside the shed. Design it so that the door is facing away from your home view.

How best to get all these features on your site? Plan for their installation when you are building your house, or when you are doing another big project and the plumber is on-site working; you can build the shed later. Just remember to hide the utility part of the building from view, so that if you're interrupted in mid-chore, no one's the wiser. There is always time to wash out a spray canister or clean some pots later!

Architecturally simple and well kept, this shed just outside the back door is a charming addition to the landscape.

A solid surface at this shed entrance is most welcomed when doing those odd jobs.

This garden shed is in full view from every part of the home, so making it beautiful is important.

The pretty door is visible from the house—but not the extra-wide door with the concrete landing, water faucet, hose, and the mess that is all part of gardening.

The garden is just beyond the shed—how convenient!

237

238 **The location of your gardening tools and supplies must be convenient to your garden.**

A basic tenet holds true here: People will walk only so far to satisfy their needs. Gardening especially is a back-and-forth scenario: many items are used and any one can be easily forgotten. Even after a project is over, putting everything away is a tiresome task. It needs to be made as convenient as possible.

So here are some thoughts: Make sure your storage area has a good access to move mowers and other large equipment in and out. If you're using a basement or garage that has another, primary function, try to keep access to the gardening materials in its own space, preferably with outside access; no one likes to park the car amid tools, fertilizers, and other paraphernalia needed in the garden. If at all possible, build a shed for this specific need—but be sure the location is convenient, and hide it or make it part of the landscape.

Basically, the needs of your garden should be considered in the preliminary plans for your house and your site. You plan for your clothes to go into a closet next to your bedroom—so plan for your garden stuff to be in its space near your garden.

A location for gardening tools was not in this house plan, but instead of gathering all that stuff in the garage for all to see each day, this simple, attractive shed was built on a side wall, convenient to water and out of view. In a few years, maturing shrubs and ornamental trees will soften its newly built look.

Discreet, tucked-in working spaces are just another way to solve the problem of how to manage gardening needs; close to the garden and easy access make life so much simpler. If no plan is made, the necessary materials will spill out and detract from the beauty of any landscape.

238

238

Unless you live in snow country, consider a detached carport or garage to open up wall space on the house for extra windows. An extra and very important benefit is being able to enjoy the outdoors before coming inside.

Natural light cannot be duplicated. When a garage is attached to the house, it takes valuable wall space from the home where windows could be added for more light. Unless an attached garage is built on the harsher northern or western side of the house, it just might be blocking the home from the warmth and cheeriness given only by the sun.

An enclosed attached garage with its large hard parking pad also takes us another step farther from any real contact with the outdoors: We go from the house to the car and back again without ever experiencing the outdoors. Looking at the weather on the Internet is *not* the same.

On the other hand, a detached garage or carport can give you extra minutes to spend walking from the house, feeling a little rain, or enjoying a cooling breeze, with a background of birds chirping, trees whistling, and frogs croaking. If the rain or hot sun is too much, a covered walk will suffice for most situations, unless, perhaps, you live in snow country.

See **Photos** *42, 252, 292*

 Workshops should be built in their own separate structure, not located in the basement.

These are some of the more important reasons a separate structure is needed:

1) Natural light is necessary for many projects and is probably not available in the basement.

2) Ventilation is easily accommodated; dust, fumes, dangerous materials, and noisy equipment are away from the house—and if someone wants to work at odd hours, he can!

3) Workshops seldom need to be heated to the comfort level of the home.

4) It's easier to get materials in and out of a separate structure.

5) You can "hide" bulky, unattractive project materials behind the workshop. (If a neighbor's view is a concern, a small fence or planting can camouflage the area.)

6) A maintained outbuilding adds to the pleasure of the landscape.

See **Plan All Essential Outdoor Spaces** *40*
Roofline Steepness *302*
Architectural Complement *42*

240

This homeowner loves working in his shop. Separating the facility from the main house keeps everyone safe and happy, especially with lots of grandkids wandering about.

Building a separate workshop, instead of using the daylight basement, eliminated viewing masses of concrete in the back garden.

The contrast of concrete and brick paving identifies the parking and walkway areas.

The cover over every door on this home is a detail often missed by many homeowners. Not only is it functional but it adds great appeal to connect the structures to the outdoors.

Structures planned for entertainment must have a restroom facility or one close by or this structure will never be used.

Many outdoor entertainment structures are quite lovely. But there is one item that *must* be available with fairly good access and that is a restroom. I have seen many wonderful sites enjoy very limited use because a restroom was not available or was located far away. Many people did not want to find themselves in an embarrassing situation, so they avoided the possibility completely by staying away.

To share a personal example, on our farm we built a summerhouse located quite some distance from our home. We anticipated going there to cook out with family and friends. The first thing we were asked was, "Are there restrooms?" Sadly, there are not. Now, we have found entertaining options restricted to picnics of limited duration. Even the most rustic cabin or funky area for a cook-out will just not be used without some sort of accommodations, especially for the ladies.

See **Photo** *267*

 A summerhouse is probably one of the loveliest additions to your landscape possible. Its beauty can be enjoyed from within the home and it will draw anyone out into the garden for even more enjoyment of the outdoors.

Occasionally an attached porch is not structurally possible, but the need is still there for a casual outdoor entertainment area, a place to keep kids from underfoot, or a place to relax, removed from the immediate household.

A summerhouse is a detached structure with a solid roof that creates space for tables, chairs, and multiple activities. A light rain will not spoil your picnic; the hot sun will be ameliorated; biting bugs will be eliminated (if it's screened); and you will smell the gardenias while eating a light supper.

Summerhouses can be built in a variety of situations: One owner built on an extended portion of his deck, providing a dynamic view of the landscape. Another added his to the edge of a patio, expanding the use of this space for entertainment. Others in homes near lakes are now able to enjoy an insect-free vista. They're often used with swimming pools too.

See **Architectural Complement** *42*
Plan for Furniture *246*
Lighting, Italian Style *336*
Photo *47*

Can anything be more inviting than this summerhouse? There's comfortable seating and you're out of the elements—but surrounded by all things natural.

Even the simplest summerhouse—with all sides open for relaxed comings and goings—make it a gardener's paradise.

Any need for some enclosure is accomplished with some plantings...only a few are necessary, but they make this space feel inviting and comfortable.

Several different, easy-to-move chairs give this place a most relaxed feeling.

243 The roofline of all outdoor structures should be fairly steep, often the same or close to the same as the one on your home; a low-angle roofline is visually unappealing.

Landscaping can't fix an unattractive roofline. Somehow the roof angle does matter—in fact a roofline can do wonders to a building of otherwise little note. We all know lower rooflines are cheaper to build and, if prefabricated, easier to move on a flat-bed truck; but once the money is spent, the lasting visual negative can never be overcome.

Locally, I have noticed the prefabricated selections of garden sheds are sometimes offering higher-pitched roofs—and seeing them sitting next to each other, it's clear the high pitched roofs look a whole lot better than the low-angled versions. Once home-owners see the buildings, especially side by side, they recognize the difference the roofline makes. This holds true for workshops and other outbuildings too. As an added note, do not select a shed with a barn-like roofline; leave the barn roof to barns.

See **Photos** *12, 197, 290, 293, 294, 295, 299*

A prefabricated utility structure with such a wonderful roof line would be a beautiful addition to anyone's landscape.

Just be sure to add a generous landing, then some steps or perhaps a ramp.

243

244 **Is your gazebo intended for use, or to beautify the landscape?** **A gazebo for using should have generous dimensions and be accessible and close to the house; one for viewing can be designed strictly for aesthetic appeal.**

As with all entertainment outdoor structures, the farther they are from the house, the less likely they are to be used. Carrying goodies and drinks out to them, and returning to use the facilities are just facts of life that cannot be ignored. Consider also the size needed to accommodate furniture: the circular shape that makes a gazebo so attractive also diminishes its functional use by cutting off corners, so you might want to plan a diameter of ten feet or more.

Removing rails and other impediments to increase accessibility, as well as keeping it at ground level, also ensure a gazebo that will be used and enjoyed for years.

Building a gazebo to become part of the distant vista is something else entirely. Its strong, definite lines become a major focal point in the landscape, and you will be less interested in its size and number of rails or steps, because its use will be limited to casual walks out into the landscape.

See **Steps** *272, 288*
Enclosure *50*
Surfacing for Endurance, Safety *196*
Plan for Furniture *246*

For many years it was a first-class playhouse; now it's a great adult retreat. The generous dimensions allow for flexibility of seating arrangements and the limited use of rails and small shrubs to their back create just the right amount of enclosure for that cozy feeling they provide.

Eliminating a low-to-the-ground wood surface as permanent flooring is usually preferable for long-term durability. The choice of this red tile is extremely attractive, and furniture moves easily over its surface.

244

245 Besides their charm, arbors or pergolas provide a destination of delicious dappled shade. **They are major transitional elements in the landscape.**

An arbor is one of the most requested structures in my line of work; it adds a dimension of beauty to a garden, but also fills some very real needs and solves some problems. The swimming pool area needs some shade for anyone wishing to join the party but stay out of the sun. The garden area needs a little space set apart for sitting; it shades a window on the sun-facing facade of the home (especially if a covered porch will not be constructed) and, of course, it's a perfect structure for those much-wanted vines in your garden.

More than this, though, arbors provide that architectural element that denotes an entrance. Many times these entrances are self-evident, but other times entrances are ambiguous. The arbor, even a very simple one, lets everyone know they are indeed invited to travel on to another dimension in the landscape.

See **Photos** *59, 328*

 246 If you plan to keep your arbor painted, be sure to pick a vine that can be pruned off but will recover quickly. **If you plan to plant a substantial vine, do not plan to paint your arbor and be sure to build a substantial structure built to withstand the vine's weight, especially when it's wet or iced over.**

A crisp white arbor is quite attractive in the landscape but its maintenance demands the choice of a light-weight vine or even one that can be cut back completely every few years to revive its vigor and to allow you to repaint the arbor. If you choose a heavy duty vine, whose removal would be nearly impossible plus undesirable, evaluate the design of your arbor. It must be of substantial dimensions as every part of the structure must support the increasingly larger plant. A strong arbor is especially important for those areas that receive cold, rainy weather; the collected weight of water or ice tests the best of structures. And, of course, no paint is recommended for the arbor.

See **Photo** *52*

Just a simple arbor invites one to enter for a walk in the woodlands.

These steppingstones are generously sized and evenly spaced. They absorb the impact of heavy traffic but also act as a lovely directional tool to the wooded garden.

Watching young swimmers is fun, and sitting under this wonderful shade makes it more comfortable.

Heavy construction is just right for a heavy vine.

Leaving this arbor unpainted allows the vine to be trimmed but not completely removed every few years.

A recessed space is often a more attractive space, especially if heavy rambunctious traffic is expected.

A 6-foot depth is needed for chairs to be comfortably situated.

No problem here: This vine can quickly recover after periodic paintings of the arbor.

With this arbor, neighborhood strollers are assured they are welcome to enter this beautiful garden; otherwise the opening would go unnoticed or be thought a mistake. No mistaking the message here!

247 The attributes of a fence or a wall often make it a better choice than plants for an enclosure or screening.

Many sites have a need to be either enclosed or screened. Both the hardscape (fences and walls) and planting materials should be considered to handle the job; in most cases, both materials will be needed. But in some instances, a fence or wall should be considered first with plants used mainly as accents.

A fence can be built *quickly*. Some situations need to be addressed right away, such as the immediate needs of small children and pets. You may not have time to wait the several years plants need to grow into the job.

A fence or wall is only a few inches to a couple of feet wide. Shrubs need a width of three to eight feet for proper spacing, and some sites do not have this much useable space.

A fence or a wall avoids the ramifications of differing cultural situations, which can run the gamut from dense shade to a wet zone to a hot dry spot.

When using plants, every site must be considered not only for the choice of plant materials but also whether they can even do the job. If the site is particularly stressful, plants can take years to accomplish the goal…if at all.

This last point is particularly important because too often plant selections are "one choice fits all." Let me give you an example: a homeowner had an exquisite garden but her neighbors did not, necessitating a screen. She had two very mature oak trees dominating most of the planting space on the side where screening was needed, and she wanted a row of plants to serve as screening. I explained that these two massive oaks would not allow much to grow; if anything did grow, it would be slowly and irregularly. The solution was to install a lovely wood fence, which immediately obstructed the unwanted view, and add some plants suited for the shade.

See **Plants Chosen for a Specific Job and Mature Size** *35, 64*
Break Up Strong Horizontal Lines *70*
Use of Ornamental Trees *78*

Attaining complete privacy in this limited landscape using a space only 6 inches wide and 6 feet tall should be considered a job well done. With no need for a heavy shrub border, gardening can then be a little of this and that scattered about for real interest and joy.

The neighbor's borrowed trees—both Ornamental and Significant—provide beauty and shade to these new homeowners. Faced with the warming rays of a southern exposure, this feature is very important for their home.

247

248 **Because of their economy of space and structural dominance in the landscape, fences and walls are excellent problem solvers. But remember, if you're enclosing any large living space, appropriate gates must be installed to ensure good circulation.**

Every landscape has multiple problems to solve. Plants might be the love of your life, but sometimes choosing to use a fence or wall has the virtue of using available space economically, while adding a strong aesthetic dimension.

For instance, a tidy fence in a small space can hide your utility elements such as gas meter, power box, or air conditioning unit. Plants might have been lovely, but there was no space for a good screen, only for an accent or two. A neat, two-rail fence can be a welcoming entrance or define the space at your front walk. Similarly, a fence or a wall makes a wonderful room divider: Your Carport Area might need separation from your back yard, and a large back yard might need some further division to make it more interesting and usable.

If the approach to your driveway is unclear, a fence can guide visitors in to the parking area, while steering them away from roads intended for the homeowner's use. Use this dominant structural feature to guide visitors straight to the front door!

One of the biggest uses of fences and walls is to enclose a back yard. Once that problem is solved, do not create another problem by eliminating gates, which are essential to guide one in a walk around the property. I have often seen this "economy" measure but a lack of gates often results in whole parts of the landscape ignored because of lack of access. What at first did not seem important becomes a big issue as the homeowner finds himself cut off by his fence.

Fences and walls come in all sizes and styles and have a dramatic effect on the landscape while solving many problems. With a little attention to details, more problems can be avoided.

See **Avoid Too Tall Screening** *68*
    Kids Love Circles *344*
    Need for Circulation *186*

The trash men love this home with its easy pick-up access through the gate. The homeowners love this situation, too, with its easy access to the kitchen but the trash cans totally out of view. This situation did not just happen—it was planned.

Plants are now used for interest, not massed to cover up a disturbing view.

248

It doesn't matter what's behind this fence. We don't see it and our time around the pool is not spoiled by whatever is there. How nice! Now our focus is on beautiful plantings and visiting with friends.

The use of simple period-style fencing quietly separates the Car Area from the Outdoor Living Space. This effectively directs the numerous visitors to walk up the spacious walkway and not across the lawn. When returning to their cars, the fence directs them to a position for a safe crossing. The extra maintenance forced by this fence is balanced by the very real purpose it fulfills in the landscape.

249 The height of a fence or wall creates a definite mood: 6 feet sends a very strong message of privacy and a definite "Keep Out," whereas a 5-foot fence is seen as a friendly barrier. **Use this "friendly" height unless the taller fence is essential.**

Where houses are close by, it might be very important for family life to have some privacy. A fence of six feet or more says "I don't want to see you or you to see me," and its message is often overpowering, especially if the enclosure is small. You might feel like you're living in a hole.

A fence or wall about five to five-and-a-half feet, however, will keep the kids and dogs in and unwanted visitors out. You will see a little of your neighbors, but the fence is more friendly. It's also important to note that in most cases the difference between five and six feet is very little, so it's just nicer to choose the more friendly height and plan on some lovely plants at strategic locations to take care of any particular problems.

The emotional resonance of a very tall fence can't be emphasized enough. Several builders once met with me at a site to discuss a problem they could not solve. A retention pond was located between the last two homes they could not sell. What to do, they asked. They had enclosed the pond with a very high, plain wood fence and wanted suggestions for plantings to hide their monstrosity; surely, this would be the answer. However, I had a different solution—and the two homes sold in less than two weeks! I told them the fence gave a feeling of a prison compound, and recommended they cut the fence down to about four to five feet. The fencing was still in place but now it was seen as an attractive feature to the two homes and not as a barrier to something terrible hidden behind it.

See **Avoid Too Tall Screening** *68*
Photos *321, 326*

The original, 6-foot-tall drab fence was trimmed and painted to complement the Tudor architecture of the home, creating a more inviting atmosphere for interesting plant choices.

The simple arbor creates a space for those who prefer a little shade sitting next to a pool.

Three- to four-foot fences and walls are used for architectural interest and to define space—usually with a goal in mind.

A fence this height can contain very young kids and, perhaps, a small dog, but will not exclude unwanted visitors. Its construction is often more open and is used to define space, not for any real privacy. Architecturally, its details become much more important since it is seen as a decorative element in the landscape, unlike fences for enclosure where one might want this item to recede in its importance.

These particular fences and walls are often constructed with a goal in mind: they might introduce an entrance, define space for a small garden, or create a focus for a particular feature. The crisp, neat appearance in the landscape is often just the touch for a great look.

See **Photos** *10, 66, 99, 131, 308, 315*

 Fences (and rails) made with iron have a special place in the landscape. They provide the strength necessary for a fence but allow the visibility so necessary in many situations. Consider this material in combination with, or as an alternative to, wood and brick.

Sometimes there is a very real need to separate—but at the same time maintain—the view essential to a landscape, and an iron fence is the answer. Plantings might be introduced to soften its angularity, but its wonderful see-through qualities still exist. This might be a perfect solution for a pool fence, where safety concerns require unobstructed visibility. A small area in the yard needs a separation to maintain a safety zone for small children—how nice to have an elegant fence that allows mother to see beyond and behind to keep tabs on everyone. A retaining wall must have a fence to keep folks from accidentally taking a wrong turn and a tumble. I especially love iron used with brick to provide a dramatic upscale separation of the front entrance to the home beyond.

Iron is expensive and is actually difficult to include in some cases, but if this material can fit into your budget, extend yourself for a strong, elegant barrier. There are now many look-alike substitutes on the market (which are not as strong but just as attractive).

See **Rails** *260*

Consider Your View with Design *46*

Photos *59, 200, 239, 289, 347*

Iron fences, rails, and gates have great structural strength; additionally they're lightweight in appearance and a wonderful alternative to wood.

Outwardly curving steps from 6 to 9 feet wide at the base present a most inviting picture.

This generous landing outside the screened door allows anyone a stable place to gather himself and his paraphernalia before entering or exiting the summerhouse. Omitting this landing creates a highly hazardous, unappealing situation.

The use of iron is extended to all fencing around the house, creating an aesthetic whole.

251

A fence or wall should not connect with the house directly on a corner unless it is an architectural extension of the home.

The beginnings of a fence or wall are usually constructed with a strong post or column; the corners of most homes might also have some strong architectural features. Trying to connect these two elements at the corner with an agreeable visual outcome is difficult. It would be better to set the beginning of the fence or wall back, even if only a foot or two.

The set-back creates a pleasing 90-degree angle that contrasts the large home and the smaller fence or wall for a more balanced result; a decorative support post will probably show off better against the blank side of the house, while a plain one can be better camouflaged in the more recessed position. This nook is also a better foil for interesting plantings than the flat monotonous surface created by a continuation of a fence straight off from the corner of the house.

Obviously the exception to this design element is when the façade of the home itself extends outward to form the fence.

 When a fence connects to your home, it must never cut off or crowd any prominent architectural feature on the structure. Instead, the joining should indicate an awareness of the architectural elements of the house and in itself be an attractive extension.

Homes can have randomly placed architectural details, but many times a set of elements makes a strong statement of wholeness, as in a chimney flanked by two windows. Any dominant feature (a long blank wall, for example) or a composition of elements should never be cut off or crowded by the joining of a fence.

Instead, locate the fence or wall to avoid or even enhance the architectural features of the home. A chimney flanked by the two windows could be framed by positioning the fence outside the perimeter of this composition. The long blank wall might be divided by a fence one-third of the way down.

A fence or wall joining the home is an extension of its beauty. Odd, disjointed attachments detract from the overall beauty of the site.

This homeowner knew to set the beginning connection for the fence back from the corner and then move out for the turn, creating a wonderful, interesting space. A low-growing plant can be set in this pocket next to the entrance gate for an interesting landscape.

This 3- to 4-foot fence with open pickets is an invitation for neighborly interchanges. A few interesting shrubs strategically planted would give any other necessary privacy.

The dramatic architectural design of this fence is a wonderful complement to the main structure. The effect is stunning.

The placement of this wall was carefully chosen. At the front corner, there was not adequate room near the edge of the window; a spot farther down toward the porch would have crowded this structure. Setting the wall between the windows, not crowding either one, was the perfect choice.

253

Fences and walls should connect perpendicular to a home; after a foot or two, the fence can then angle for the needs of the situation.

This design element might not seem like such an important detail but fences and gates make strong statements, and odd angles create an uncomfortable effect.

On one job, the homeowner explained to me where his pool fence would be. The space was tight and left few choices, but I emphasized that the fence connecting to the house at such an awkward angle was quite displeasing. He kept asking why, and my answer was because aesthetics are important. We react to certain definitions of space; often people say, "I know when I *see* something that it is pretty, but I do not know how to get there." This element of design is just another part of "How To Get There." If the space *feels* wrong, it probably is.

 Fences and walls built to enclose a space should not have any angles less than 45 degrees.

A constricting, sharp angle offends the senses and sends a message of entrapment. If your property line or area to be fenced creates such an angle, it's best to cut off this point; otherwise the fence seems like a pointed arrow leading nowhere. If the excluded area will be used, install a gate.

Consider this advice *before* you have your fence installed; fencing is expensive and the final results should be appealing. A very tight angle is not.

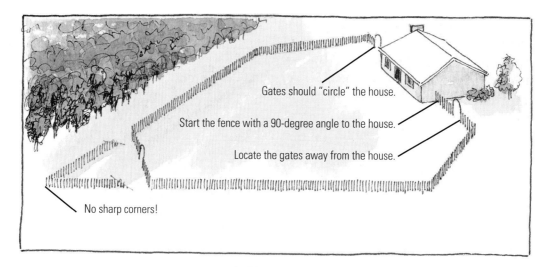

Gates should "circle" the house.

Start the fence with a 90-degree angle to the house.

Locate the gates away from the house.

No sharp corners!

Avoid sharp angles.

256 Aesthetically, a fence or a wall makes a wonderful backdrop for flowers, shrubs, and trees. This crisp, permanent element creates definition while a lot of greenery seems overbearing, even unruly.

Flowers and bushes tumbling all together can become too much. Isn't there something that can tie a mixed shrub border or a flower bed into a more agreeable whole? Yes: a nice fence.

A dear friend who had an incredibly beautiful garden comes to mind. Her site was limited and was adjacent to neighbors who did not share her hobby. No matter how beautiful her garden, the visual effect was compromised by the next-door view. Her lovely shrubs and flowers melted into the green conglomeration next door. My suggestion of an artistically designed four- to five-foot fence was tossed about for several years but she just couldn't pull the trigger. Finally, she installed one. What an immediate transformation! She could not believe how crisply this architectural feature framed her beautiful plantings, giving them a wonderful definitive background. Her plants took on a whole new dimension, as different ones became more beautifully visible with such a lovely fence at their backs.

A beautiful, smart fence or walls are particularly important for many flower sites. They become a wonderful frame, setting off the glory of the plantings—and more important, they remain all year as the garden's beauty waxes and wanes.

See **China Cabinet Element of Design** *76*
Foliage in Plants *83*
Creating Rooms in the Landscape *164*
Photo *89*

A country setting is expected to be very casual, but even here the crispness of this zig-zag fence does wonders for the landscape. It creates a great foil for any plants this homeowner wishes to introduce. If one removed the charming cabin and this whimsical fence, the plantings would not have the same dramatic effect, but together they create an aesthetic whole.

256

257 A formal garden should be on level ground with its fence on a level plane. **If the terrain is not level, change your design to a more informal one, with the fence rambling up and down as the land dictates.**

The boundaries of a formal garden are usually square or rectangular; inside it, every kind of geometric shape could be used for a simple or intricate effect. If this formal motif is desired, the outside enclosure (fence, wall, shrubs) and the interior space must be on the same level. If the chosen spot for this garden slopes and undulates here and there, the formal motif will never work. Instead, an informal rambling design should be used.

See **Size of Fence or Wall** *309, 310*
    Iron for Visibility *310*
    Use of Evergreens *84*
    Photos *44, 130*

258 Fences and walls should not enclose your utility meters.

Fences and walls can enclose dogs and kids, and create a secure place against intruders and unwanted visitors.

The utility person, however, just wants to do his job. Going inside this enclosed space to read meters contradicts every reason for the fence or wall. Dogs can escape or become a nuisance; the safety and security of the family is compromised; and no one wants a surprise visit by the utility person in his private space. Just leave this person out of your picture by keeping him outside your fenced area. He will greatly appreciate it.

As an interesting aside, modern technology is changing this need of utility staff to have direct access to your meter each month.

This gardener could not find enough iron fencing so the suggestion was to continue the formal design with some evergreen shrubs that would mature at the same height as the fence. The concept of this formal garden works because it is on level ground, and the surrounding shrubs and fencing are also on level ground. To the left side the land falls away to more informal gardens, with meandering bed lines fitting in with the natural flow of the land.

259 An open entrance within a garden—one without a gate—should have elements added both to create beauty and to indicate its function of directing traffic.

Many entrances do not need a gate, only an opening for traffic, and these openings may have design elements added to help direct traffic through a specific space. Just as important, the results should enhance the landscape. The ideas are boundless: large urns, an arbor, dramatic specimen evergreens or ornamental trees, decorative posts (perhaps with lights)…and on and on.

The homeowner might want to designate the entrance to a woodland walk, so perhaps a large boulder or concrete creature would work. Another constructs an arbor to stand between two of her garden rooms, adding immeasurably to the beauty of both sites. A lovely fence might be constructed to divide a pasture from the farm lawn, leaving an opening for traffic.

Whether simple or quite dramatic, a garden becomes more inviting with some attention to spaces leading from one area to another.

See **Arbors** *304*
Containers *156, 158*
Ornamental Trees *78, 99*
Use of Symmetry *92*
Lighting *334*

There's no gate, but this transition space is wonderfully accented by two beautiful urns sitting on lovely brick pedestals.

These containers are so dramatic they could be left unplanted for lower maintenance.

Even for a side garden, this walk is generous in width.

The steps have garden dimensions—a small riser and a wide tread for an easy glide up to the next garden space.

259

259

In clearing an overgrown
backyard, these lovely
brick and granite
materials were put to
good use as pavers and
edging, creating a
beautiful link to this now
gracious space. The old
light column provides
dramatic interest, and
with the addition of the
little angel statue and a
few planted urns, this
entrance is quite
effective.

The bed lines are drawn
in broad strokes,
accenting existing
Significant Trees and
creating depth and
mystery in an otherwise
large, rectangular yard.

260 **Power meters need to be accessible for service personnel but that does not mean they should be located front and center, especially at any side entrance. Minor changes in their placement will eliminate this eyesore.**

The placement of power meters and all other necessary utility items should be addressed as soon as possible in the building process. They are often placed where they are easily seen and they become eyesores. Once they are positioned, there is no way to camouflage their presence.

A good builder will make sure these items are not six inches from your back door, too high to be concealed by plants, too close to an architectural feature such as a door or window trim, or surrounded by concrete, which makes any attractive visual remedy virtually impossible.

Do not assume important utility decisions will be handled to your liking by installers. In your home, you do not look straight into the laundry room; neither should you be greeted every day by any utility features on the outside.

 261 **Always locate gates and openings away from structures so that they create their own space; locate them next to the house only if there is no other option.**

A gate is the grand entrance to your private world—so leave plenty of space around it for materials to help frame and add interest. Even the smallest amount of space between the gate and the house can be of immeasurable importance, particularly because a walkway located away from the house creates a lovely space for plantings.

Obviously, certain constraints can force the gate to be located next to the house; if this must be, set the gate back a foot or two from the corner.

Most homeowners have a hard time pulling away from the home to set out their landscape (in fact, many look like they are circling the wagon). Once they have broken through this imaginary circumference, a real joy of discovering the *whole* property begins. I often see the placement of gates as one of the major hardscape decisions that are nearly impossible to change; if thought is given to this one feature, many other positive decisions will fall into place.

See **Illustration** *314*

261

Some formal evergreens and other neat elements such as the brick wall are necessary ingredients for a pleasing composition that includes flowers.

This 4-foot decorative wall creates an inviting garden enclosure.

The pretty planted containers are a beautiful added whimsy, but if a busy summer of traveling is planned, leave the containers unplanted and the landscape will still be lovely.

There's very little space for this elegant gate, but setting it back just a few feet away from the Car Area, and away from the main structure by just 2 feet, gives it a proper setting to show its beauty.

There's no question this gate was designed with appropriate surrounding space! Imagining this same gate positioned next to the house seems impossible, yet this is often done, with the resulting walk next to the house and all planting beds eliminated. By setting a gate away from the structure, the walk is also set apart, allowing the landscaping to bring great beauty to the home.

A full 6-foot solid brick wall was an excellent choice to give complete privacy.

A decorative concrete flowerpot is low maintenance. It never dies, wilts, or is out of season!

262 Benches that seat two to four people, especially ones with a back, can be an architectural delight and perfect for many situations—but for day-to-day sitting needs, an individual chair is best, especially one with arms.

Benches have their uses, but if you're sitting down for some conversation with a friend, most people prefer to converse at an angle of about 45 degrees—not shoulder-to-shoulder, as one would sit on a bench.

Maneuverability is the key; they should be able to be turned and moved to fit any conversational situation. To work best, seating should be lightweight; this explains the ubiquitous plastic lawn chair! For your beautiful patio, there are plenty of high-end choices that provide the same flexibility—but no matter how much you care to spend, an easily moved seat for each person is the best choice in nearly every case.

Individual seats that are heavy and bulky are much less appealing—too many of these bulky seats crush social situations.

See **No Built-in Benches** *261*

263 All seating must be selected for comfort.

The patio is the culmination of the house and garden experience. Everyone wants to spend time there relaxing, reading the paper, eating a meal, or visiting with guests. But uncomfortable seating will end that vision. Too often a homeowner gets caught up in a décor and will select seating that is really not comfortable. It's like digging into a beautiful dessert to find it tastes terrible—I've seen the same reaction by people taking a seat on a beautiful patio to discover a torture chamber instead.

Spend time *sitting* in the seat you intend to purchase—not looking at it. If your reaction is that it is not comfortable, that reaction will not improve over time. Move on until you find a seat you can imagine sitting in for a stretch of time, enjoying the outdoors.

See **Photos** *247, 325*

Two comfortable armchairs and a small table combine for a perfect spot to take a break and look out over the vista. Moving them to a different view (or if the late-afternoon sun is in your eyes) is quick and easy.

A level, firm, solid surface is important for these chairs to be welcoming.

The wonderful canopy of these Significant Trees creates a perfect sense of enclosure, so necessary for someone to feel comfortable in a space.

262

From the very casual to more formal situations, individual chairs, preferably with arms, create a more inviting and comfortable seating arrangement.

The backs of these chairs face a downhill slope, but the large shrubs create the necessary enclosure to feel comfortable seated there.

The job description for any plant for these urns is "tough"; just as important, the decorative appeal of these urns makes them just as attractive when empty, especially important when winter comes.

I've sat in these chairs (not the little folks chairs!) and they fit the body—how nice!

A two-rail fence sends a small, polite message separating this Outdoor Living Space from the Guest Entrance walkway.

The corner of the house has only low plantings to soften the space; they don't overpower or obscure the walkway to the Guest Entrance.

263

Your selection of seating will determine how formally—or how informally—you wish to present your Outdoor Living space.

The arrangement and choice of seating sets the tone in an outdoor entertainment area. If all the furniture is identical and formally set up, the tone of the entertainment will be considered formal. Many people like a controlled situation, and find this preferable.

To create the opposite mood, mix it up. A large cushiony chair (perfect for a nap!), a funky bench, several different rockers or maybe a glider to get someone into a necessary state of motion encourage a casual atmosphere.

The furniture you choose will send a strong message about your personality and your expectations for an evening's visit. There is no right or wrong!

See **Recessed Decks and Porches** *259*

    Power of the Sun *57, 242*

    Porch, Transitional Space *252*

 Because of their size, noise, and water effusion, air conditioning units should be located away from any outdoor seating area or where windows will be open.

Have you ever gone to bed with the window open, expecting to hear crickets or a little rain—only to hear the drone of the air conditioner? Or perhaps you want to sit outside on the patio, but the closely situated unit drowns out conversation, while water trails across the pavement. Are the bottom steps leading from your deck compromised by a constant wet muck?

Most builders are quite aware of this concern, but don't take it for granted that yours has come up with the best solution for your site. Contractors make lots of decisions, and this is one that often falls through the cracks, leaving the homeowner a landscaping problem to solve. Talk to your builder and address this situation *at the beginning*, because construction details could make any changes later on impossible (or, if possible, expensive).

See **Plan Ahead for Utilities** *60*

    Fencing, Problem Solving *307*

    Too Much Concrete *218*

Different chairs (even a bed) for every need were chosen for this informal setting. Someone asked this homeowner if anyone actually used the bed. The answer: "Anytime of day or evening, rain or shine, you'll find someone stretched out enjoying the surrounding vista and the sounds of nature!"

265

The kids might travel around this way as they play, but otherwise this "dead" zone is wonderful for lining up every utility this home will use. Notice the extra detail of extending a solid wall to block this view before beginning the open iron fence again.

Behind the carport and away from everything, these air conditioning units can't even be seen. What good planning!

These air conditioners are nowhere near the front entrance, back patio, bedroom windows, or the opposite side yard. Here they can drone away, drip water—and also be easily camouflaged by shrubbery.

265

266 The placement of trash cans, gutters, and downspouts are often overlooked during building, leaving them as eyesores to address later. **Plan for them now!**

Folks, trash cans are here to stay. Finding a good place for them *after* the home is built can be difficult, while planning an out-of-sight, enclosed niche is easy. (This is particularly important where animals routinely prowl for treats.) Identify a space—perhaps with other utility items such as spigots, hoses, and air conditioners—and construct a firm, level surface that can be screened by fencing or plants.

Gutters and downspouts are another utility item that creates a state of shock just when the homeowner doesn't think he can stand another. Have you ever seen gutters and downspouts shown on a house plan?

Yet at the very end of construction, a truck drives up and those incredible columns out front now have a downspout front and center, that beautiful limestone corner piece has a metal line coursing right down its side, the overrun is an unwanted waterfall, or downspouts pour water all over the sidewalk (or worse, flood plantings, causing them to struggle and perhaps die). Water is a powerful and destructive force. Asking questions isn't just for aesthetics, but also for the integrity of your home (think of the problems of water in the basement). So get answers. Now.

See **Fences, Problem Solvers** *307*
Drainage Issues *17*
Plan for all Utilities *60*
Photo *17*

This is a simple but quite effective solution; neither drivers on the street nor the homeowner can see the trash can. The fence might even keep a few dogs out.

266

This downspout is buried under the walk to emerge at a drainage area below, so water does not spill over the walk during every rainstorm. Every homeowner should have this item listed in his contract, because its placement is totally integrated with the pouring of all concrete, and cannot be done afterwards.

Placement of water faucets is often dictated by your local county code office. If it's not, tell your contractor you want one on every side of your house (but not in places where keeping a hose would be offensive to the landscape).

Here again is the combination of function and beauty so often found in landscaping. No land can succeed without water, so you'll need a faucet handy. But plan to locate them in unobtrusive spots: Why have a faucet right next to your front door when it could just as easily be around some corner in a little nook? Why is it one foot from your garage door when just a few feet down it would have been easily hidden, along with that coil of hose? Why is a faucet located right on the patio?

This is actually a hard nut to crack in the planning stage, but their exact placement is done near the end of building a home so be ready to make some decisions. These little concerns become big ones when the overall landscape is being addressed.

 All power and telephone lines need to be noted before anything is planted under them. Plants that mature at a height under 15 feet should be acceptable; anything planted under a power line that matures over that height is going to be cut back by the power company. These mutilations create an ugly landscape.

In most regions of the country, the acceptable mature height of plants under power lines is about fifteen feet; check with your power company to be sure. Branches that intrude in the space of the power lines create a hazard that must be maintained. In other words, any tree that is growing into the power line space will be mutilated over the years; in winter, when the leaves are gone. In other words, any tree that is growing into the power line space will be mutilated over the years; in winter, when the leaves are gone, this now ugly silhouette becomes quite visible and the mutilation is particularly unsettling.

This is just another "heads up" situation: Look *up* before you make your selection.

The previous plantings under this power line had been chopped back over many years and had become quite disfigured. These new plantings were set back, which allows them to reach their intended mature height. Their beauty will never be destroyed by power maintenance crews.

269 **Consider the locations of electrical outlets and conduits for future electrical lines when planning your house.**

Why use messy extension cords if you can avoid it? If you don't plan for the conveniences necessary for your lifestyle, you may not be able to plug in that wonderful rotisserie for your grill, and outdoor lighting might be a headache instead of a blessing.

When a house is designed, a schematic drawing is made for all electrical wiring. You will naturally be concerned with the fixtures and outlets inside your home, but take the time to consider your outdoor electrical needs before it's too late. Consider also putting conduits under walks and driveways during their construction; they come in quite handy when the lighting person shows up and needs to run electrical wires to the other side of the concrete.

See **All Essential Uses, Plan Ahead** *40*

Lighting *334, 336*

270 **Totally ignore all utility elements such as fire hydrants, street signs, water or power concrete markers, and the like.**

Beside the fact that *by law* most of these items cannot be obscured (and, in fact, if your house is on fire, the fire hydrant needs to be quite visible and accessible!), in reality no one notices these items. They are "invisible"— we all see these utility elements in our day-to-day living, but we have learned to not see them.

Landscape as if they are not even there. Your bed lines should enhance your home; if they are unattractively contorted to include such objects, you've essentially created a bull's eye around them. Instead allow them to be in your lawn or part of your planting bed standing there quite alone. The human eye will not "see" them.

This funky picture is just to remind every homeowner to think electrical for your outdoor landscape.

Note the location of the septic system—including tanks and the septic field—before any landscaping plans are made. **Keep a schematic of the plan on file for future reference.**

Most homes are on a public sewer system. But many still use a septic system, and if so, there are important considerations. For example, invasive plants should not be planted near the hook-up and septic tank area due to potential problems with their roots; and since septic tanks must be cleaned out periodically, access to this area is very important. Additionally, heavy equipment used by landscapers can destroy a tank and piping, so you should stake the area to highlight its presence.

The placement of the tank and field can also have a dramatic impact on your landscape plans. Swimming pools, tennis courts, grading for a special garden area, or even the location of an outdoor entertainment structure could all be affected by the initial placement of the septic system. Be sure to go over this with your contractor, preferably before the system is placed.

 All outbuildings including barns should present their pretty side to any view from the homesite. **The entrances to outbuildings should face away from the homesite.**

All working and storage areas are inherently messy. No project, pieces of equipment, nor all the other working items can ever present a pretty picture in the landscape. Yet these outbuildings can be some of the most appealing elements in a landscape, often built with attention to many details of interest. It is only their placement in relationship to the homesite that needs to be addressed. The planning process is the time to note your visual space and consider other essential factors (drainage, parking space, fences, woods, and so forth), to position outbuildings so they present their best side to your homesite.

If you have an open storage space with no sides at all, this problem also needs to be addressed. Perhaps you are confident the items will be kept aesthetically pleasing, such as a nicely stacked pile of firewood, or the items in view will be several pieces of equipment that just need a cover. Otherwise, if you know this space will be a major workspace, plan to move this open storage behind another building or position it out of sight elsewhere. This will make everyone happy because while work buildings are beautiful, their insides are not.

See **Photo** *75*

Entrances to workshops and working areas should be sited to avoid any exposure to the north. Position them to face a more southern exposure.

Working on equipment and projects is often done outside in all kinds of weather. In the colder months, this work can be a more pleasant prospect when the working space faces the warming southern exposure and the building helps shield the homeowner from cold northern winds. For the hotter summer months, a Significant Tree could be planted to take advantage of its cooling shade.

The value of a more southern exposure was demonstrated to me on a visit to a famous horse farm where all barns were built into the north side of a hill. The day was cold, but the horses were being bathed and groomed most comfortably. I have visited other barns that were always unpleasant no matter the weather or time of year. A northern exposure is especially irksome as the wind constantly blows in leaves, dirt, and other debris. Work areas are particularly affected by the sun's warmth in winter and natural light year-round. So look to the sun.

See **Power of the Sun** *57*

 Lighting parking areas, walkways, and potentially dangerous situations— including the outdoor cooking area—is essential. It's the best way to give night-time visitors the welcomed clues they need. The use of motion sensors is particularly effective in most situations.

Very often, landscaping decisions are made during the day, and some dangerous situations are just not identified. However, there are certain locations where strategically placed lights will give both the homeowner and the visitor all the clues they need to maneuver in some degree of safety.

The use of motion sensors is particularly effective for many of these outdoor situations. Visitors get light before they reach the front door, a homeowner feels safer when he steps outside at night and doesn't need to wonder later if he turned out the lights. Needless to say, an unwanted visitor will not like to be highlighted moving around your property.

Lights are particularly desirable near steps, a drop-off, a dock, alleys—anywhere where it's important to know where to step next. While you have the option, try to anticipate these problem areas and install the biggest safety factor…light.

See **Photos** *51, 135, 213, 226, 239*

The pierced brick wall drastically blocks the view—of the Guest Parking area.

Facing directly south and thus generally uncomfortably hot, this space was designed only as a passageway down to the major entertainment space.

The chairs are for occasional use only.

Can you see it? A little light set in the brick column illuminates the top step. In fact, all steps in this landscape are lit.

274

If someone suggests putting soft lighting in some of your specimen trees, do so.

It is called "moonlighting." With many schedules as packed as they are these days, your nights might be the only time you have to enjoy the garden. Full moons come around, but clouds, late moon risings, and anything less than a full moon limit that ethereal look—this feature extends the opportunity to view your garden that gives incredible pleasure.

Extravagant? Yes, but well worth the effort and money.

Lighting overhead or on tall poles (called cafeteria style) is great for maximum visibility. Lighting with lower bulb wattages and at eye level (Italian style) creates a soft effect where details are more blurred.

Lots of light, especially overhead, sets the tone for a particular style of entertaining. This includes ceiling-fan lights or lights on posts surrounding an Outdoor Living Space, and it produces a lively effect. I call it "cafeteria style" lighting. On the other end of the spectrum, the Italian style includes lights lowered in height (at eye level and below) and wattage: candles on tables, torches on short poles, soft up-lighting in nearby trees. Italian style lighting will produce a much more relaxed and intimate atmosphere.

This otherwise dark corner will come alive with the addition of that little light at the base of this small tree. Also notice the addition of small walkway lighting to the left, which is carried throughout the garden and invites late evening strolls.

276

All lights at this pool are Italian style. Notice the lights on the surrounding wall pointing downward and located only 5 feet high.

The pool's interior is lit at night and candles are set on the tables when the homeowners entertain.

The post light was lowered to only 2 feet, so it gives off a glow instead of an overall illumination. Even the selection of the bulb wattage was lowered to reduce its glare.

Consider this same pool with only post lights and spotlights from under every eave of the house. The existing situation is for soft entertainment; the other is great for lots of small kids running about, when cafeteria-style lighting might be more appropriate.

276

The original cafeteria-style lights on these two columns are important to the landscape because they illuminate both the entrance and the interior of this courtyard. Without some lighting, this landscape would not be so appealing after dark.

The beginning of the wall is set back about 1 foot from the corner.

An iron gate replaced the original one of wooden construction, which created too much enclosure to be comfortable.

Symmetry of plantings and keeping the number to a minimum result in low maintenance.

Wide, firm footing should be installed for ease of walking, especially in a shady area.

An irrigation system should replicate the average rain pattern (of a good year) for your region. Otherwise, plant deaths increase dramatically because they receive excessive, unnatural amounts of water.

Periodically, Nature provides too much or too little rain—making plants (and gardeners) happy or unhappy as the case may be. But even with normal variables, there is usually a normal rainfall pattern which provides enough water for plants to thrive.

Observe the normal rain patterns for your region. Here in central Georgia, our pattern is this: it usually rains, is dry for several days or even a week or two, and then rains again. During some years the dry periods are too long; during other years, everything seems to rot because there is too much rain. Other regions have primarily dry (out West), while others seem more like a rain forest (such as Florida).

If your landscape design is based on plants regularly grown in your region, irrigation should be set up to mimic your region's normal rainfall. In Georgia, we receive approximately forty-two inches a year, scattered throughout the year in amounts of one to three inches, followed by dry weather. Therefore, irrigation in Georgia should *not* be timed for every two or three days, should *not* provide inordinate amounts of water at these times, and should *not* distribute small amounts daily, which would keep plants and the soil soggy.

Plants adapt to their climate and soils—water is part of this adaptation. When irrigation tips the balance (always too much), plants suffer. An excess of water literally suffocates the root systems.

I chuckle at every irrigation system I see installed. I know each person is thinking, "By George, I paid for it and I am going to use it!" Water sprays all over, the run-off flows into the streets, and it makes lawns so soggy they cannot be walked upon. Guess what? Soon, the plants are turning black. Very expensive plants.

An irrigation system should be viewed in the same way as fire insurance. It's there when you need it but just because you paid for it doesn't mean you have to burn down your house to get any benefit. Think about what Mother Nature has devised for your area and follow her lead.

 Overhead watering is not inherently bad.

Overhead watering is supposedly bad because it's believed it will promote diseases. Actually, what encourages diseases is too much watering to the extent that plants are never allowed to dry out either at their roots or on their foliage. By reducing irrigation to what your region's normal rainfall is, and spacing the timing to follow Nature's natural pattern, any disease problems can be blamed on something else—but not on overhead irrigation.

See **Soil Must Percolate** *21*
　　　Watering Guide *26*

Irrigation systems need to be designed as simply as possible and with visible sprinkler heads because any system carrying water has the potential to break or leak, and cause great damage.

It is the nature of man to experiment with all kinds of unique stuff. That can be good, but when irrigation systems are installed, the whole scheme should be as simple as possible for most homeowners so that as problems crop up, easy solutions will be at hand. If the system is simple, the identification of any problems can be quite straightforward. If it's not a simple design the situation can become quite perplexing—even if the same person who installed is the one you call to fix it.

Currently in my work, I see two kinds of irrigation systems available: the visible and the invisible. In the visible systems, the sprinkler heads can be seen, so you can see what is happening—or what is not happening, or what is happening in a crazy way. Appropriate action can be taken.

Irrigation systems that are invisible employ designs in which emitters are attached to a web of small tubing running along the surface. You cannot see when or if it is working. This design is intended to conserve water by minimizing evaporation. However, if a critter chews on these tubes, or the gardener accidentally cuts them, or the emitter quits working, no one can see the tubes pouring water into the ground unchecked. That means some plants are flooded while some are getting no water at all.

By their very nature, irrigation systems *will* have problems. But when the problems are not visible, discovering them is almost an accident; some really bad results can occur in the meantime.

Just keep it simple. Your irrigation man does not need to become your bosom buddy.

 If you plan an overall landscape that will have a specific design and if you also plan to install an irrigation system, coordinate the two.

Very often irrigation systems are installed before landscape designs have been finalized. Naturally, the two often do not have the same goals, and costly adjustments must be made. A conscientious irrigation installer will ask the homeowner about his intentions regarding his landscape and will advise him to wait if a design is in the works.

If a homeowner plans to hire a professional landscape installer, I often suggest that person coordinate with the irrigation installer. These two professionals are usually working on top of each other and there is a great need for good communication. Hopefully the responsible party will be easier to handle if a line gets cut or other problems arise.

Homeowners often rush the end of construction by the need to water a newly installed lawn. But it's worth taking a little time to sort out the irrigation situation before more serious problems arise and money is wasted.

281 Ideally, a detailed schematic drawing of any irrigation systems should be required.

In most cases, an irrigation system is installed using a drawing showing the placement of the controlling values, lines, and heads. But too often this drawing is not done or the details are so carelessly marked that it is extremely hard to use when the need arises. Additionally, irrigation systems may already be installed by builders or the previous owner; all records, if any existed, are lost to the new owner of the property. The problem becomes more complicated when additional irrigation lines are installed or corrections are made. It is quite obvious this has become a problem in the industry. But any new owner must work with the situation as best he can.

Anyone installing an irrigation system should get as detailed a drawing as possible of the location of the lines, outlets, and values. This can be filed with other papers relevant to the home site and pulled out when the situation demands.

282 The need for irrigation usually increases when you choose plants that are outside the norm for your area. **Because water restrictions are becoming more prevalent, out-of-region plant choices need to be reduced if not eliminated.**

Every area has or will be faced with water shortages or restrictions. Not only does my region have long periods of drought, but we make huge demands of the current water supply; demand can only increase in the future. One after another, communities have been clamping down on excessive water use, which naturally affects irrigation of your landscape. Many regions already have quite severe restrictions, forcing quite obvious adaptations.

When installing a landscape, the wise use—and even the availability—of water needs to be considered. My clients already are asking, "Do these plants have any special watering needs?" I am delighted when a client asks because it demonstrates an awareness of this problem. Of course, they might be thinking of their water bill, but they know restrictions are already in place and do not want plants that cannot be maintained.

The old saying "No man is an island" is never truer than when it concerns water. The cumulative effects of inappropriate plants that need inordinate amounts of water are not good for our society. Do your part.

See **Mulching** *24*

Site Plants Where They Grow Best *27*

Plants – Check for Problems *30*

Having Fun

Grass and Kids

A lush, green lawn is probably the first goal of many homeowners. The effect of a wide expanse—or even a small oasis—of green lawn is one of the most inviting aspects of a beautiful landscape. Grass and kids are sometimes at odds, so getting it established right the first time leaves more time for the real outdoor fun.

Many children have fond memories of where they grew up—but never remember a perfect landscape with a perfect lawn. What they remember are walks in the woods, grilling hamburgers, picking flowers for a favorite teacher, or sitting around the outdoor fireplace roasting marshmallows. A little landscape planning will make for a lifetime of memories.

283 **All kids love to run in circles. Provide as many circular paths as you can.**

Kids running in circles in the house can drive Mom crazy, so give them circles outside. One area is the driveway, or the pad just outside the garage or carport (if it tilts, this won't work, so it must be level).

One customer had a peculiar site situation so when I laid out the drive, the result was a large oval around a dominant tree. I told him his four children would probably spend more time in that area than any other place. When I returned to do some more work, the parents burst out laughing, telling me they could not get their kids to leave the worksite because of the wonderful circular pattern in the drive. Their cars were full of bikes, trikes, and skates for their visits during construction. The kids had not wanted to move; now they could not wait.

There are many other circular paths in the landscape: around the house, around the back yard, or out one door and in the other. Children will run around the swing set, around the pool, around the patio, around a tree. Designing landscapes should recognize this need for kids, so watch for long narrow decks with only one exit; paths in woods leading to a dead end; and structures such as fences and walls that restrict runabouts. Remember, when planning the landscape, start walking and keep walking until you have determined all of your circular paths. Your kids will love you for it even though they might not mention it for twenty years!

See **Siting the House to Relate to Your Needs** *39*
Fourth Room, Outdoor Living Space *169*
Circulation *186*
Gates *307*
Daylight Basement – Barrier to Outdoors *263*
Photos *187, 197*

Two bridges, not one, create a wonderful circular path that numerous grandchildren travel when visiting. On the other side is a delightful picnic table; then kids travel back around to the summerhouse and up to the swimming pool.

284 **Official court or field sizes for any sports activity are not necessary for children to play, and could hinder the inherent idea of "playing for fun."**

Forget "official." If the kids want to play official, let them go to the school to play or join a team. Your home is for kids to play.

I took this advice when designing a field for kids to play ball. Over the years, kids had congregated in and around this ballfield. Some were little, some a little older, and then some were big—a real mix that would continue to evolve throughout the day as kids had to leave or just wanted to watch. The rules changed too. For the little-bitty kids, everyone threw a soft ball and cheered dramatically. The bases changed depending on how "serious" the game was.

Most interestingly, my huge flower bed ran all along one side of the field. Without my ever saying one word about it, if the ball flew into the bed, all play stopped until the ball was carefully retrieved—all without stepping on the flowers.

Croquet anyone? How about a little volleyball? Badminton is old-fashioned, but I still have customers who love it. In the back yard, regulation sizes might be important to adults, but kids prefer to play a game of fun and are fully capable of adapting an area to their needs. So don't get hung up on official dimensions. If your landscape cannot accommodate those measurements, just move ahead with what you have and your kids will figure something out.

See **Level Places to Play** *17, 53*

During grading of this landscape, this area was specifically marked out for kids to play. The area was leveled, friendly shrubs were planted all around, and a generously sized grassy path was planned at the other end for another exit. No one bothered to take measurements for any specific game—the space was what was available and the kids adapted joyfully.

285 **Locate children's activity areas where parents will be most available to observe safety as well as appropriate behavior. Swimming pools are especially hazardous and need special considerations.**

Every playset, swimming pool, or other designated activity area comes with some built-in hazards, so monitoring children's safety and behavior is important. Children often trip and tumble, so someone needs to be close enough to be able to react right away.

Swimming pools should be viewed as a definite hazard, much more so than a lake or pond with their sloped shores and weeds found at their edge. A small child can easily tumble into a swimming pool; sadly, statistics show more than half of the drownings that occur in family pools are children under four.

With this in mind, I strongly recommend any landscape plan should include a fence separating the pool from the household. Entrance gates should be kept to a minimum (one), should have a child-proof latch, and should be easily visible to monitor traffic into the pool area. There are many attractive ways to fence a pool, and the peace of mind afforded by them is invaluable.

See **Iron Fencing and Gates** *310*

How wonderfully attractive—and safe! With the use of this iron fencing, these homeowners have a clear view of their pool. Further, with only one gate to monitor, they can easily control all traffic when the pool is unattended.

285

Ball playing is best in a "bowl-like" situation or on a large flat field. Ball playing will not succeed in areas where the ball disappears down a slope, into a ravine, or into the street.

Balls are just about the one object every person in this world can relate to: we throw them, dodge them, hit them, catch them, and bounce them. But one thing balls do best is roll away. If the play activity is located where a ball cannot easily be retrieved when missed or it gets blown away to roll down a long hill, all activity ends immediately…and is often never taken up again. I worked with one homeowner who built a large deck for a basketball court, but it overlooked a very steep hillside. He explained that he was installing huge nets to prevent balls going over the edge. I suggested he spend his money for a YMCA membership but he moved ahead. He later told me it took only two balls—the second one went over the net—before his kids abandoned the court. Not another game was played there.

Successful areas for ballgames are enclosed by fences, *upward* slopes, or a large, friendly shrub border. A dramatic downhill side, even when the playing area is flat, can be a game-stopper; this is the time to consider a large bank of soft shrubs in your landscape plans. If games are an integral part of your life, take the terrain into account.

See **Level Places to Play** *17, 53*

 All kids love bridges, low walls, large rocks, sloping lawns for going down fast…and messy places to play.

Landscape decisions are made for many reasons—it's pretty, it retains sloping earth, it feeds the birds, and so forth. Kids see other uses: a wall becomes a place to hide, or jump off; the slope becomes a summer water slide; a tree is something to climb.

Anticipate this in your landscape design. Let a bridge lead you out and around the property. If a wall is needed, one seventeen inches high gives kids a place to sit or hide behind. At my house, I placed large boulders along the lawn; I imagined the grandkids hopping from one to another. And they do.

A good messy place is probably the best thing going for kids. Don't give over the entire landscape to total destruction; just provide a place to make mud pies. The kids will be grown soon enough, and new grass can be started after they leave. A lot of my work comes from customers whose kids have grown and left the household, so they've turned their attention to the yard.

Once kids are grown, they may ask about a specific plant or how you did this or that, but they'll remember most the freedom they had to run about, enjoying the landscape as their personal kingdom.

Kids like to sit right outside the home. It is a little private, it gives a sense of freedom, but it is still close to the center of the household where Mother is just inside (as is lunch). This area needs to be designed for this most important activity.

The landing needs to be as spacious as possible, but more important, the steps need to be broad so children, with all their "stuff," can remain even if Mom needs to pass by. The treads also need to be deep, which allow for a really comfortable sit-and-play station. Even as the kids get older, this area will remain a gathering place.

Architecturally, the spacious landing and gracious steps add greatly to the beauty of your home, but you'll love the way the kids congregate close to home.

See **Photos** *158, 289*

Children play in many different ways. An action-packed, battery-powered figure can be lots of fun, as can skates and bicycles. But running after a salamander or a cricket, scooping up tadpoles, or mounting butterflies at the end of their all-too-brief life can be just as exciting.

Every time my grandkids visit, all activities seem to pale next to chasing some critters, digging others up, or capturing still others with lots of squeals until they are finally put into some container to watch at close range. Next, the kids add little sticks or grass or perhaps some water is provided. Most of these creatures are quickly released; some are watched in their own environment (especially great if it's a gooey bog). If you find a critter that's dead, you can preserve it in some alcohol to observe at close range.

Have safe and appropriate containers readily available to foster this activity. Perhaps the kids in your life will develop another important link to our natural world.

290 Large timbers placed close to a playset only become a hazard. **Remove them or lay them farther out on the periphery.**

A child coming off a swing or a slide carries a certain amount of momentum, and if bordering landscape timbers are placed too close, a child has to adjust very quickly to avoid this hazard. Most customers tell me the timbers are to keep the mulch in a tidy space under the playset. Beside the fact that kids aren't into being tidy, removing or moving the timbers farther out would be better for their play. Too many times the space allotted is just not big enough. Watch your children, and if you need to, adjust the size of the area.

291 If the swing set is in an area that supports grass, then use grass as your surface instead of mulch.

Swing sets on a homesite are quite different than ones used on a school playground—the grass at school takes a pounding, but it will survive at your home. Furthermore, grass is soft and cool—much more pleasant than dark mulch that traps heat. So if the area has a good stand of grass, then by all means let your kids enjoy it; there might be a dead spot at the base of the slide or at the hit point under the swing, but who cares!

How relaxing and beautiful at playtime. Why would anyone want railroad ties in such a beautiful landscape?

290

Lovely grass and lovely times with children playing outside. Designing a "box" using coarse, rough materials and the continual upkeep of mulch is just not necessary in most situations.

Kids love to plant. Let them have their place in the landscape.

Given the opportunity, kids love to plant a seed or take a little flower, dig a little hole, and plug it in. The anticipation of its growth is part of an imaginary world of wonderful things that will happen. The plant will become a giant bean stalk, the big blue flower seen on the package, or maybe something to eat.

Consider two different scenes I've witnessed at my nursery. A child came up to the mother with a beautiful seed package, perhaps costing a dollar. "No darling, we don't need that. We don't have any place to plant it and you will never take care of it." The small child then turned to some small potted annuals for sale. She asked if she could buy that for the garden. The same reply from the mother. I saw the light go out in her face. She retreated and said no more.

I have other customers who routinely come in with their children to select something to plant. It is amazing to hear the dialogue between the parent and child as they exchange all kinds of chitchat about each plant. They recount successes and failures, and all kinds of really neat stuff they have done with their gardening. These kids display a joy of life participating in this wonderful interchange with their parent.

Children do not see the garden as we do. They do not envision perfectly planned out color and texture schemes. They do not see their little plant as contrary to the overall beauty their parents desire. They just love the act of planting and watching something grow. There's room for both.

Selecting a type of grass is limited both by your region and by your immediate homesite.

Check with your Extension Service, ask at your local nursery, look at your neighbor's lawn to see how different grass types are doing. Usually the choices for a lawn are fairly limited for any particular region, so it's best to get some good information about what each type grass needs for good performance. Then, after assessing your particular site, make the best choice for your situation.

I happen to love fescue, but if I moved to south Georgia, I would not persist in my personal preference. I would look at neighboring lawns and ask around until I could settle the grass type that would do best on my site. Just remember, every region has a variety of choices, so select a grass that does best where you live and move ahead with other landscaping chores—which should be a lot more fun than struggling with the wrong grass!

See **Use Local Sources** *90*
  Avoid Invasives *31*
  Planting Zones *28*

There is no grass that will be healthy and lush if it's planted on an ill-prepared bed.

Often after construction, warm-weather sod is laid on soil that's barely been raked. If the soil is rather sandy, the roots can penetrate it, but if there is hard-pan clay, the only way the roots can move far enough below the surface to avoid stressful situations (such as extremely cold winters or long droughts in summer) is if the soil has been thoroughly broken up. Be wary of a low bid for this work—it might not be such a bargain if the grass doesn't grow.

Good soil preparation is even more important for cool-weather grasses, as their roots need to be able to grow deeply into the soil. Obviously, if the land is hard, no amount of seed, fertilizer, or water will make the grass grow well…if at all.

Your soil might be a good, loamy, loose soil and a great deal of preparation might not be necessary, but after heavy construction, even the best soil is often dense, heavy, and compacted. Take the time to prepare the soil properly, to ensure a successful lawn that can stand up to environmental stresses.

See **Need for Soil Percolation** *21*
 Site Plants Where They Grow Best *27*

 The needs (fertilizer, water, weed control, maintenance) of every grass are very specific. Be sure to identify your lawn type, as this will determine what it needs and when it needs it.

Everyone knows lawns need to be fed and watered, but where should you begin?

Identify your lawn: Not only is there a big difference between warm-weather and cool-weather grasses, there are big differences within each of these groups! In every category—including watering, fertilizing, weed control, maintenance—each grass is very specific. To treat any one of them the same could spell trouble (if not death) for your grass.

Since there is an obvious difference between the growth pattern of warm-weather and cool-weather grasses, there is also a big difference in how one feeds them. Fertilizing either during dormancy (or when under stress, such as drought) will cause terrible damage. Remember, cool-weather grasses are growing all fall, winter, and spring when it is cool; warm-weather grasses are active only during spring, summer, and fall.

Did you know that the most landscaping questions asked by homeowners are about lawns? Join the club. Identify your particular lawn and compile information. If you are deciding on a particular lawn for a new site, do your homework. Make a folder. Write stuff down. Collect data. Good information will save your lawn, your money, and your time.

See **Use Local Sources** *90*

296 **Grasses are either a single plant or a continuously expanding plant. Since each has benefits and downsides, educate yourself about their growth habits to help you use them wisely. This can prevent difficult landscape problems down the road.**

Simply put, grasses can be many *single* plants, each growing from a single seed. These individual plants may reseed if they're not kept mowed. Or grasses may be a type that *continuously extends* outward by means of underground runners. The latter may or may not be able to reseed, but its growth habit usually determines where it will grow, not its reseeding abilities. Each grass type has landscape value, but an informed decision should be made before choosing the type that's best for your situation.

Single Plant: Many regions have favorite lawn grasses. In Georgia, it is fescue. Fescue actually grows over most of the United States, but in the more temperate regions, it flourishes in winter; in snowier regions, it peaks in summer and fall because it's covered by snow in winter. There are many other single-plant grass options. Deciding which variety of a single-plant grass to grow for your location is actually made quite easy by the U.S. government's extensive research. The USDA tests many selections, then provides this information to growers who in turn cultivate the best available grass for your lawn.

Since this type grows from an individual seed, this makes it a good choice for a non-invasive lawn grass. Yes, a seed may sprout in your flower bed here and there, but it is easily weeded. In more temperate regions these grasses remain green all year; perhaps if you are less compulsive about a weed-free lawn, your green weeds can join the crowd and will not be so conspicuous during the winter! I also find single-seed lawn grasses have a softer texture for walking.

Another positive attribute is that removing single-plant lawn grasses is easily accomplished. Many landscapes, especially after new construction, might not be finalized and changes are to be expected either for future projects or just changes in the plan. Because single-seed grasses' rooting systems are not a tangled web of innumerable starting points for regrowth, one application of an herbicide to kill a particular section

of grass can have you starting over in no time.

The downside to single-plant lawn grasses is that their seeding is seasonal. Germination is controlled by specific temperatures, especially of the soil, and of course the rain must cooperate. Putting down seeds in the wrong season just won't work unless there is a freak weather system to accommodate you. These grasses also demand a well-prepared planting bed to establish a deeply rooted plant that can withstand summer droughts.

Continuously expanding lawn grasses: These grasses grow by means of underground runners that extend in all directions, creating a dense mat. Their growth habit allows them to be grown in large fields, harvested in sections, then transported to landscape sites to be laid out for an "instant" lawn. In some regions, these grasses are sold by plugs which expand outward to eventually cover a lawn. These grasses are particularly effective for construction sites where the homeowner is tired of all the mud and is needful to immediately control the situation. This is especially true if the homeowner has just moved in and dirt is being tracked in with every step. In some regions, the ability to install an "instant" grass solves many problems.

A problem arises when the runners invade planting beds, especially ones with beautifully prepared soil for flowers or small plants. Once these runners have gotten in the bed amongst the flowers, absolutely nothing can remove them without Herculean efforts. If only one little piece with a node is left behind, an even bigger and better clump of grass will emerge right in the middle of your daylily patch. These runners will also grow over concrete edgings and form mats of grass, covering walkways and anything else in its path.

Continuously expanding lawn grasses are fine for the compulsive gardener who will stay on top of edging. Using a weed eater along each edge of a planting bed and along every walk or curbing is an essential maintenance chore every week or two in the growing season. These grasses are also great in some regions on large farms, where flower beds are not an issue and only a big tractor will be mowing. No one cares where grass grows in this situation, and in fact its expanding nature might be desirable.

Another downside of continuously expanding

lawn grasses is that they are winter dormant. For these months where lawns are still very much part of the landscape and not covered in snow, the lawns turn a soft brown color, but any weeds that appear will stand out since they are green. Therefore maintaining a "perfect lawn" takes on a whole new dimension. Many people will use a lawn service for the exacting applications necessary to reach this goal.

To me, though, the major problem with these grasses is not their use, but their misuse in inappropriate situations. One is the application of these grasses in sod form to control erosion on large bare slopes that cannot be safely mowed or maintained. The solution is temporary; as the years go by, this grass (or any grass) will not stand up to the pressure of a continuous water flow, allowing the erosion to begin anew. In the meantime, the slope must be kept mowed, endangering lives on heavy machines. Use this lawn grass on your lawn, and plant any slopes with trees and shrubs.

Another problem occurs when laying this type of grass over too much lawn area. This eliminates the planting of trees and shrubs, which are necessary for future enjoyment and maintaining an ecological balance for the property. When the homeowner wishes to add cooling trees or beautiful shrubbery, he finds that removing this dense grass is nearly impossible. The mat created by this type of grass is very difficult to dig and remove. Any part left will rejuvenate, creating even more grass. Herbicides can be used, but even still, unless every living part is killed, these grasses will return to grow again.

Consider the pros and cons of each type grass offered in your region. If your grass is already established, learn how to take care of it and how to deal with any future adjustments necessary for a successful landscape—adding trees, shrubs, flower beds, and such. If you are a new owner, by understanding the grass you have chosen, then you are in the driver's seat to make the best choices for its location.

See **Illustrations** *174, 175*

Invasive – Number One Maintenance Chore *31*

Mortared Solid Borders *182*

Slopes *32*

Significant Trees, Erosion Control *108*

 Grass should be grown where it will grow. It needs light and must be away from the competing root systems of large trees.

All grasses need light to grow even though some types need less light than others. Grass also competes poorly with other, more demanding root systems. Before trying to grow grass where it will not grow, the homeowner should look at his property and assess the available light and other plant materials that will compete with his grass.

New construction on a heavily wooded site presents the biggest challenge. The trees have been naturally growing tall and skinny, but after major clearing for construction, they mature and spread out in this new sun-bathed environment; their branches begin to shade the grass below more and more. Any damage done to their root system forces trees to quickly recover, depriving even more grass of water and nutrients.

I often hear how beautiful the lawn was when the homeowner first moved in—but now it's doing so poorly. When I look at it, it's clear the grass is doing quite well out in the open but is doing poorly only next to the now-maturing trees.

The solution? Grow grass where it *will* grow. Nature has the upper hand, so just go with the flow—move your grass line out to where nature indicates. Similarly, don't plant grass where it never gets real sun. Large trees create a dense shade over this intended lawn area today, tomorrow, and forever, and no matter how much you might want grass here, it must have light to grow. It's time to switch your thinking to shade-loving groundcovers.

This is the rule: if your grass is not growing in a shady situation, it is not your fault—so move along to the next stage. Plant something else or mulch the site.

See **Bed Lines – Site Away From Trees** *171*

Natural Litter *106*

Our Primal Needs

Water, Fire, and Critters

Water and fire are two of the most compelling elements on earth. Water carries an allure that touches everyone, while fire adds drama to the landscape. A fireplace soon gathers everyone around where, in hushed voices, talk becomes casual and amiable and bedtime is pushed back.

Yet the need for creatures in the landscape far surpasses all others. No matter how small and seemingly insignificant, even one small dog, a rabbit, butterflies…or something larger, like a horse…adds a dimension that far surpasses its apparent weight compared with the whole. And no matter how beautiful the landscape, creatures—large or small, wild or domesticated—are the touchstones of our lives.

298 **Locate small ornamental ponds near major sitting or viewing areas. This not only means it will be enjoyed, but assures that maintenance issues are noticed and handled promptly.**

A small ornamental pond is intended for intimate viewing. The homeowner will actually name his fish and be distressed when some raccoon or heron has dinner at their expense. Plants are added around and within the pond and fussed over and enjoyed for all their qualities. Even more importantly, the homeowner wishes to hear the sounds and see the motion of the water from a fountain or waterfall.

Occasionally I've seen an ornamental pond built away from any real living space. There might be many reasons why this happens; usually because the setting looked so perfect for a pond and everyone had good intentions for regular visits. But in the real world, the visits become less and less—and the pond is neglected more and more.

I remember one pond tucked behind an auxiliary building; our visit noted a dead pump. How long had that been the situation, and how many fish had died as a result? Another pond was so far down in a forested garden area that it was seldom visited; it was clogged with leaves. Still another was just below the homeowner's deck—but it could only be seen when they stood up and looked straight down. This family was missing a lovely visual just ten feet below their sitting space.

So when you are walking about looking for the perfect pond location, think first about where you will be spending most of your time outside, as well as your special viewing spot from inside the house. Then consider the presence of sunlight, traffic flow, the lay of the land and any other relevant factor before siting your pond.

See **Low Maintenance – Combination of Many Projects** *13*
Consider View from Home *46*

This pond could have been sited in a side garden or even in the front landscape. But by being near the patio that's used daily and visible from the main inside living space, its beauty and soothing sounds can be enjoyed every day—and if trouble arises, nothing will be missed.

298

This breathtaking combination is sited in full view of where the home-owners enjoy sitting daily.

A dark bottom gives an illusion of depth but also hides litter until clean up time.

298

Choose as natural a setting as possible for an informal pond. However, a pond should never be sited in the path of a natural water runoff.

Building a pond is an artistic endeavor. Just as an artist cannot tell you why a specific painting is appealing, no book can tell you why a particular pond is so beautiful. But here are some tips:

- The water should travel *down the natural grade* of the land. Many times I see ponds inverted because the homeowner built up the earth in an unnatural way, directing the view of the water back toward his visual space. But unless there is a mass of plantings to camouflage this odd site, it always looks odd. Instead, keep reviewing sites until the lay of the land suggests that the pond would already be there if only Nature had gotten there first.

- Unless you are in a specific rock-collecting situation, the stones chosen should be *subtle* and of many *different sizes.* The rocks should be laid in a manner of a natural repose; a too-sharp angle that suggests man has intervened interrupts the beauty of the site. (Note that placing rocks requires a really strong back and good help; this is when you'll learn you seldom lift a rock, you slide it.)

- *At no time should a pond be sited where a natural drainage occurs during rainstorms.* In most situations, homeowners go to a site of natural drainage first, thinking this runoff water will become a part of their "natural" pond—but a rainstorm will flush out plantings and fish, leaving behind a big deposit of silt. I have seen an extreme rainstorm actually tear out a whole pond, lifting the liner completely out. Identify any drainage situations and instead choose a location where no water will enter the pond except what you put there or which falls naturally from rain vs. runoff.

See **Natural Materials** *48, 81*

Mimicking Mother Nature is often very hard to do…but try.

This gentle slope between a summerhouse and the back porch is a perfect setting for a "natural" waterfall and pond.

300 Water features in formal shapes must be in an open, sunny space because cleanliness is essential for these designs. **Also, any surrounding formal plantings need all-around sun for their success.**

The inherent qualities of a formal design demand that they be kept very clean and neat, so place them out in the open away from plants that may litter the water, to keep maintenance to a minimum. This is especially important for water features with bottoms painted a clear cool color or with inlaid designs, as unsightly debris destroys the effect (an alternative is to plan on a very dark or even black color for the bottom, to camouflage debris until cleaning can be accomplished).

Any formal plantings need to be selected with some careful thought. First, think *evergreen* for year-round interest, then think *tough* because formal plantings do not need unsightly gaps, and last, think *habits of the plant,* so the plants will be part of the solution and not part of a problem, perhaps by littering the area unnecessarily.

See **Evergreens** *84*
Symmetry *92*
Formal Garden – Level *316*

This watery centerpiece is sited in surroundings with generous sunlight for a completely satisfactory outcome.

The extra-wide walkways are in keeping with the expansive landscape.

Formal garden designs always need a completely level space to be effective. Symmetrical plantings need identical cultural sites to succeed.

Dimensions for a table and chairs were planned for— not a hopeful afterthought.

Small ornamental ponds for fish and plants are best situated in good sunlight and away from dense, littering trees. If trees are present, they must be maintained for proper balance of sun and shade.

Many times the potential location of an ornamental pond is limited. You know you want it fairly close by and visible from your homesite. But be sure to consider the presence of trees when choosing a site, as leaves and branches can make this pond more of a maintenance item than you anticipate.

Many homeowners complain of spring cleanings that require donning heavy waders to pull out masses of rotting leaves from the bottom of the pool. Remember: A natural running stream will continually wash itself out with alternate heavy rains, especially in the springtime. This cannot happen with your pond—you are the one doing the cleaning

As you've read, there are many references to thinning, pruning, limbing up, and general information about trees. I have noticed many ponds over the years that were sited near surrounding trees. Sometimes there were too many trees at the beginning when the pond was dug; other ponds were placed close to trees that continued to mature; eventually, they grew over the ponds. In most cases, the effect of trees in relation to the beauty of the pond was not noted in time. But once a homeowner removes excess trees, thins others of branches, or limbs up others to obtain a higher canopy to reach a plateau of dappled shade, he is overjoyed by the results. However, since nature never stops, pruning, thinning, and limbing up must continue over the years to maintain that wonderful balance of sun and shade for the desired goal of the perfect pond.

Of course, the additional maintenance chores of keeping the pond clean never go away either, but now the pond can give the homeowner an element in the landscape rarely equaled by any other landscape feature.

See **Sun, Shade** *56*

Site Plants Where They Grow Best *27*

Thinning, Identify Trees *100*

Trees – Continual Maintenance *104*

Prune to Expose Beauty *114*

Limbing Up *123*

Photo *356*

302 If the land for a lake can be manipulated with heavy equipment, choose a graceful, meandering shoreline rather than a formal shape like an oval. **A disappearing shoreline, especially for a small lake, is especially appealing.**

The mystery of any lake is greatly heightened by a wandering shoreline. The eye follows the edge as it reaches out, continues to follow the line back to a hidden cove, and perhaps is surprised by a disappearing bend that gives a sense that the lake continues on forever.

Work out these critical details with the installer beforehand to be sure you are both on the same page. One operator might have a good clean edge with as symmetrical a shape as possible as his primary goal, while another might know just how to enhance the site to its maximum beauty. My experience has been that homeowners with a bowl-shaped lake often lament its uninspiring outline and ask for advice how to make it look more natural. Of course, draining a lake to make adjustments is a very costly endeavor, so be sure your installer knows just what you want.

See **Multiple Focal Points** *54*

Planting Beds – Create Mystery *172*

Many people ask this homeowner just where the pond goes around this bend. In fact it goes nowhere but the illusion of depth and mystery is obvious.

An open gazebo with comfortable chairs on a firm surface draws everyone to sit and visit . . . like a magnet.

Over the years, the trees in this field were limbed up until all dangerous lower branches were removed.

The combination of an open and closed shoreline creates a perfect habitat for wildlife.

This beautiful Ornamental Tree has found a perfect spot to show off its beauty close by, not out in the field beyond.

302

Get professional advice before building any pond or lake that requires a dam. In many locations, regulations must be followed before any construction can proceed.

I see pond construction projects with all kinds of variables; however, the approach taken usually falls into two different categories.

The first type of homeowners decides to build a lake and proceeds. They hire large equipment operators to move earth, build a dam and spillways, and install piping systems. Unfortunately, the installer does not always have the qualifications to determine if the site will support this lake.

These are some of the results I have observed: The soil was too porous and the water continually drained out. The available soil for building the dam was not a quality that would make for a solid dam. The drain field was not determined, so when heavy rains came, the overflow could not be accommodated safely. Or the source of water was inadequate, leaving the lake chronically low.

The second type hires professional engineers or qualified installers. They test the soil and perform other engineering studies to arrive at answers that should address all the problems the first type of homeowner hoped would just be resolved with good luck.

Good luck still has to be on your side, however. Many properly engineered lakes still develop problems; even with all our technology, the interaction of water and soil is a mysterious subject. But to take on such an expensive project with such important repercussions without the use of the best available resources would be foolish, if not illegal, so be sure to take the appropriate steps before proceeding.

See **Never Share a Project, Few Exceptions** *45*

 Any body of water, no matter how small or large, carries the possibility of stagnation and mosquito problems. Fish and moving water are the most important solutions to mosquitoes.

Many people view the lake at my home and immediately ask about the mosquito problem. "I don't have any," I reply. My lake is dynamic with spring-fed water and hosts many fish that love mosquito larvae. The stream coming from the lake is always running, so of course no mosquito larvae can live there.

The mosquito larvae thrives in stagnant water, even as little as one-half teaspoon! Beds of ivy, old cans, clogged gutters, and other debris can become a community to millions of pesky mosquitoes. Another culprit is an ornamental pond containing no fish and no movement. You can add fish for personal enjoyment, but they also will feast on insects larvae such as mosquitoes. If there are no fish, some movement added by sprays, bubblers, or cascading falls will take care of the problem.

A combination of some clean lake shoreline alternating with areas left for a more natural growth pattern solve two goals: safe access and visibility to the water plus a natural connection to wildlife habitat.

A lake with perfectly clean edges results in a rather sterile environment. The water has its beauty, but no life seems to blend from the surrounding elements. No one will see birds flitting in and out of adjacent shrubs or perhaps a fox or rabbit making its home in the protection afforded by natural growth. The wildlife that does appear seems out of place in such a manicured environment.

Many people who keep such neatly manicured ponds do so because of the fear of certain animals, but rest assured, few creatures enjoy the company of noisy humans and seldom pose any danger to the homeowner. Actually, it is usually the other way around!

A totally unkempt lake is just as unpleasing. If left to nature, the edge quickly grows up into an impenetrable mass, and the view of the lake is obstructed if not obliterated. This also prevents access for boating, fishing or swimming.

However, anyone can tell you that keeping the edge of a lake clean is a continuous maintenance chore, so a combination of natural and manicured edges is a reasonable solution, letting the land itself dictate. Areas out of reach of easy maintenance (and away from the family's immediate activity) become overgrown, creating natural wildlife habitats, while areas within the homeowners' domain are kept neat. Seeking a balance with both options will give any landowner the best of all worlds.

 Do not fence a retention pond unless required by code or insurance. Sometimes modifying the design can eliminate this undesirable feature.

Retention ponds should pose no more of a hazard as any other depression that collects water from time to time. However fences continue to be installed on a regular basis. Aesthetically, these fences do more damage to the landscape than any other feature. The very nature of a fence is to contain and shut out; the psychological effect is one of imprisonment or danger.

For example, I once worked on a large shopping center site that has a big retention pond at its entrance. A very tall chain-link fence topped with barbed wire was installed, (although absolutely nothing could be more unappealing to a shopper than to see this prisonlike situation). The owners realized the problem, and the solution was to remove the fence to allow the naturally growing pines, poplars, and native shrubs to become part of the overall landscape. Thus no attention was drawn to what was an otherwise innocuous situation.

Retention ponds are engineered by man, but the results should mimic the natural beauty of nature.

Retention ponds have become unnecessary eyesores in the landscape—yet there is nothing unnatural about wetlands or floodplains, which are simply natural retention ponds! In fact, wetlands are often quite attractive, if not stunning, such as the Everglades and the marshes along the Georgia coast, or the lowlands next to rivers. This is a complex, irregular world where nature has evolved, over centuries, ways to manage water.

But for some reason, because retention ponds are engineered, they are usually dug with great precision into perfectly shaped bowls and ringed by a perfectly planted hedge, thus creating a bull's-eye that draws unwanted attention to an unattractive, engineered solution to a natural event—water and erosion.

A better alternative is to create the retention pond to mimic nature. The shoreline can be graded in a more casual manner and the plantings selected for a more natural look. The goal should be to allow the retention pond to become a part of a whole landscape, rather than to stick out as a separate unattractive entity. Use Mother Nature as a model, relax the whole design, and plant as nature would.

This retention pond was dug in the front and to the left of this business and in full view to all customers. After these plantings were established, the area appears only as a shrub border—not a deep pit of dubious visual beauty.

This planting also created a haven for lunching employees, plus serves to screen the not-so-pretty loading docks behind it.

Tables are set on concrete and not on the wet, cold ground.

Significant trees were planted for their many benefits, but most important here are shade and the sense of an inviting space they've created.

Outdoor fireplaces become major elements in the landscape. Design and site them for safety, aesthetics, and utilitarian needs. Then enjoy them!

Obviously, any fire creates a hazard, so build accordingly. Outdoor fireplaces *not* designed correctly for good combustion are particularly vulnerable to winds kicking up at inappropriate times, spitting out embers onto nearby planting beds. Just like an indoor fireplace, every precaution needs to be addressed before their construction.

Fireplaces should be architecturally appealing and complementary to the homesite. Repeat the same materials and architectural style; this is not the time to pick a design out of a landscaping book that has nothing to do with your style of home (a home-on-the-range style does not pair well with French Tudor).

Plan all utilitarian considerations before you build, such as these elements: a wood box if using wood as fuel; an ash can with a tight lid for clean up; necessary tools; a grill with storage for any necessary items; and a flat space for parking trays of food. With good planning, an outdoor fireplace will add lots of enjoyment to your landscape.

See **Architecturally Complement Home** *42*

Enclosure *50*

Fourth Room, Outdoor Living Space *169*

Power of the Sun *242*

All in One Place and One Level *243*

Measuring for Furniture *246*

The Grill *248*

Plan for All Your Patio Needs *250*

When a homeowner tells you of spending two to four evenings a week enjoying the outdoor fireplace, there is no doubt this landscape decision was a correct one. Wood was chosen because this homeowner enjoys the fun of building a fire and cleaning up is an acceptable activity.

Any fire hazard is greatly reduced because this fireplace faces a large stone patio.

With both a wood box and a grilling surface, this setting is not only stunningly beautiful but also practical.

309 A fire can either be wood burning or gas.
**Choose one based on the availability of fuel
and how it will work with your lifestyle.**

Nostalgia can be a compelling factor for having a
wood-burning fire instead of "artificial" gas.
However, several factors come into play: Do you have
a good supply of wood now and for many years
ahead? Do you have enough leisure time to allow for
the extra time you'll spend both building and putting
out the fire? Are you willing to put up with the continual cleaning chores wood fires create?

There are so many safety issues associated with
fire, and even more with wood fires. Regardless of
whether you choose wood or gas, the end product is
the wonderful ambience a fire provides. Pick the one
to suit your lifestyle and begin adding some great
evenings to your life.

This weekend hideout has
the added convenience of a
gas fireplace.

The fireplace was sited off
to one side to keep the
view to the lake open.

A small wall was extended
on either side to create a
small sense of enclosure
for the cozy feeling.

Easy exits are provided
allowing, ensuring this
patio is not a dead end.

A fire box in a moveable apparatus is convenient; a fire pit in a permanent ground setting is not.

A fire box is a contraption that stands alone, moves about to adapt to the situation, and can even be stored away after cleaning—a major consideration when choosing the right one for the changing seasons of your landscape. Fire boxes come in a variety of styles, from Mexican stucco to sleek metal; aesthetics and safety (place on a noncombustible surface, and make sure the fire's out at evening's end) are the only concerns.

A permanent outdoor fire pit is altogether different: ashes must be removed (wet ashes are a mess), and access to those ashes can be inconvenient. Think this one through before building a permanent structure. Be sure you're willing to devote the energy it takes to maintain, since you don't want to look at a pile of ashes on your patio every day.

See **High Maintenance Projects** *13*

Movable and easy to clean, this fire box has drawn many friends and neighbors over to share a relaxing evening.

The surrounding garden is bordered by a mortared wall with many exits to all other parts of the landscape.

Significant trees create a comforting canopy and soft enclosure. The Ornamental Trees close by add interest in the landscape.

If a dog is an integral part of the homeowner's life, the landscape design (mainly hardscape decisions) must integrate the dog's needs within the design.

Every dog owner has a routine with his animal. Even if another, previous dog has died, the owner can tell me how he wants the new dog to integrate within the family—in at night, outside during the day, only outside to walk, in and out at will, on the deck or not, and so forth. In each case, in-and-out access should be addressed when the home is being built so that decisions can be made upfront.

When building a new home, sit down with your architect or builder and plot out the doggie door, the door to "let him outside," the pen and its gate, and the gates to the back yard. Don't think these problems will solve themselves once you move in! I can think of many jobs with dog problems that King Solomon could not have solved except with a tacked on, convoluted result—but a little thought upfront would have made the solution attractive and less expensive. Thinking ahead saves a lot of headaches when trying to integrate dogs and their needs with the creation of a lovely outdoor space for the family.

This dog owner planned ahead. The added porch has an attractive rail and gate, keeping this space separate from the rambunctious needs of his little friends. The spacious deck has an arbor, giving the dogs shade, while a little house sits in the corner and a doggie door enters to a special place inside the home. A second fence keeps the dogs in a smaller back yard with plenty of plantings on the outside, where their playful antics are not a problem.

If a dog is destroying the landscaping, give him his own space—either by installing "silent fencing" or constructing a dog run.

Dogs (and children!) present every landscaper an emotionally charged situation. For every dog that poses no problem to the landscape, there is a dog with the digging ability of a backhoe or one that can chew nails in two (and does). The former just needs some directions as to where to go and play, and "silent fencing" might be the answer. The latter needs his own space separated from the landscape (if, indeed, a landscape is desired). A well-constructed dog run will satisfy everyone.

Silent fencing can be used within a fenced yard to train a dog to keep out of certain areas, especially at the vulnerable, early plant growth stages. Most dog owners know that even a well-trained dog might find it hard to stay out of newly dug, sweet smelling dirt. Silent fencing can be moved around as projects come and go, giving new landscaping a chance to thrive. Dogs have to be trained for silent fencing to be effective, but some dogs will literally shock themselves crazy crossing the fence line; if so, try a dog run.

Dogs like a defined space, so a *dog run* is a great solution. However, this defined space should be with a fence, never with the dog tethered by a chain to his collar. A tethered dog becomes vicious. The enclosed area should be large enough for the dog to run— that's why it's called a dog run. Dog runs are also nice auxiliary sites in which to keep dogs while entertaining, or during any activity in which he might interfere; it gives him his own space without compromising space within the home.

Dog runs must be placed so that at some spot the dog and the owner can see each other; if the dog can watch all the activity from his pen, he will be quite content, but a hidden dog can develop personality or anxiety problems. Additionally, the owner must be able to see his dog when he comes home or is outside—not only for the social interaction with the dog but also to monitor the animal's situation for food, water, and health problems.

Some shade and shelter should be provided, of course. And all dogs love some concrete surface—it is clean for the homeowner and cool on the dog's underside. The gate should be located within easy access for feeding and letting the dog out for playtime. Add a pleasant walkway, some attractive shrubs or other plantings, and the dog run can certainly be compatible with a beautiful landscape.

Every dog owner should consider the choice of their dog and its needs and decide if it is compatible with the available outdoor space plus the desires of the homeowner for a beautiful landscape. Many landscapes are compromised, or completely ruined, because these two desires are not compatible or the homeowner is unwilling to address any solutions arising from this conflict such as installing a dog run or silent fencing. I have observed many situations where the homeowner had a "digging dog," but once an appropriate dog run was sited or silent fencing was in place (and the dog was trained), the landscape was able to progress. Any homeowner who has a well-mannered dog should be thankful.

See **Focal Points** *54*

Plants for Specific Job *64*

Avoid Unnecessary Height in Screening *68*

Evergreens *84*

Symmetry – Avoid Here *92*

Significant Trees – Shade *96*

Choosing a dog compatible with the available space for play is a critical step toward having a doable landscape.

This dog and this landscape get along! How nice and also how cute.

This Significant Tree is limbed up quite high to allow more light to reach the lawn area.

Meandering shrub borders create interest in any landscape.

Large, closely spaced steppingstones create a practical path and direct traffic at the same time.

312

313 **Critters—especially birds—need only a few basic considerations to thrive in your landscape.**

Every creature has essential fundamental demands for survival—basically, appropriate food and shelter. Some adapt better than others. Consider the following suggestions for creating a year-round habitat based on the natural environment supplying all of their needs.

1. *Plant a wide variety of flowers and shrubs that bloom and seed throughout the seasons.* Critters will respond, knowing their dinner will always be ready at your home plus they'll have great places to perch, nestle down at night, and perhaps set up housekeeping. Organizations can give very detailed lists to attract specific animals, but just getting a variety of plants out there will accomplish this goal. Conversely, a limited array of typical evergreen foundation shrubs whose blooms are routinely sheared off will cause critters to bypass your home.

2. *Plant a variety of trees that grow to different sizes.* The demands of critters are quite variable: one wants to be high, another on the ground, one likes this seedpod, another likes certain grubs under tree bark. Your goal is to provide a cafeteria addressing all the different tastes or habitat demands various creatures have. In my area, the nuthatch runs up and down our tree trunks all day; migrating robins spend hours on the ground but love to perch in nearby small trees and shrubs; and hawks position themselves on the highest tree top for a good hunting view. A lone tree or two in the landscape can be very dramatic, but critters will quickly move on without ample food and shelter.

3. *Water is essential to all living creatures.* Birdbaths might seem like ornamental trappings—but ask the bird who stops over for a drink and a little wash-up in still, shallow water. He will only want to suggest that it be kept clean and full, especially during long periods of drought. Other creatures will also be seen taking a drink from time to time. Of course, ponds, lakes, and streams will draw an even wider variety of wildlife.

4. *A more relaxed landscape is a magnet for creatures.* A lawn on which few or no chemicals are used will yield delicious critter meals—a real smorgasbord. Undisturbed leaf litter under your trees harbors abundant bugs and stuff for snacks, while an old dead tree can be a wonderful apartment complex with its own indoor cafeteria. A part of the lake left natural attracts ducks and otters seeking refuge for raising their families. If you are lucky, a gaggle of wild turkeys might take up residence. They will be wary of a lurking fox or coyote nearby. Conversely, a routinely sprayed and manicured lawn, mulch beds cleaned and replaced with perfectly clean new mulch each season, every dead tree or branch removed, and shrubs trimmed on a regular basis will not become a great attraction for many creatures. It's just a tradeoff.

5. *Alternate open fields or lawns with wooded and shrub areas.* In and out, in and out—creatures are always on the move, going from open spaces for different food supplies and back into the woods and shrubs for cover. From the largest farm to the smallest suburban lot, the opening up and closing off with plants will provide a habitat for many creatures. Some neighborhoods are planted with few trees or shrubs, leaving just open expansive lawns, but most wildlife will not find this limitless grassy landscape very appealing; nor will homes in deep sunless forests with the underbrush cleaned away attract many critters.

So, mix it up! A habitat filled with a variety of flowers, trees, and shrubs, with ample water sources and a mix of open areas and forest sites will make your site perfect for a large array of critters you'll enjoy observing.

See **Job Description for Plants** *64*

Plant Year-round *67*

Local Sources *90*

Litter, Natural Mulch *106*

Photos *107, 364*

A combination of tall trees, understory trees, shrubs, and plenty of natural foods is a siren call for birds and many kinds of other critters.

Three broods of bluebirds one summer was a major prize. This homeowner is still trying to figure out how Mr. and Mrs. Bluebird can fly so fast into that hole and avoid a head-on collision!

The beauty of the landscape benefits with the wonderful variety of plant materials.

313

314 **Practically every landscape has a statue of some creature—if not lots of them!— tucked about or prominently displayed. Since live animals are often not visible, these fake critters do their part for the homeowner's sense of well-being.**

Wildlife is often quite elusive, yet their presence is essential to how man relates the outdoors. Catching a glimpse of a rabbit or a frog in the garden is fun, but wouldn't it be nice to see them more often? Seeing a deer from time to time is exciting, but why not have one permanently displayed somewhere? A concrete statue might be second best, but it helps man relate to the outdoors.

The art world is awash with wonderful selections to complement every garden. Adding a croaking frog next to a walk is just plain funky. Placing a deer family off in the meadow is rather restful. A large dog statue at your front door could be very elegant. Little bunnies nestled around some planted containers are so whimsical.

Throughout the ages, man has tried to capture the spirit of wild creatures by drawing or making their image in a permanent form. An appearance of the real McCoy is often all too brief; their images are the next best thing.

See **Focal Points – Place From Viewing Site** *53*
Focal Points, Multiple *54*
Containers *158*
Photos *137, 138, 316*

Permanent creatures give year-round pleasure. Do you know a child who plays with frogs like that?

Man has drastically altered the balance of nature for animals in the landscape. Try to understand the complexity of the problem and become part of the solution.

…Deer are beautiful, but what do you know about them other than you like seeing them in your meadow?

…Trout introduced to streams might make good fishing, but are there important long-term implications you should know?

…Coyotes are being killed, but is there good data to support this strategy?

…Prairie dogs were almost annihilated because their holes were supposedly breaking the legs of grazing cows. It was found that cows were fine with the holes—and now the loss of the prairie dog habitat has proved disastrous to hundreds of other critters.

…A bug is chewing on your plant. Will spraying the whole backyard with insecticide cause more harm than good?

…Bird feeders give endless joy to homeowners but studies are finding their use can promote transmission of diseases, as well as cause window collisions. Should you learn more about how to manage your avian community?

…Bringing home an unknown critter that finds its way into the surrounding landscape has unleashed monumental havoc to the environment in many cases; what have you unknowingly unleashed?

A simple backyard landscape can be just as vulnerable as the largest national forest when the balance of nature is upset. I've seen gypsy moths defoliate entire trees in a friend's garden in New York. I've watched chipmunks take over another's crawlspace. On a larger scale, walking catfish, choking mussels in the waterways, and a devastating rodent in Louisiana are ongoing environmental horror stories.

The stories go on and on, with purposeful, accidental, or "just not caring" issues that impact the lives of animals that have no voice on these matters.

Recently, an entire cactus family in Mexico is threatened by a moth that was introduced on another continent to eradicate unwanted cactus. It seemed like such a simple solution to a local problem. But what was good for one situation is a disaster for another: now the same moth is poised to wreak financial havoc on Mexico's economy—because Mexico's seventh largest cash crop is cacti.

We have made countless changes to the land, causing subtle as well as dramatic problems in our environment. As responsible stewards, we should attempt to correct these problems—while knowing that each is complex and often not well understood. As landowners, our part is to be aware, and question everything before we impact the environment. Simplistic solutions might not be the best and can create even *more* problems. Man has the intelligence to study, test, and evaluate information to start unraveling the secrets of the natural world, and we should do so. So read!

316 Anticipate that some critters are pests. Acknowledge their ability to invade your location, and plan accordingly.

Considerable anguish could be avoided if man could view animals as he views a new baby in the house. Both are really cute, but one chews on the carpet while the other spits up on it—and neither care that it is your Persian rug!

Deer: Select plants they will absolutely not eat, and don't plant the ones they absolutely love. In between are many plants whose mature leaves are not so delicious as the younger tender ones, and will thrive if protected for a time. As a tree or shrub matures, the bark will toughen up to resist deer's chewing and rubbings. If you are lucky, the excitement of exploring the new freshly planted shrubs wears off after a time, and their path will sometimes turn out of your yard.

I've seen newly planted camellias chewed to a stalk but on old farms, camellias are massive giants never touched by deer. My young apple trees were pawed and rubbed nearly out of the ground, but our old pear trees stood unnoticed. One big leaf magnolia disappeared twice; the third time they left it alone, and now it's twenty-five feet tall. A customer had an existing row of Indian hawthorn growing for many years so I repeated them across the driveway. The deer ate the newly planted hawthorns three times but never touched the ones ten feet away!

Deer have become epidemic in our present environment. Their natural predators were eliminated many years ago, leaving them to multiply unchecked, with their numbers increasing from thousands to millions—and they need to eat. The havoc wrought on understory plants is doing irreparable harm to the ecosystem, with the loss of native plants and the animals they support.

A homeowner's landscape is very important, but the problem of deer infestation has many more profound effects with far-reaching implications for the extended landscapes of our nation.

Woodpeckers, squirrels, chipmunks: Using wood as an outside material can invite several different guests into your home. The cedar siding on my home certainly was wonderful protection against rot but not against woodpeckers; after they drilled the holes, squirrels moved in. When I built again near woods, I chose concrete siding this time. Now the woodpeckers can drill their heads off and not reach pay dirt. It sounds mean, but I really prefer them to use our nearby trees instead. Every day, I spot squirrels looking for some kind of entry into the house. But I'd prefer them to go to their nests in the trees.

Many new materials are available that address some of the ravages of critters. Homes built in thick woods seem to be even more vulnerable to unwanted guests. No matter how aesthetically pleasing some materials appear, their ability to stand up to nature must be the first consideration—because even with the best choices, woodpeckers, squirrels, chipmunks and such would love setting up house with you if given half a chance.

Raccoons and possums (even bears): They *love* garbage. Even though your own dog could be the culprit, put trashcans in a secure place with secure lids. Don't put meats and oils in your compost. Don't feed your animals outside unless it is strictly controlled. Any time wild animals are encouraged to regard a homesite as a place to find food, your family is in jeopardy—perhaps from minor problems, but some can be quite serious.

Termites: Wood and dark places are their favorite combo. Remove any loose wood from under your house. Never mulch with wood chips next to your foundation. Check with the termite people to get a recommendation for proper mulches. Never permanently store firewood next to your home. And have your home routinely inspected—leave nothing to chance with this destructive invader.

Snakes: Noise bothers snakes. If you plan to work in a certain cluttered area, make considerable noise and rattle bushes before moving in for the job at hand. Snakes react to noise by moving on to quieter locations. Bites occur when they are startled; so give them a chance to leave. Their first preference is to leave for their own protection.

One particular gentleman, who was my assistant for several years, was built of steel but afraid of snakes, so when a new project started taking us into quite a thicket, he rattled metal objects, brought out a noisy chain saw, and so forth. We would see an occasional tiny garden snake, but usually this was because they were accidentally picked up with mulch or brush and had not had time to just scoot away.

Many homeowners are afraid to walk their own property. My suggestion is to make plenty of noise if your plans are to hang around for yardwork; if you're only going for a walk, just do so. On the other hand, if a homeowner tells me he will not walk outside because of the fear of snakes, and I see ivy consuming the yard, I know snakes might be a consideration. But, I am much more concerned that an invasive exotic plant needs to be removed from the property and the land reclaimed for human use. When this is done, the fear of snakes hiding in the landscape will be gone and many more problems will be solved!

Bees and wasps: These insects come in all sizes and temperaments. Many people are highly allergic to their stings and should be afraid of their presence, especially if they disturb a wasp nest, step on yellow jacket entrances, or knock down a hornet's nest. Obviously, if any of these pests put you in harm's way, preventative measures need to be taken.

Others—like the paper wasp or carpenter bee—make a mess and can be destructive, but eradicate them only if you must. Remember they are often beneficial, if not ecologically essential, to the landscape in many ways.

Bees hovering in and around flowers cause me no concern. I have brushed against these indolent creatures for years and watched them move lazily from flower to flower. My presence means nothing to them. Sometimes a bee will be "busy as a bee" on a flower I'm cutting for an arrangement, but a soft brush and it will move on over to another meal site.

Coyotes and foxes—vs. chickens, cats, and small dogs: This is not a good mix. If you have the first, plan on the second group doing some disappearing acts unless you make sure they are protected by tight enclosures or kept inside. As more people move closer to natural areas, these encounters are part of everyday life. Living with nearby wildlife is a balancing act you must consider when buying property near these "wild" areas, if you have pets.

Ducks, geese, swans: These favorite birds are often introduced to the family pond or lake. Before you make that decision, please check out their habits and personalities. Both wild wood ducks and mallards call my property "home" each year. There are enough areas for them to nest and hide, while their wildness keeps them away from the open shores of my pond.

I often see aquatic birds like Canada geese take over a shoreline and adjoining open spaces (meaning your lawn)—turning them into muddied guano patches. Some of these birds have aggressive temperaments and should be enjoyed only at a distance. A swan pair is the epitome of elegance swimming in your lake but they are mean, aggressive creatures up close.

If these factors are acceptable, fine, but if the ducks, geese, or swans become destructive, reclaiming the situation can be fairly shattering emotionally and financially.

The gathering of the clan.

Index

even versus odd number of plants, 88

evergreen plants

    in flower and plant beds, 151

    screening with, 30, 69, 84

    symmetrical plantings, 93

    year-round interest, 84–85, 118, 151, 362

F

fences

    angles, 314

    benefits of, 306, 315

    characteristics of, 131

    connection to house, 312–314

    to control traffic, 307–308

    defining property with, 12, 99, 182–183, 307–308, 324

    formal versus informal plantings, 316

    gates, 307, 310–311, 314, 319–321

    grade of property and, 17

    height of, 309–310

    maintenance of, 34

    materials for, 81, 310–311

    near parking areas, 214

    outdoor living spaces, 50–51, 57, 66

    planting in front of, 315

    screening with, 68, 306–308, 326–327

    swimming pools, 347

    utility meters and, 316

    visual statics, 80–81

fertilizers, 25, 151, 353

fields, barren, 102–103

fire hydrants, 332

firepits, 370

fireplaces, 357, 368–370

fish, 358, 360, 363, 365, 377

flower and plant beds

    borders, 80, 133, 143, 180–185

    color from, 20, 138–139

    design and arrangement of, 76–77, 78, 91, 129, 132–134, 155, 176–179, 182

    fences and walls in, 315

    fertilizing, 25, 151

    irrigation, 26

    lines of, 87, 96, 170–175

    location of, 12, 34

    maintenance of, 20, 204

    mass plantings, 150

    mixed borders, 76–77, 78

    number of plants, 88

    preparation of, 21

    raised, 161

    repeating plants and forms, 91

    shrubs and trees to enhance, 151, 171–175, 179

    site choices, 130–131

    size of, 87, 132–133, 178–179

    year-round interest, 151

flower arranging, 146–148

focal points, 53–55, 248

foliage, 20, 83, 134

forest, climax, 102–103, 109

formal plantings, 53, 88, 316, 362

foundation plantings

    choosing plants for, 12, 33, 65, 84

    choosing to not plant, 176

    evergreen plants, 84

    height of, 35, 65, 171

    purpose of, 176

    vertical elements, 70–71

fox, 374, 379

front doors, 231–232, 234–235

front walks, 91, 225–230

front yards, 130

furniture, 242, 246–247, 250, 301, 305, 322–325, 362

G

garages and outbuildings. *See also* car areas

    design and planning, 40–43, 168, 197, 292–293, 298–299, 333–334

    detached garages, 12, 298–299

    plant colors to complement, 86–87, 157

    site choices, 75

    visual statics, 80

gardening as art, 155

gardening tools, 296–297

garden sheds, 294–297

gas meters, 60

gates, 307, 310–311, 314, 319–321

gazebos, 54, 303, 364

geese, 379

grade of property, 17–19, 53, 101, 180–181, 263

grafted plants, 22

grass. *See* lawns and grass

grasses, ornamental, 91

gravel, 36, 190, 192–193, 198, 227

grills, 248–249

grooming plants, 153

groundcovers, 20, 171

guest entrances

 clues to direct visitors to, 164, 205, 212, 231

 design and arrangement of, 164–166, 174–175, 177, 201, 205

 division from car areas, 164–166, 167–168

 exits, 205

 front doors, 231–232, 234–235

 front walks, 225–230

 parking areas, 205–211, 216–218, 219, 221, 226–227, 229–230

 surfaces for, 194–195

gutters and downspouts, 60, 329–330

H

hardiness zones, 28–29

hardscape elements, 42–43, 46, 251, 265

hedges, 80

herb gardens, 137

herbicides, 36

high maintenance, 25, 30, 31, 34, 36, 38, 192

houses

 building and landscaping costs, 61

 complementary design, 42

 debris, construction, 17–18

 exits, 39, 59, 263

 hardscape elements, 42–43

 low-profile homes, 70, 101, 171, 176–177

 outdoor space allocations, 40–41

 plant colors to complement, 86–87, 157

 relationship to outdoors, 39

 site choices, 44, 45–47, 57–59

 site clearing, 15–16, 100, 105

 sun and shade situations, 56–59

 views from, 44, 45–47, 53, 72–77, 130–131, 253–255, 266–267, 283, 285

humidity, 29

I

informal plantings, 88, 316

insects and bugs, 365, 377, 379

invasive plants

 borders to contain, 182–183

 choosing to plant, 31, 134–136, 137

 lawn grasses, 31, 182–183, 197, 354–355

 septic systems and, 333

 threat to landscape from, 37, 102–103

iron fences, rails, and gates

 aesthetic security from, 238, 239, 260, 310–311, 338

 examples of, 59, 221

irrigation

 frequency of, 26, 339

 method for new plantings, 26

 systems, 339–341

 trees and shrubs, 22–23, 26

Italian style lighting, 336

J

jointly-owned projects, 45

lakes, 364–366

landing areas

 doors, 222–224, 226, 232, 234–239, 243, 311, 349

 pads, 226

 steps, 222–224, 236–239, 280–281, 285, 286–288

 street parking, 213

landscape contractor, 61

landscape designer/architect, 40, 42, 61

landscape personality types, 121

landscape plans, 101

lawns and grass

 chemical spraying, 374, 377

 children and, 343–352

 connecting to foundation, 176

 establishment of, 343, 353, 355

 fertilizing, 25, 353

 grass choices, 352–355

 invasive plants, 31, 182–183, 197, 354–355

 mowing, 34

 under trees, 171, 179, 355

 walkways and paths, 192

 for wildlife, 374

 wooded sites versus, 15–16, 355

power lines, 331, 332

power meters, 60, 316, 319

prairie dogs, 377

primary forests, 102

project sharing, 45

propagation, 105

property
    boundary lines, 60
    building site clearing, 15–16
    design and arrangement of, 174–175
    grade of, 17–19, 53, 180–181, 263
    outdoor rooms and functions, 164, 174–175
    size of, 12
    use of, 13–14
    water drainage, 17–19

pruning trees and plants
    benefits of, 71–73, 104
    grooming, 153
    limbing up, 42, 73, 81, 87, 101, 122–123
    procedures for, 112–113, 118–119, 122
    purpose of, 114, 115
    shearing versus, 115–116
    thinning, 51, 65–66, 73, 87, 100, 123
    timing of, 124–125
    topping trees, 120

publications, 90

putting green, 41

R

raccoons, 378

railings
    decks, 260, 264
    design choices, 260
    materials for, 239, 256, 260, 310–311
    safety, 238
    steps, 238–239, 249, 289

raised beds, 161

repeating designs, 91

resources, local, 90, 150

restroom facilities, 300

retaining walls, 19, 180–181, 214

retention ponds, 366–367

roadside plantings, 140

rooflines, 197, 293, 302

root systems, 111, 152, 154

S

screening plants
    air conditioning units, 328
    borrowed views, 44
    enclosure, 50–51, 170
    height of, 68–69
    plant choices, 94
    shrub borders, mixed, 94
    symmetrical plantings, 93, 94

seating and sitting areas
    base materials, 269, 322, 367
    benches, 167, 184, 235, 322
    built-in on decks, 261
    for children, 349
    furniture, 242, 246–247, 301, 305, 322–325, 362
    importance of, 52, 131
    walls used for, 41, 268

seedlings, 38, 87, 104

septic systems, 333

shade. *See* sun and shade

shared projects, 45

sharing plants, 149

shearing trees and plants, 114–118, 121, 123

sheds, 80, 169, 294, 297

shopping for plants, 67

shrubs. *See also* ornamental trees and shrubs; pruning
    trees and plants
    choosing, 63
    color from, 20, 83
    erosion control, 108, 180
    fertilizing, 25
    in flower and plant beds, 151, 171–175
    growth habits, 121, 178–179
    irrigation, 22–23, 26
    mulch placement, 22, 23, 24
    planting guides, 22–23
    shape of, 82
    shrub borders, mixed, 94
    site choices, 53
    texture of, 83

significant trees
    availability of, 109
    benefits of, 96–98
    climate control, 109
    excuse for not planting, 97, 98

plantings next to, 228
steppingstones, 188–189, 304, 373
through woods, 198–199
tilting, 198, 225
visual statics, 80, 81
width of, 14, 191, 225–227, 230, 362
walls
angles, 314
benefits of, 306, 315
child-friendly landscapes, 348
connection to house, 312–314, 338
to control traffic, 268, 307–308
defining property with, 307–308
drainage and, 19
gates, 307, 310–311, 314, 319–321
height of, 41, 268, 309–310
materials for, 81, 83, 180, 320, 321
near parking areas, 214
outdoor living spaces, 50–51
planting in front of, 184–185, 315
retaining walls, 19, 180–181, 214
screening with, 306–308, 326
as seating, 41, 268
utility meters and, 316
visual statics, 80
wasps, 379
water drainage
bed preparation and, 21

grading and, 17–19
planting guides, 22–23
underground drains, 17, 18
walls, 19
water faucets, 331
water features
formal designs, 362
lakes, 364–366
mosquitoes and, 365
ornamental ponds, 358–363, 365
role of in landscape, 80, 357
watering, 339, 341
water line markers, 332
weed control, 36
wildflower gardens, 140–141
window boxes, 157, 224
winter landscapes, 56, 64–65, 84–85, 118–119
woodpeckers, 378
workshops, 298–299

Y

year-round interest from plants, 67, 84–85, 118–119, 151, 362
year-round shopping, 67

Z

zone maps, 28

Landscape Terms

Amender Any substance used to change the composition of soil that is either too dense to allow water to percolate, or too loose allowing water to drain too quickly for proper absorption. Amenders come in bags or in bulk, can be gathered locally, and can be organic, inorganic, or both. Examples include cow manure, horse manure, composted refuse, worm castings, peat moss, small granite rocks, and expanded shale. NOTE: Some amenders may introduce undesirable invasive weed seeds to your garden.

Annual Plants (usually flowers) that must be planted each year. Some annuals are not genetically programmed to live for extended periods; others cannot sustain life through extreme winter or summer temperatures.

Beauty Any landscaping decision based on its aesthetic appeal. Examples include concrete colored to coordinate with the home; a fence built with attention to artistic and placement details; plants chosen for the color and size of their blossoms; chairs chosen for color and design. Every decision affects the aesthetic appeal of a landscape when its elements come together.

Biennial Flowers that require a two-year cycle to set seed and bloom the following year. Gardeners should limit placement of biennials to areas that can accommodate their need for undisturbed space.

Collar The swelling at the juncture where a branch grows from a tree. This area has special cells for healing and a wonderful identifying mark to tell anyone cutting a branch where to cut. This collar should always be left on for the pruning cut to heal quickly and well. To prune farther out the branch either leaves a dead stub or causes the branch to grow out more. Cutting the collar off will force one to cut into the main branch, hindering the healing process.

Color A high priority for landscapers. Novice gardeners may expect their landscape to look like the landscapes at local commercial sites or like magazine photos. In reality, most of these areas are gardened intensively; pictures tend to capture a garden at its height of color. For most landscapes, color comes from flowering shrubs and trees, annuals, and the varying textures of different plantings.

Deciduous Plants that lose their leaves in the winter. This occurrence varies by region and, sometimes, a winter's harshness.

Drainage How water enters and leaves your site. Drainage problems may be created by the hardscape of the home site itself, which may then pass water on to another downhill site. Drainage may be controlled aboveground with correct grading coupled with plantings and rocks, or by the use of underground pipes. Incorrect drainage control is the number one problem in most landscapes and can compromise the integrity of the home.

Evergreen Plants that retain their foliage throughout the year. Many evergreens molt in late winter as fresh foliage emerges. Old foliage will turn and fall off even as new growth appears on the tips and fills out for the season, hence the name "evergreen."

Focal Point Any plant or object that arrests the eye if only for a few seconds. Man enjoys a vista of interest. If various focal points fulfill this need, the landscape will succeed. If there is an absence of focal points or they are of a negative quality, the landscape will diminish in its appeal.

Functional A functional landscape is imperative to successful design. Decisions should be based on efficiency and maximum utility. For example, concrete is permanent and should not be slippery; a fence should block a view of the neighbors; plants may create a noise buffer; chairs should allow one to sit comfortably; electrical meters may be easily accessed to allow lights to be plugged in for reading. Every landscaping decision affects the functionality of its combined elements.

Guest Parking An area that, ideally, allows visitors to park their cars with easy access to the front entrance and out of the way of the homeowner and other guests.

Hardscape Elements in the landscape that are "hard"—concrete, brick, stone, iron, wood and other materials used to create patios, decks, porches, fences, walls, paths, and driveways.

Inorganic Any substance that never lived. (An example would be rocks.)

Invasive Any plant that *quickly* spreads by way of seeds and/or roots into areas where it is not wanted. Planting an invasive plant in a personal garden can ruin the joy of a site; either the invasive overwhelms existing plantings, or the effort to maintain control becomes oppressive. Invasives in the general environment choke out desired plantings and can create other problems. Not all invasive plants are equal in creating a destructive outcome; some are only an annoyance.

Level A location in the landscape that is perceptibly flat in order for it to be put to good use but which has a slight slope for adequate run off.

Limbing Up Removing the lower limbs of any plant. Because plants grow by adding on to their top rather than stretching upward, any low-growing branch will remain at its original height and may eventually become an eyesore, a mowing hazard, or an obstacle to proper light.

Low Maintenance The number one request by every homeowner, which is the reduction of hours spent maintaining the landscape. The amount of maintenance a landscape requires is determined in the initial planning stages by its location, its design, and the growth habits and cultural requirements of the plants chosen for the landscape.

Mulch A layer of litter on the ground, either placed there for new plantings or provided by nature in the form of dead leaves fallen from existing plants. A layer of mulch plays a critical role in the health of plants.

Native Any plant that existed in a region before change caused by the introduction (either intentional or accidental) of nonnative plants. The value of native and nonnative plants to the landscape is determined by the qualities of the individual plants and not by their origin.

Organic Anything that lives and then dies. Decomposition occurs very quickly when water is present; in arid areas, the process takes longer.

Ornamental Tree A smaller-sized tree that is best used in relationship to other trees or sited in relationship to features in the landscape. If planted out in the open with no context to other features, these smaller trees become lost and diminish the landscape.

Percolate In nearly all planting situations, soil should allow water to pass by the roots of the plant as though it's passing through coffee grounds. The water should be available long enough to be used by the roots of the plants but not so long as to suffocate them.

Perennial Perennials are flowers that are relatively permanent in the landscape. To remember this term, think "permanent." Because of the complexity of the flower world, just how permanent can vary, but a perennial should last many years. Some perennials die back to the ground each year and reemerge each spring; others stay alive aboveground throughout the year.

Region The area where certain plant materials survive and thrive. When you select plant materials for your landscape, the Planting Zone Map can help you choose plants suited to your region. A good look around at the plants common to successful landscapes and gardens may also provide ideas.

Shade A term to describe the amount of light needed by certain plants. Like the need for sun, the amount of shade varies by location. Forests can provide both full shade or areas of partial shade, where some sun reaches the forest floor. A building may cause complete shade; an arbor can provide partial shade.

Significant Tree A tree that grows to a large size. The use of significant trees in the landscape anchors the home to the site. Some create a canopy; some are giant cone shapes; others may be towering palm trees. In more arid regions, the trees can be rather scrubby but still be the largest specimen available.

Slope or Bank Any area that cannot be mowed safely.

Succession of Growth A region's natural succession of plant materials that help regenerate an area. These natural plantings often have trashy qualities which prevent the appearance of more desirable plants. For the homeowner, understanding the succession of growth for his landscape will help determine which plants to eliminate and which to keep and thin as the plants naturally appear.

Sun A term to describe the amount of sunlight needed by certain plants. Like shade, the amount of sun needed varies by location. A landscape may have a cooler site created by shade from nearby trees, or a site exposed to the morning (eastern) sun and shaded from the hot western sun; a site under hot sun with uninterrupted western exposure; or even an all-day blast with absolutely no shade. It's preferable to monitor the amount of sun a site receives before planting, but plants will quickly let you know how much "sun" they prefer.

Stub That part of a branch left from an incorrect cut. Rather than leaving a smooth, upward-growing branch as properly cutting back to the collar leaves, an improper cut leaves a dead stub or a one that sprouts unsightly whips (growths). Improperly cut branches are one of the most detrimental elements to a beautiful landscape.

Thinning The partial removal of plant material when a plant or site is too crowded for maximum health and beauty. This might include thinning branches from a shrub or tree that have grown too dense, or thinning a grove of trees located too close together for any one to develop beautifully and with full vigor.

Topping Cutting off the tops of large trees (usually those growing under power lines or endangering structures). Unfortunately, unless performed by an expert, the result may mean the health of a tree quickly deteriorates, posing further danger to the site. Aesthetically, topping irrevocably alters the tree's winter silhouette, destroying the beauty of the landscape. In most cases, a tree should be completely removed and any new plantings chosen for their height at maturity.

Trash Tree A trash tree is any tree in the landscape that creates severe problems through its susceptibility to disease, weak growth, invasiveness, fruit or leaf litter, et cetera.

Trash Wall An undesirable growth of natural plantings occurring along property lines and at the edge of forests. Despite some positive attributes—screening from neighbors or providing cover for forest critters—the results are often detrimental to the landscape. In the home landscape, unwanted trees and undesirable shrubs pose long-term hazards. On larger properties, trash walls may block desirable views or access.

Gardening Terms

Acid soil soil with a pH lower than 7.0; also referred to as sour soil.

Adventitious originating from an unusual or unexpected position.

Alkaline soil soil with a pH greater than 7.0; also referred to as sweet soil. It lacks acidity, often because it has limestone in it.

All-purpose fertilizer powdered, liquid, or granular fertilizer with a balanced proportion of the three key nutrients—nitrogen (N), phosphorus (P), and potassium (K). It is suitable for maintenance nutrition for most plants.

Annual a plant that lives its entire life in one growing season. It is genetically determined to germinate, grow, flower, set seed, and die the same year.

Apical bud the bud located at the tip of a branch or stem.

Apical dominance the tendency of a leader or central shoot with an apical bud to inhibit the development of side shoots on a stem or plant.

Balled-and-burlapped describes a tree or shrub, usually field grown, whose soilball was dug and wrapped with protective burlap and twine for sale or transplanting. "Balled-and-burlapped" is commercially referred to as B&B.

Bare root describes plants that have been dug without any soil around their roots. (Often young, dormant shrubs and trees are purchased through the mail; they arrive with their exposed roots covered with moist peat or sphagnum moss, sawdust, or similar material, and wrapped in plastic.) "Bare root" is commercially referred to as BR.

Barrier plant a plant that has intimidating thorns or spines and is sited purposely to block foot traffic or other access to the home or yard.

Beneficial insects insects or their larvae that prey on pest organisms and their eggs. They may be flying insects, such as ladybugs, parasitic wasps, praying mantids, and soldier bugs, or soil dwellers such as predatory nematodes, spiders, and ants.

Berm a narrow raised ring of soil around a newly planted tree or shrub, used to hold water so it will be directed to the root zone. (Also a mound of soil used to create an elevated landscape effect for planting of trees and shrubs.)

Bract a modified leaf structure on a plant stem near its flower that resembles a petal. Often it is more colorful and visible than the actual flower, as in dogwood.

Bud union the point at which the top scion or bud of a plant was grafted to the rootstock; usually refers to roses and ornamental trees.

Butterfly the process of scoring (cutting vertically into the root mass) the solid mass of roots of a rootbound plant in order to spread them out for planting.

Canopy the overhead branching area of a tree, usually referring to its extent including foliage.

Cold hardiness the ability of a perennial plant to survive the winter cold in a particular area.

Composite a flower that is actually composed of many tiny flowers. Typically, they are flat clusters of tiny, tight florets, sometimes surrounded by wider-petaled florets. Composite flowers are highly attractive to bees and beneficial insects.

Compost organic matter that has undergone progressive decomposition by microbial and macrobial activity until it is reduced to a spongy, fluffy texture. Added to soil of any type, it improves the soil's ability to hold air, water, and nutrients and to drain well.

Corm the swollen energy-storing structure, analogous to a bulb, under the soil at the base of the stem of plants such as crocus and gladiolus.

Crown the base of a plant at, or just beneath, the surface of the soil where the roots meet the stems.

Cultivar a CULTIvated VARiety. It is a naturally occurring form of a plant that has been identified as special or superior and is purposely selected for propagation and production.

Cure to dry or heat fresh cuts of corms, rhizomes, stolons, and tubers. Time required varies from a few hours to several days.

Deadheading a pruning technique that removes faded flower heads from plants to improve their appearance, abort seed production, and stimulate further flowering.

Deciduous plants unlike evergreens, these trees and shrubs lose their leaves in the fall and releaf the following growing season.

Desiccation drying out of foliage tissues, usually due to drought, or wind, or in the case of seashore plantings, to salt spray.

Division the practice of splitting apart perennial plants to create several smaller-rooted segments. The practice is useful for controlling the plant's size and for acquiring more plants; it is also essential to the health and continued flowering of certain species.

Dormancy the period, usually the winter, when perennial plants temporarily cease active growth and rest. Go dormant is the verb form, as used in this sentence: Some plants, like spring-blooming bulbs, go dormant in the summer.

Endophyte a naturally occurring fungus (found in certain species of grasses) that improves drought-resistance and resistance to some aboveground feeding insects.

Establishment the point at which a newly planted tree, shrub, or flower has become adapted to its new growing conditions. This may be indicated by the production of new growth, either foliage or stems, and may indicate that the roots have recovered from transplant shock and have begun to grow and spread.

Evergreen describes perennial plants that do not lose their foliage annually with the onset of winter. Needled or broadleaf foliage will persist and continues to function on a plant through one or more winters, aging and dropping unobtrusively in cycles of two or more years.

Fall the drooping lower flower petal of an iris.

Flare the point where roots begin to spread from the base of the stem or trunk.

Floret a tiny flower, usually one of many forming a cluster, that comprises a single blossom.

Foliar of or about foliage—usually refers to the practice of spraying foliage, as in foliar feeding or treating with insecticides and fungicides.

Germinate to sprout. Germination is a fertile seed's first stage of development.

Girdling the growth of a root in a strangulating manner around the base of a shrub or tree trunk. The root can physically strangle the plant by cutting off the flow of manufactured food to the roots.

Graft (union) the point on the stem of a woody plant with sturdier roots where a stem scion or bud from a highly ornamental plant is inserted so it will join with it. Roses are commonly grafted.

Hardscape the permanent, structural, nonplant part of a landscape, such as walls, sheds, pools, patios, arbors, and walkways.

Herbaceous describes plants having fleshy or soft stems that die back with frost; the opposite of woody.

Humic acid the end product of decaying matter. The black liquid which acts as the substance that holds soil particles together as well as apart, gives soil its dark color, improves its nutrient-holding capacity, and improves aeration and drainage.

Hybrid a plant that is the result of intentional or natural cross-pollination between two or more different kinds of plants of the same species or genus.

Leader candle the central, upright growing main stem of a single trunk tree.

Low-water-demand describes plants that tolerate dry soil for varying periods of time. Typically, they have succulent, hairy, or silvery-gray foliage and tuberous roots or taproots.

Melting-out the physiological dieback of turfgrass, usually during summer, caused by heat, drought, oppressive humidity, and certain diseases.

Mulch a covering over the surface of the soil used to reduce compaction, conserve moisture, reduce runoff of water, prevent erosion, stop weed growth, and reduce soil temperature fluctuation. It may be inorganic (gravel, plastic, fabric) or organic (wood chips, bark, pine needles, chopped leaves, etc.).

Naturalize (a) to plant seeds, bulbs, or plants in a random, informal pattern as they would appear in their natural habitat; (b) to adapt to and spread throughout adopted habitats (a tendency of some nonnative plants).

Nectar the sweet fluid produced by glands on flowers that attracts pollinators such as hummingbirds and honeybees for whom it is a source of energy.

Organic material, organic matter any material or debris that is derived from plants. It is carbon-based material capable of undergoing decomposition and decay.

Peat moss organic matter from peat sedges (United States) or sphagnum mosses (Canada), often used to improve soil texture and as bulk in soilless potting mixes. The acidity of sphagnum peat moss makes it ideal for boosting or maintaining soil acidity while also improving its moisture-holding capacity and drainage.

Perennial a flowering plant that lives over two or more seasons. Many die back with frost, but have roots that survive the winter and generate new shoots in the spring.

Petiole the stalk of a leaf.

pH a measurement of the relative acidity (low pH) or alkalinity (high pH) of soil or water based on a scale of 0 to 14, 7 being neutral. Individual plants require soil to be within a certain range so that nutrients can dissolve in moisture and be available to them.

Pinch to remove tender stems and/or leaves by pressing them between thumb and forefinger. This pruning technique encourages branching, compactness, and flowering in plants, or it removes aphids clustered at growing tips.

Pollen the often yellow, powdery grains produced by the anthers (male parts of the flower). They are transferred to the female flower parts by means of wind or animal pollinators to facilitate fertilization and seed production.

Raceme an arrangement of single stalked flowers along an elongated, unbranched axis.

Rhizome a swollen energy-storing stem structure, similar to a bulb, that lies horizontally in the soil, with roots emerging from its lower surface and growth shoots from a growing point at or near its tip, as in bearded iris.

Rootbound (or potbound) the condition of a plant that has been confined in a container too long, its roots having been forced to wrap around themselves and even swell out of the container. Successful transplanting or repotting requires untangling and trimming away of some of the matted roots.

Root flare the transition at the base of a tree trunk where the bark tissue begins to differentiate and roots begin to form just before entering the soil. This area should not be covered with soil when planting a tree.

Root-prune to cut outwardly spreading roots of a tree or shrub in preparation for transplanting.

Scarify (a) to scratch or nick the seed coat (outer covering) of a seed to facilitate penetration of water and free oxygen for germination; (b) to immerse seed in acid, bleach, or hot water.

Self-seeding the tendency of some plants to sow their seeds freely around the yard. It creates many seedlings the following season that may or may not be welcome.

Semievergreen tending to be evergreen in a mild climate but deciduous in a rigorous one.

Shearing the pruning technique whereby plant stems and branches are cut uniformly with long-bladed pruning shears (hedge shears) or powered hedge trimmers. It is used when creating and maintaining hedges and topiary.

Slow-release fertilizer fertilizer that is water-insoluble and therefore releases its nutrients gradually as a function of soil temperature, moisture, and related microbial activity. Typically granular, it may be organic or synthetic.

Standard (a) one of the erect central petals of an iris flower; (b) a plant grown with a round, bushy top or head of branches atop a single, upright stem.

Stolon an aboveground stem growing on the soil surface from which roots and new plants are produced at intervals along its length.

Succulent growth the sometimes undesirable production of fleshy, water-storing leaves or stems that results from overfertilization and/or excessive moisture.

Sucker a new growing shoot. Underground plant roots produce suckers to form new stems and spread by means of these suckering roots to form large plantings, or colonies. Some plants produce root suckers or branch suckers as a result of pruning or wounding.

Transpiration the giving off of water vapor and liquid water through the aerial parts of the plant. It is the cooling system for a living plant.

Tuber a type of underground storage structure in a plant root or stem, analogous to a bulb. It generates roots below and stems above ground (example: dahlia).

Variegated having various colors or color patterns. The term usually refers to plant foliage that is streaked, edged, blotched, or mottled with a contrasting color, often green with yellow, cream, or white.

Whip a young seedling or sapling or grafted tree without lateral branches.

White grubs fat, off-white, wormlike larvae of Japanese and other kinds of beetles. They reside in the soil and feed on plant (especially grass) roots until pupation, when they emerge as beetle adults to feed on plant foliage and flowers.

Wings (a) the corky tissue that forms edges along the twigs of some woody plants such as winged euonymus; (b) the flat, dried extension of tissue on some seeds, such as maple, that catch the wind and help them disseminate.

Xeriscape gardening water-efficient gardening that makes use of drip irrigation and drought-adaptable plants.

Jane's Landscape Checklist

Few properties have a perfect shape or size. And even if you can sketch the outlines of your property, a drawing really doesn't answer the question of what is important to *you*. But you can facilitate the landscape design process. Use this list as an overall list of goals or check off what you would like or need and concentrate on those items. It will help guide you and your landscape architect or contractor in the right direction. When you visualize your goals, then the whole picture will come together.

✓ Check the option of including a covered space (versus a deck) if an outdoor living space is planned

✓ Select land for goals (entertaining, play, et cetera)

✓ Select architect and contractor who understands basic ideas for proper land use

✓ Estimate costs for both house construction and outdoor needs

✓ Identify special attributes of the property and confirm their presence at the end of construction (trees, landscape features, et cetera)

✓ Identify all trees for health and attributes

✓ Plan all uses of land including parking and exits, and all outbuildings

✓ Identify the four rooms in the landscape (be sure to separate utility areas from outdoor living space)

✓ Check the position of the sun throughout the day and how it may influence the house design

✓ Identify all exits for access to the outdoors

✓ Contracts to include proper drainage, including burying drains

✓ Contracts to include no debris left after construction is complete

✓ Contractor to identify locations of all utilities

✓ Site all outdoor structures for correct exposure to the sun and for viewing from the home

✓ Contractor to build the home with even risers and treads for all steps

✓ Contractor to make all parking and outdoor living spaces level

✓ The front walk to be a minimum of 5 feet wide, drawn broadly and leading to visitor parking

✓ Plan to include all doors leading to the outside to have a generous landing and cover (if possible)

✓ Consider the role of all pets (and plan the house design to fit this need)

✓ Plan the placement of the grill

- ✓ Check the option of including a covered space (versus a deck) if an outdoor living space is planned

- ✓ Consider the impact of the sun if a deck is planned

- ✓ Plan attached outdoor living spaces to be recessed

- ✓ Plan all steps from attached living spaces to lead to the garden

- ✓ Check deck design for rails to fit your needs

- ✓ Trim out all support posts and unsightly structural elements

- ✓ All hardscape items to be simple and complementary to the home

- ✓ Attach all fencing to the house following these simple rules: perpendicular to the house, set back from the corner, and avoid bisecting architectural features

- ✓ Set all gates away from the home (few exceptions)

- ✓ Include some level spaces for the outdoors

- ✓ Consider the view from inside for all planned outdoor living spaces

- ✓ Plan additional structures to fit different needs such as workshops, sheds, or for entertainment

- ✓ Check the roofline for all structure for a pleasing angle

- ✓ Site all outdoor structures for correct exposure to the sun and for viewing from the home

- ✓ Identify needs for Significant Trees in the landscape (such as shade or framing)

- ✓ Site all Ornamental Trees as accents to other elements (never plant them alone)

- ✓ Identify all trees to make decisions for clearing and saving

- ✓ Walk the property and check the house plan for proper circulation (no dead ends!)

- ✓ Draw bed lines to solve problems

- ✓ Draw bed lines in broad strokes with lawn mowing in mind

- ✓ Identify each plant to use in the landscape to solve goals—privacy, shade, beauty

- ✓ Plan for few objects to be scattered about the lawn

- ✓ Select chosen plants for mature size, not its size at purchase

- ✓ Check plants for where it grows best—appropriate for your planting zone and your property site

- ✓ Avoid all invasive plants, even certain lawn grasses

- ✓ Check plant selection to include evergreens and some plants with structural interest or foliage texture

- ✓ Use only natural materials for the landscape

Meet Jane Bath

Jane Bath is one of America's premier landscape designers. During her twenty-five-plus year career, she has designed more than 4,000 landscapes in the Atlanta area, including residential, commercial, and retail sites and public gardens. Bath's design for the perennial garden at Barnsley Garden was featured in *Southern Living* as well as on the cover of *Southern Heirloom Gardens*. Bath discovered the perennial that was eventually named for her, 'Bath's Pink' dianthus, which is still ranked as the one of the Top Ten most-often sold perennials in the United States. In addition to her extensive landscape design business, Bath owns and operates a plant nursery, and is a popular and prolific speaker.

Jane lives with her husband, Nick, on a farm in Bogart, Georgia.

Cool Springs Press is devoted to state, regional, and national gardening and offers a wide selection of books to help you become a better gardener. CSP publishes books about your state or region, using local experts who live and garden in their respective areas.

Visit the Cool Springs Press website at www.coolspringspress.net to check out our other great titles (and it's more than just gardening!) You'll be glad you did.

COOL SPRINGS PRESS
A Division of Thomas Nelson Publishers
Since 1798